THE SECULAR LITURGICAL OFFICE
IN LATE MEDIEVAL ENGLAND

MEDIEVAL CHURCH STUDIES

Previously published volumes in this series are listed at the back of the book.

VOLUME 36

THE SECULAR LITURGICAL OFFICE IN LATE MEDIEVAL ENGLAND

by

Matthew Cheung Salisbury

BREPOLS

British Library Cataloguing in Publication Data

Salisbury, Matthew Cheung author.
The secular liturgical office in late medieval England. -- (Medieval church studies ; 36)
　　1. Liturgics--England--History--To 1500.
　　2. Liturgics--England--History--Sources.
I. Title
II. Series
264'.00942'0902-dc23

ISBN-13: 9782503548067

D/2015/0095/17
ISBN: 978-2-503-54806-7
Printed in the EU on acid-free paper

For Andrew Hughes

CONTENTS

List of Tables   ix

Acknowledgements   xiii

Abbreviations   xv

Introduction   1

Chapter 1. Studying the English Office Liturgy   11

Chapter 2. Liturgical Analysis   37

Chapter 3. Textual Analysis   105

Chapter 4. The Regulation and Transmission of Secular Liturgy   171

Conclusion   223

Bibliography   233

Handlist 1   245

Handlist 2   250

Index   255

LIST OF TABLES

Table 2.1: Secular responsory series compared. 43

Table 2.2: Responsory series of the Cluniac group. 49

Table 2.3: Responsory series of the Guisborough group. 51

Table 2.4: Responsory series of the Coldingham/Battle group. 53

Table 2.5: Responsory series shared by the Triduum monastic group. 56

Table 2.6: Relations between kalendars of the 'Chichele' group. 67

Table 2.7: Kalendars with closest relations. 68

Table 2.8: Normative kalendars extrapolated from Sarum,
Benedictine (OSB) and York sources. 73

Table 2.9: Dedication feasts indicated in kalendars. 91

Table 2.10: Relics feasts indicated in kalendars. 92

Table 2.11: Regional feasts for Gloucester. 93

Table 2.12: Regional feasts for Hereford. 94

Table 2.13: Regional feasts for Worcester. 95

Table 2.14: Regional feasts for the South East. 96

Table 2.15: Regional feasts for London, Surrey, Sussex. 96

Table 2.16: Regional feasts for East Anglia. 97

Table 2.17: Manuscripts Containing 'Synodal' Feasts.................... 99

Table 2.18: Synodal observances in Norwich/East Anglia manuscripts
    organized by feast. 100

Table 2.19: Synodal observances in Norwich/East Anglia
    organized by kalendar.. 101

Table 3.1: List of manuscripts from which full texts
    have been transcribed. 108

Table 3.2: Manuscripts containing 'Adv-Short'......................... 110

Table 3.3: Manuscripts containing 'Adv-Long'. 111

Table 3.4: Types of variants shared between Harley and Sloane........... 113

Table 3.5: Variants shared between BL Addl 59862,
    Camb. Dd. X. 66, Addl 3474–5, and Bodl. Bodley 976.............. 114

Table 3.6: Monastic manuscripts from which transcriptions were made.... 117

Table 3.7: Responsory series (in parallel) from BL Addl 49363
    and Addl 43405... 118

Table 3.8: Sources of lessons for Advent Sunday in Sarum, York,
    Hereford, and monastic breviaries................................. 120

Table 3.9: Divisions of lessons from Isaiah in three York breviaries........ 121

Table 3.10: Divisions of lessons from Isaiah in two Hereford breviaries, ... 122

Table 3.11: Order of sungtexts for the two monastic breviaries
    with the monastic cursus and Bodl. University College 9 126

Table 3.12: Orders of sungtexts for Thomas Becket
    in the three secular Uses. 128

Table 3.13: Six Sarum manuscripts with similar lessons for Thomas. 129

Table 3.14a: Orders of sungtexts for the Office of the Dead
    in the three secular Uses... 134

Table 3.14b: Divisions of lessons for the Office of the Dead
in the three secular Uses.. 136

Table 3.15: Manuscripts from which the Office of the Dead
was transcribed.. 137

Table 3.16: Sources from which the proper Office for William
has been transcribed.. 145

Table 4.1: Kalendars containing the *nova festa*. 191

Table 4.2: Feasts to be observed in the diocese of London (1245–1259)... 195

Table 4.3: Groups of manuscripts studied by Reames.................... 205

ACKNOWLEDGEMENTS

I am grateful for the erudition and support of Dr Cristina Dondi and Prof. Richard Sharpe, the supervisors of the doctoral thesis upon which this volume is based.

Funding for aspects of this study came from Worcester College, Oxford; the Colin Matthew Fund, St Hugh's College, Oxford; and the Scottish Borders Council. Prof. Elizabeth Eva Leach and Prof. Robert Saxton opened the door to teaching. Another grant administered by Prof. Andrew Hughes allowed me to arrange for the digitization of the Arundel antiphonal, for which work permission was granted by the Lady Herries of Terregles. Staff members from many libraries and other institutions were good enough to assist me in the study of a great many manuscripts, and offered hospitality and assistance in many ways. I thank all who were helpful, and especially Dom David Foster OSB of Downside Abbey; Jan Graffius of Stonyhurst College; Dr Kate Harris of Longleat; Rachel Hosker and staff at the Heritage Hub in Hawick; Dr Dorothy Johnston of Nottingham University Library; Enrica Lozzi of the Alessandrina Library, Rome; Vanessa Mitchell of Blackburn Museum, who tracked down a particularly recalcitrant newspaper article; Catherine Newley of Colchester Castle Museum; Sarah Rodger of Arundel Castle Archives; Abbot Geoffrey Scott OSB of Douai Abbey; and Peter Young of York Minster. Like many others before me I am especially thankful for the help of the staff of Duke Humfrey's Library, still a collegial haven, and (during the recent exile of manuscript studies) all at the Special Collections Reading Room.

This published version shows the valued influence of the examiners of the thesis, Dr Benjamin Thompson and Prof. Sarah Hamilton. I am also grateful for discussions of the subject and this study in its intermediate stages with colleagues, especially with members of the AHRC Interpreting Medieval Liturgy Network, led by Prof. Hamilton and Dr Helen Gittos. Prof. Nigel Morgan shared unpublished information. For commiserations about performance texts

I thank Prof. Elisabeth Dutton. In the years since the completion of the thesis Prof. John Harper has offered encouragement and support, and also commented on the complete text. Finally, I have been privileged to have become better acquainted with Prof. Richard Pfaff, whose friendship and guidance have been as valuable as his important work on the English liturgy. While wisdom from others has tempered many wayward thoughts, any faults in the present text are mine alone.

My parents provided moral — and material — support. The Revd Dr Jonathan Arnold was a true friend. In addition to many kindnesses, my wife Dr Jennifer Rushworth proof-read the text, prepared the final copy, and suggested many of the epigraphs. Every page shows her influence. Prof. Andrew Hughes supplied the idea, and, guiding me in the spirit of Proverbs 22. 6, helped in ways too numerous to mention. This book is dedicated to his memory.

Matthew Cheung Salisbury

Feast of St Columba 2013
Worcester College, Oxford
Raw End Farm, Halifax

ABBREVIATIONS

Addl   Additional

Aug.   Augustinians

BL   British Library

Bodl.   Bodleian

BVM   Blessed Virgin Mary

C&S   *Councils & Synods, with Other Documents Relating to the English Church: AD 1205–1313*, ed. by F. M. Powicke and C. R. Cheney (Oxford: Clarendon Press, 1964)

Camb.   Cambridge

CAO   Hesbert, René-Jean, *Corpus Antiphonalium Officii*, Rerum Ecclesiasticarum Documenta Series Maior 7–12, 6 vols (Rome: Herder, 1963–79)

Dugdale   *Monasticon anglicanum: A History of the Abbies and other Monasteries, Hospitals, Frieries, and Cathedral and Collegiate Churches, with their Dependencies, in England and Wales*, ed. by William Dugdale, rev. by John Caley, Henry Ellis, and Bulkeley Bandinel, 6 vols (London: [n. publ.], 1817–30) [All citations are from volume 6]

Haddan and Stubbs
              Councils and Ecclesiastical Documents Relating to Great Britain and Ireland, ed. by Arthur W. Haddan and William Stubbs, 3 vols, new edn (Oxford: Clarendon Press, 1964)

HE   Bede, *The Ecclesiastical History of the English People*, ed. by Judith McClure and Roger Collins (Oxford: Oxford University Press, 2008)

Oct.	Octave
Ord.	Ordination
OSB	Order of St Benedict
Pfaff, *LME*	Richard W. Pfaff, *The Liturgy in Medieval England: A History* (Cambridge: Cambridge University Press, 2009)
PL	*Patrologiae cursus completus: series latina*, ed. by Jacques-Paul Migne, 221 vols (Paris, 1844–64)
RC	*Regularis Concordia Anglicae Nationis Monachorum Sanctimoni- aliumque* [The Monastic Agreement of the Monks and Nuns of the English Nation], ed. by Thomas Symons (London: Nelson, 1953)
Reg. Chichele	*The Register of Henry Chichele, Archbishop of Canterbury, 1414– 1443*, ed. by E. F. Jacob, 4 vols (Oxford: Oxford University Press, 1937–47)
Tr.	Translation
UL	University Library
WC	*Concilia Magnae Britanniae et Hiberniae, a synodo Verolamiensi AD 496 ad Londinensem AD 1717*, ed. by David Wilkins, 4 vols (London, 1737)

Abbreviations Relating to Sungtexts

Liturgical texts are often referred to in the following format, MR3, i.e., the third responsory of Matins. See Andrew Hughes, *Medieval Manuscripts for Mass and Office: A Guide to their Organisation and Terminology* (Toronto: University of Toronto Press, 1982), inside front cover.

V = Vespers, M = Matins, L = Lauds

A = Antiphon, E = Canticle antiphon, L = Lesson, R = Responsory, V = Verse

MRV6, then, represents both Matins responsory 6 and its corresponding verse.

INTRODUCTION

> In pre-mechanical printing there is no such thing as a duplicate.
>
> Bent Juel-Jensen, cited in the *Bodleian Library Record*

John Flood has reported an episode from the history of liturgical books, in which 'as late as 1485 or 1487 we hear of nervous or incredulous clerics [...] laboriously checking hundreds of printed missals individually to see that they really were identical'.[1] This story may be easily dismissed as an entertaining anecdote through which the modern reader, endowed with the unassailable truth that every copy of an edition of a printed book is identical, can enjoy yet another laugh at the expense of the ignorant medieval mind. But any humour ought to be dampened by the fact that modern descriptions of English liturgical manuscripts, the books which contained the texts and chants for Mass and the Divine Office, are often founded on equally irrational assumptions. This study, which examines manuscript witnesses of the Office, the daily round of canonical hours of prayer, is based on the axiom that all such manuscripts ought to be considered as individuals. This premise, and this premise only, will allow the definition of constitutive criteria for each of the several English liturgical Uses (patterns of observances, texts, and ceremonial used in a particular region or diocese), namely the baseline characteristics found in manuscripts associated with each Use. It makes possible the recording and analysis of the distinct and diverse contents of individual manuscripts, illustrating how and why individual manuscripts may have been created or modified, and how service books and the rites they transmit were altered over time. These analyses will show that

---

[1] John Flood, '"Volentes sibi comparare infrascriptos libros impressos...": Printed Books as a Commercial Commodity in the Fifteenth Century', in *Incunabula and their Readers: Printing, Selling, and Using Books in the Fifteenth Century*, ed. by Kristian Jensen (London: British Library, 2003), pp. 139–51 (p. 139).

liturgical books reflect a wide range of influences on their contents, and on the worship of the medieval English Church. I contend in what follows that the sometimes dramatic differences between manuscript service books indicate:

1. That a set of constitutive elements for each of the several secular liturgical Uses of late medieval England can be quantified with reference to a large number of surviving, complete witnesses;

2. That the dominant such Use, known as the Use of Sarum because of its emergence in the late 1200s from the liturgical practices associated with Salisbury Cathedral, was subject to an abundance of simultaneous but dissimilar influences as it spread throughout the south of England: some of these sought to standardize liturgical practice, perhaps in response to criticism from Wycliffite or other circles or to the need to streamline the Office based on the proliferation of detail and additional observances; others reflected regionalizing influences, witnessed by the introduction (or re-introduction) of local preferences, especially in rubrics and lessons;

3. That local adoption of authoritative prescriptions concerning liturgy was affected by numerous, often unidentifiable factors, some of which can be characterized using the manuscript evidence. In particular, the surprisingly regional character in some witnesses of the Office is consistent with the diocesan bishop or other local figure being the authority for the conduct of liturgy, a proposition supported by evidence from diocesan and provincial statutes and other documentary evidence;

4. That each manuscript witness of the English liturgy must, consequently, be treated as a unique witness, a practice that has not yet found widespread adoption.

The present state of affairs is stereotyped as follows. Once a manuscript has been assigned by some procedure to a number of useful categories (say, a breviary, with notation, of the liturgical Use of Sarum), it is often deemed unnecessary by cataloguers to study the contents in greater detail. The texts and music contained in such books are understood to conform to the standard ones for the region, or for the Use, to which the book has been assigned: for instance, Falconer Madan's tests for liturgical Use, based on incipits of two texts, 'suffice to differentiate nearly all local Uses.'[2] Here lies the conceit: the notion that such standard versions of the contents existed wholesale in liturgical manuscripts.

[2] Falconer Madan, 'The Localization of Manuscripts', in *Essays in History Presented to Reginald Lane Poole*, ed. by H. W. C. Davis (Oxford: Clarendon Press, 1927), pp. 5–23 (p. 22).

This is an incorrect and hardly defensible impression, originally formed on the basis of inadequate methodology and ideological preoccupations, but it is one that is rarely questioned.[3] To give a central example, the properties that identify specific English liturgical Uses have never been defined with reference to more than a few of the surviving sources, perhaps because the identification of such properties is made difficult by the variation among the witnesses of any category of liturgical book. Comparative studies of complex sources which take into account more than a few criteria are, by their nature, triggers for confusion.

The potentially tedious and unrewarding work of assessing the differences among scores of books already assigned to convenient categories has often been displaced by a need to compare single witnesses of different liturgical Uses, for the more immediately fulfilling purpose of discovering the origins of the Christian liturgy.[4] Such work is a natural outcome of liturgical research, and often the sole purpose for which it is undertaken. But these projects have been ill served by their limited sample size, for reasons to be outlined here. Any impressions of a liturgical Use, at least for the Divine Office, have been clouded by inadequate comparisons of single manuscripts or printed books, framed as representative sources of different liturgical traditions, and by the employment as exemplars of modern editions, usually transcriptions of early printed liturgical books which themselves do not always reflect the manuscript tradition. That consultation of the antecedent manuscripts is a rare undertaking may be interpreted as a result of the availability of such editions: Sherry Reames has suggested that scholars take for granted the uniform nature of the liturgy and therefore believe that 'there is nothing to be learned from the manuscripts that cannot be learned faster and more conveniently from the printed versions'.[5] After all, the objec-

---

[3] Chadd points out the 'striking' amount of difference 'for a text purporting to represent a uniform Use', in 'Beyond the Frontiers: Guides for Uncharted Territory', delivered at Frontiers of Research in Medieval Music, Dartmouth College, USA, summer 1988 (revised typescript dated October 1999, unpublished).

[4] The most obvious and recent published example is René-Jean Hesbert's *Corpus Antiphonalium Officii*, Rerum Ecclesiasticarum Documenta Series Maior, 7–12, 6 vols (Rome: Herder, 1963–79), discussed below, the publication of which was accelerated in order to serve the task of liturgical revision during and after the Second Vatican Council. Richard Pfaff has thoughtfully and dispassionately discussed the issues surrounding the division of 'liturgical studies' into two approaches, one 'largely theological and pastoral' and with its origins in the Liturgical Movement; and one principally philological and medieval. See Richard Pfaff, 'Liturgical Studies Today: One Subject or Two?', *Journal of Ecclesiastical History*, 45 (1994), 325–32.

[5] Sherry Reames, 'Lectionary Revision in Sarum Breviaries and the Origins of the Early Printed Editions', *Journal of the Early Book Society*, 9 (2006), 95–115 (p. 95).

tives of those who describe medieval manuscripts, and indeed of scholars who need to use liturgical material, among them musicologists, hagiographers, and literary specialists, would be best served by just such a uniform version, but such a generic *ordo* is not capable of being generated from the surviving manuscript evidence.[6] Reames notes that there are so many 'surprising divergences' from the standard printed editions that the idea of the fixity of Sarum must be questioned entirely.[7] Consequently, I propose that the consideration of as many manuscripts as possible, in as much detail as possible, is the only way to address central questions: how the contents of liturgical books were constructed and modified, how they betray ecclesiastical influences, and most importantly, how a liturgical Use may be defined. This must be carried out by examining either a number of sections of relatively few witnesses, or studying limited contents in a more substantial number of witnesses. In all cases a cumulative assessment of the character of a book, based on multiple criteria, should be made.

'Use' is a key category that supplies an identity and perhaps even an origin for a liturgical book. Were the texts and chants to be as uniform as scholars have believed, the identification of key characteristics of the Sarum and York Uses would be as simple as comparing the synoptic Gospels in parallel columns. Sometimes, this has been done.[8] But despite the frequency of application of the concept of a Use, it is impossible to abstract the contents of, for instance, all books of the Use of Sarum such that 'the third lesson at Matins of the second Sunday after Epiphany' is a single, identifiable text in every witness of a Use. This study will suggest that until the advent of printing, no such absolute, uniform text or chant repertory existed for any secular English Use. Indeed such texts

---

[6] This is an observation that is even more valid for the Kalendar and for other sections where local preferences were accommodated. To give one striking example, in a study of lessons for saints' days in manuscripts and printed books associated with Sarum, Sherry Reames has shown that the surviving books associated with Sarum Use can be grouped into over a dozen textual traditions. See Reames, 'Late Medieval Efforts at Standardization and Reform in the Sarum Lessons for Saints' Days', in *Design and Distribution of Late Medieval Manuscripts in England*, ed. by Margaret Connolly and Linne R. Mooney (Woodbridge: Boydell and Brewer, 2008), pp. 91–117 (p. 92).

[7] Sherry Reames, 'Unexpected Texts for Saints in some Sarum Breviary Manuscripts', in *The Study of Medieval Manuscripts of England: Festschrift in Honor of Richard W. Pfaff*, ed. by George Hardin Brown and Linda Ehrsam Voigts (Turnhout: Brepols, 2010), pp. 163–84 (p. 163).

[8] For instance, William Maskell, *The Ancient Liturgy of the Church of England: According to the Uses of Sarum, Bangor, York, & Hereford and the Modern Roman Liturgy Arranged in Parallel Columns* (London: William Pickering, 1844), a work that is still being referenced in the literature.

and chants as were transmitted in the printed editions, as Reames has suggested for the lessons, do not always represent the prevailing tradition in the surviving manuscripts. Instead, English manuscripts of the liturgical Office transmit varied, strong features that allow the development of textual families within a morass of less useful variation. The existence of variation in the sources is the enabler of their historical value, and the fact that this variation has hitherto been ignored has furthered the assumption that the sources are not much good save for reading and consulting the apparently uniform texts which they contain.

* * *

This study identifies key characteristics of each of the three secular Uses of Sarum, York, and Hereford: in every case, books of the same Use are most reliably linked not by their ceremonial, rubrics, presentation of feastdays in the Kalendar, divisions of psalmody, or other such genres, but instead by their sungtexts,[9] a subset of which may be used to construct summaries known as 'responsory series'. Kalendars and the contents of the Sanctorale can also, cumulatively, supply confirmation. In addition to the principal transregional Uses, I also lay out some local patterns according to the hagiographical evidence. But since all manuscripts are subject to a range of influences during manufacture, all 'breviaries of the Use of Sarum' are different, unlike printed editions of the later twentieth and twenty-first centuries.[10] If nothing else more blatant, each manuscript copy has a signature of apparently trivial variants, sometimes known as 'minor encoding habits',[11] that can, with some work, supply very useful information about where a book was produced, where it was used, and the ways

[9] Literally *texts that are sung to melodies*: a term coined by Andrew Hughes. See his *Medieval Manuscripts for Mass and Office: A Guide to their Organisation and Terminology* (Toronto: University of Toronto Press, 1982), p. xv.

[10] As David Chadd wrote, 'the designation "Sarum missal" is one which covers a multitude of phenomena.' See Chadd, 'Liturgical Books: Catalogues, Editions and Inventories', in *Die Erschließung der Quellen des mittelalterlichen liturgischen Gesangs*, ed. by David Hiley, Wolfenbütteler Mittelalter-Studien, 18 (Wiesbaden: Harrassowitz in Kommission, 2004), pp. 43–74 (p. 46). Andrew Hughes and I have propounded the idea, related to one of the principal arguments of the present work, that each early printed liturgical book must be treated like a manuscript: see our *Cataloguing Discrepancies: The Printed York Breviary of 1493* (Toronto: University of Toronto Press, 2011).

[11] William J. Paisley is responsible for my use of this term, which was initially applied to attempts to infer authorship from such habits: see his 'Identifying the Unknown Communicator in Painting, Literature and Music: The Significance of Minor Encoding Habits', *Journal of Communication*, 14 (1964), 219–37.

that the text and music therein contained have been transmitted. These are all matters of general scholarly interest. The analysis of individual manuscripts produces inferences not only about the *manufacture* of books, one by one, from the character of their variants, but also about the development and change of the rites contained in the manuscripts. Both types of inference are valuable for assessing the effects of deliberate change on the manuscripts and their contents, and how the extant witnesses confirm or deny the received historical narrative about the development of medieval English worship.

Perhaps some of these statements are truisms. But they have been neglected by every historian or musicologist who, for example, has made reference to the text or music 'of the York Use' with the implication that some *Urtext* is retrievable, or who has neglected to record the shelfmark of some breviary from which he has transcribed some contents on the understanding that it is a single copy of a uniform liturgical pattern, or who has made assumptions, methodological or otherwise, based on the presumed existence of a concrete and invariant canon of texts.

I set out to determine, in a more comprehensive survey than had yet been carried out on the surviving manuscripts (encompassing data from one hundred and seventy-seven breviaries, antiphonals, and other manuscripts for English use in British and Irish libraries), whether *any* consistent identifying characteristics could be identified for the several English liturgical Uses of the Middle Ages. In a few words, David Chadd had already outlined the necessary method: to identify the differences between sources, and then to assess the relative significance of those differences.[12] This deceptively simple procedure was, of course, complicated by the manifold variations in every manuscript consulted. It was clear that the first step must be to collect afresh pertinent, representative data from the manuscripts in order to make reasoned conjectures about their relation to antecedent archetypical texts and their dissemination and enactment. The second stage must be to determine for each single source, by means of analysis of its texts, to which known sources it may be related. These types of enquiry, repeated for every manuscript, make possible reasonable comments on the corpus as a whole. It must then be ascertained, or at least asked, whether standard versions or standard components of any medieval English Use ever existed. If not, one ought to ask in which of their complex components were manuscripts apparently of some given Use most consistent. Questions whose answers are of broad import present themselves: What are the parameters that

---

[12] Chadd, 'Liturgical Books', p. 43.

we should employ to diagnose the Use of an unknown manuscript? How was a liturgical Use understood by its contemporaries? I will suggest that, owing to the possibly multifarious influences on the contents of different sections of a service book, the assessment of the Use of a book must be based on a cumulative assessment of all sections and of different types of content, rather than relying on one or two diagnostics as has been the case. Through analysis of the surviving, complete sources, I lay out a series of 'constitutive criteria' for each of the three secular Uses against which future comparative analyses of manuscripts can be made.

Far from being worthless, or merely a textual minefield for which the critical apparatus of a synthetic, majoritarian text would be impossibly extensive,[13] the variants found in individual sources contribute to our understanding of their manufacture and practical use. Analysis of the hagiographical evidence across a wider range of manuscripts supplies insights into the origins and movements of saints' cults and the adherence of local centres to episcopal prescriptions; these patterns are surveyed in chapter 2. Textual variants are studied in chapter 3, and an attempt to reconcile the variants with the historical developments which may have precipitated them is in chapter 4. The manuscripts taken as a whole demonstrate that the liturgy of the medieval Church in England was neither static nor prescribed, but a varied experience shaped by local practice.[14] The extant sources vary in a surprising range of aspects, but within individual Uses some contents are absolutely consistent. It would seem that some changes to liturgical texts were deliberately applied or enforced, in attempts to create or preserve specific traditions, and that others simply reflected contemporary trends in the transmission of text and music, and varying adherence to authority.[15] To distinguish between these two possibilities an informed knowledge of the complete picture, in all available sources, was required. Each manuscript of the liturgical Office needed, therefore, to be treated as an individual, a unique witness.

The first chapter of the present volume addresses the historiography of liturgical research, assessing previous work and exploring the origins of the present methodology. A brief history of the conventional understanding of English lit-

---

[13] Analyses for chapter 3 required the preparation of an edition too extensive and convoluted to appear here.

[14] Among others, Eamon Duffy has questioned the received narratives about the lay experience of religion, particularly on a local level, in *The Stripping of the Altars: Traditional Religion in England 1400–c. 1580* (New Haven: Yale University Press, 1992).

[15] The application of systematic philological methods is problematic: see Stephen G. Nichols, 'Philology in a Manuscript Culture', *Speculum*, 65 (1990), 1–10.

urgy is supplied, a necessary foundation for what follows. The background for liturgical and liturgico-musicological research is then thoroughly documented, showing that the limitations of the present resources are a result of a decades-long dependence on the need to fit sources into identifiable categories. Another observation, clear from the first part of this Introduction, is that manuscript sources have been treated like printed books. Their contents, once established as to Use by some means, usually by consultation of one of the modern editions, are assumed to be invariant from the model. Any component of a liturgical book, then, say the 'Sarum litany', the 'York hymn at Corpus Christi', or the 'Sarum saints', as so often in the imitable and influential catalogues of M. R. James among others, are considered as immutable from copy to copy as a literary work. It may be the case that there was a group of saints whose feasts were frequently observed in Sarum manuscripts (and chapter 2 does indeed present a 'normative Sarum kalendar'). But I suggest that while on a practical level these 'Sarum saints' may have been the principal influence on the construction of any single manuscript kalendar for 'Sarum Use', there were undoubtedly other influences such as regional observances and the local reaction to province-wide promulgations of saints, which have ensured that no two kalendars are identical. One is reminded of the 'ideal copy' of descriptive bibliography, an artificial version that ought, paradoxically, to be at least as correct as the best real copy. It is no wonder that the reprints from single editions of liturgical texts, such as Procter and Wordsworth's reprint of the 1531 Sarum Breviary, have been the sole resources on which modern scholars can rely.[16] More optimistically, I also survey the useful inheritance from the past two hundred years of serious liturgical scholarship. There has been a shift towards quantitative methods of comparison and the compilation of large quantities of data within which individual sources and traditions can be compared. The exhaustive research carried out throughout the twentieth century supplies the modern student with a huge corpus of material with which to compare observations for the English books. Although the project of an archetype or *Urtext* is now discredited, the raw data now available are unparalleled. In the final section of chapter 1, I discuss the data and methodologies inherited by modern scholars, enumerate their benefits and shortcomings, and show how the present research is founded on improved forms of similar methods. Most recently, Nigel Morgan and Sherry Reames have compared dozens of manuscript Sanctorales in order to produce

---

[16] *Breviarium ad usum insignis ecclesiae Sarum*, ed. by Francis Procter and Christopher Wordsworth, 3 vols (Cambridge: Cambridge University Press, 1879–86).

inventories and descriptions of the hagiographical lessons for saints. Andrew Hughes, Richard Pfaff, David Chadd, and others have defined new methods of examining the sources, either compiling complete texts from a handful of manuscripts, or comparing hundreds of copies of the same liturgical observance. The next step, it would seem, is to carry out research in both directions.

In the second chapter, therefore, I examine the key sections of every manuscript. Kalendars, Sanctorales, responsory series, and other data are compared in order to identify, situate, and document the contents of the manuscripts, and give some account of their structure and variety, with the aim of identifying some reliable characteristics of Sarum, York, and Hereford books. The emphasis here is on the presence or absence of items (sections, saints, texts: is there a Kalendar? is Thomas Becket in it? Are his proper texts in the Sanctorale?) throughout entire volumes, with minimal demand on word by-word analysis. Responsory series, perhaps representatives of the contents of the Temporale and Sanctorale, are relatively stable. By comparison, the saints in kalendars across the corpus of manuscripts are much more likely to vary, apparently dependent on local practices, and it is possible for the first time to characterize the kalendars of manuscripts of several geographical regions *within* a Use by listing saints whose feasts appear most frequently, with a view to establishing where certain local saints were observed, and to what degree the official promulgation of saints in the late Middle Ages bore fruit in manuscript service books.

The third chapter embarks on a more detailed examination of the texts of four liturgical observances: Advent Sunday, the feast of St Thomas Becket, and the Office of the Dead are studied across all three Uses, and a case-study for York alone, documenting an observance restricted to one region, examines the office for St William of York. Based on the analyses of entire books, a subset of manuscripts is selected for word-by-word and pitch-by-pitch transcription and editorial work. At this level of detail, demonstrating the practical differences in contents across the books and the liturgical year, the amount of variation is magnified, with the proper texts for William's feast (which were of extremely limited distribution) in ways varying as greatly as Advent Sunday. It is shown that the Sarum manuscripts alone are subject to a range of influences, only one of which can be completely associated with the eponymous cathedral.

Some sources, like the Sarum Ordinal and Customary (Salisbury Cathedral MS 175) consciously transmit the liturgy of Salisbury Cathedral. Many of these date from the late thirteenth century or later, some time after the assembly of the early Sarum Ordinals. Others reflect the extensive promulgation of a liturgical pattern easily associated with Salisbury through its sungtexts, but with other aspects deliberately modified to make it usable in the widest range of venues. Interest in harmonizing and reforming the generic 'Sarum' liturgy has been, not necessarily correctly, associated closely with Henry Chichele, archbishop of Canterbury 1414–43. During his archiepiscopate there is evidence that several large institutions, including Chichester and St Paul's cathedrals, and many smaller bodies adopted Sarum, and the evidence for Chichele's personal actions in this regard are evaluated in chapter 3. In any case it has been suggested that fifteenth-century clerical authorities favoured a revision of the increasingly unwieldy, elaborate, and impractical Office, perhaps in response to Wycliffite criticism.

Other influences reintroduced local variation, mostly expansion on the generic pattern in light of new developments. The unifying feature of these manuscripts is the interest, shared by different constituencies, in creating a version of the Sarum Office which retained or inspired a local character, especially as concerned specific rubrics and lessons.

The fourth chapter examines the historical context for liturgical developments in medieval Britain, in order to contextualize the results from the liturgical and textual analyses. How and when were saints imposed on the liturgy? Indeed, how was the Use of Sarum imposed? The gradual adoption of the Sarum pattern is upheld by documentary evidence; and the imposition of saints and feastdays across the province of Canterbury is shown to support the important role of diocesan and local prescriptions. The final section explores matters of the transmission of text and music, in written form, in medieval sources. Amongst the conclusions, links are drawn between the trends in variation and potential reasons for difference.

On Music

To ignore the melodies to which much liturgical text was set is to ignore the element that makes 'sungtexts' unique and, by consequence, to ignore half of the evidence that a codex can supply. The melodic data were collected from all witnesses of the textual analysis which contained music. These data, some of which have been analysed, are awaiting publication in other venues. This study, for the sake of brevity and simplicity, does not treat the data fully and indeed makes only a single significant excursus into the musical, in the section discussing the texts and music of the Office of St William.

Chapter 1

STUDYING THE ENGLISH OFFICE LITURGY

The presence of the original is the prerequisite to the concept of authenticity.[1]
Walter Benjamin, *The Work of Art in the Age of Mechanical Reproduction*

This chapter introduces liturgical manuscripts as historical sources and illustrates the complex structures they contain which allow the individual witnesses to be compared profitably. It summarizes the work done to date in the field of 'comparative liturgy', and establishes that there is a clear gap in scholarly activity: existing, conventional methods of describing such manuscripts are not sufficient to document the variation and discernible patterns, the very causes of their historical significance. The tasks that remain to be done — the elucidation of the constitutive characteristics of each English Use and the analysis of divergent contents in comparable manuscripts — are outlined and the method of the present study explained in light of existing scholarship.

The Influence of Liturgy

The liturgy of the medieval period affected culture in many ways. Conceptions of time and of the day in the Middle Ages were, unconsciously or otherwise, given structure by the liturgical day and year. Cults of saints could be spread, and later tracked, by their appearance in liturgical volumes. The repetition of formulae and the theological truths imparted by liturgical texts were no doubt a contributing factor to the internalization of Church doctrine and were them-

---

[1] Walter Benjamin, 'The Work of Art in the Age of Mechanical Reproduction', in *Illuminations*, ed. by Hannah Arendt and trans. by Harry Zorn (London: Pimlico, 1999), pp. 211–44 (p. 214).

selves reflective of piety. The continual practice and presence of the liturgy in the public and private spheres ensured that the central tenets of religion and the fundamentals of catholic theology which they propounded, such as the doctrine of the purgation of souls by the prayers of the living, were frequently endorsed and brought to mind. Perhaps as a consequence, the texts of the liturgy had an great influence on medieval literature, causing readers and writers to be familiar with liturgical forms and with the Scriptural and especially psalmodic texts which the liturgy brought to particular prominence. The influence of liturgical texts and themes on literary works, both canonical and local, has been well documented. A series of articles by Ronald L. Martinez gives a strong case for the liturgical inspiration behind elements of works by Dante and Petrarch; among English works, a recent study by Penny Granger investigates liturgical references in the N-Town Plays.[2] Similarly, the influence of liturgical music on other religious and secular forms in the Middle Ages requires no comment: sacred polyphony of all varieties owes its existence to antecedent plainsong forms. More obviously, liturgical manuscripts ought to be seen as key sources for insight into the practical activities of the medieval Church: if nothing else, they give some sense of what was deemed important to record in a permanent way about what went on in church, and how the relationship between text, memory, and performance should to be understood.[3] In more recent times, accounts of elaborate and sometimes esoteric liturgical acts, especially processions, represent one of the most prevalent and colourful topoi in scholarly writing about the Middle Ages, especially to illustrate aspects of daily life. But, as Cyrille Vogel has indicated, there are difficulties with interpreting these rites, however florid, as sources for the history of Christian civilization.[4] These problems are functional rather than intellectual.

---

[2] See Ronald L. Martinez, 'Dante's Forese, the Book of Job, and the Office of the Dead: A Note on *Purgatorio* 23', *Dante Studies*, 120 (2002), 1–16, and 'Mourning Laura in the *Canzoniere*: Lessons from Lamentations', *Modern Language Notes*, 118 (2003), 1–45; also, Penny Granger, *The N-Town Plays: Drama and Liturgy in Medieval East Anglia* (Woodbridge: Boydell and Brewer, 2009).

[3] See Leo Treitler, 'Written Music and Oral Music: Improvisation in Medieval Performance' and 'Oral, Written, and Literate Process in the Music of the Middle Ages', both collected in his *With Voice and Pen: Coming to know Medieval Song and How it was Made* (Oxford: Oxford University Press, 2003), pp. 39–67 and pp. 230–51 respectively.

[4] Cyrille Vogel, *Introduction aux sources de l'histoire du culte chrétien au Moyen Âge*, Biblioteca degli Studi Medievali, 1 (Spoleto: Centro Italiano di Studi sull'Alto Medioevo, 1966), p. 9.

The Structures of Liturgy

One of the principal factors which has constrained meaningful research with a large group of manuscript sources of the liturgical Office is the structure of such books. Without a clear sense of the function, or of the underlying principles of the liturgy which determine the contents, it is difficult to arrive at an assessment of which components of a convoluted breviary or antiphonal may be of any help in distinguishing unique from ubiquitous contents. Further, catalogues which include liturgical manuscripts are not normally designed with such complex, idiosyncratic structures in mind, and thus omit or incompletely document some of the detail. A one-line summary stating that some manuscript contains a 'Sarum kalendar' is not ideal. As a result of more or less summary description, many manuscripts do not appear particularly interesting, and can be overlooked, especially if they do not contain illuminated sections or musical notation. By contrast, manuscripts such as BL Stowe MS 12, an impressive fourteenth-century illuminated Sarum breviary from Norwich, have attracted considerable interest and interdisciplinary attention to their contents and presentation.[5]

All Sarum breviaries have the same function, it is to be hoped, but each one contains a 'signature' of material which distinguishes it from the corpus and allows the circumstances for which it was written to be probed. Knowing where to find this signature must be the result of work with as many sources as possible, conscious of the way all such books are structured and with a keen eye for substantive difference. While succeeding chapters will help to define ways by which this signature may be detected, this section outlines some general principles for understanding the structure and function of different textual components of the Office and of service books generally, indicating where difference, if it exists, can be recorded usefully.

All English Office books conform to the Western Roman liturgical pattern and more specifically to the Norman strain which was one of the principal influences on English worship after the Conquest.[6] Most of the manuscripts

---

[5] For an introduction to the Stowe breviary, see Sherry Reames, 'Origins and Affiliations of the Pre-Sarum Office for Anne in the Stowe Breviary', in *Music and Medieval Manuscripts: Paleography and Performance, Essays Dedicated to Andrew Hughes*, ed. by John Haines and Randall Rosenfeld (Aldershot: Ashgate, 2004), pp. 349–68.

[6] I discuss the impact of the Norman pattern on English liturgy in *The Use of York: Characteristics of the Medieval Liturgical Office in York* (York: Borthwick Institute, 2008). Although the effect of the imported Norman liturgy seems to have been significant, Richard Pfaff questions the stability and consistency of the purported antecedent pattern: see 'Lanfranc's Supposed Purge of the

considered here are designed for the *secular* cursus rather than the *monastic* cursus; that is, the pattern of liturgy which existed in cathedrals, collegiate chapels, and parish churches, which was distinct from the pattern used in English religious communities in the structure of individual services. For instance, nine lessons were the maximum in secular Matins, as opposed to the twelve of the monastic service. The Kalendar and the extent of proper material included for each observance were more likely to vary substantially in monastic sources and less so in secular ones. In general, one impression from the work in this study was that while English secular liturgy tended to adhere to a diocesan model, it seems that monastic communities had greater flexibility in liturgical practice, both in terms of the observances celebrated and the patterns of text used. In a recent thesis Jesse Billett has argued that on the basis of 'monastic tradition', the abbot of an English Benedictine community would have had the freedom to promulgate whatever liturgical features he deemed appropriate, at least until the late tenth century.[7] It is conceivable that this principle may have continued, or that the distinctive practices of each monastery were maintained or reflected in later liturgical forms.

In every case, it is important to distinguish between the 'standard' and 'newly-composed' Offices around which the liturgical year was organized. The 'standard' Christological observances, many of which are common to all parts of the Western Church, have a well-established pattern of texts and chants of considerable antiquity. It is most interesting to observe the fresh expressions or interpretations of these texts which were developed by medieval practitioners. 'Newly-composed' observances are, for the present study, those whose existence and proper texts are both medieval in origin. They form an additional set of feasts which sometimes coincide with the ordinary Office. These new chants and texts too demand exploration. As Richard Pfaff has discovered with respect to the so-called *nova festa*, the Transfiguration, the Visitation of the Blessed Virgin, and the Holy Name of Jesus, sometimes the introduction of newly-composed observances in liturgical books does not correspond with the official introduction of the observance, whether this is caused by the promulgation of a feast or the canonization of a saint.[8]

Anglo-Saxon Calendar', in *Warriors and Churchmen in the High Middle Ages: Essays presented to Karl Leyser*, ed. by Timothy Reuter (London: Hambledon, 1992), pp. 95–108.

[7] Jesse D. Billett, 'The Divine Office in Anglo-Saxon England, 597–c. 1000' (unpublished doctoral thesis, University of Cambridge, 2009), p. 22.

[8] Richard W. Pfaff, *New Liturgical Feasts in Later Medieval England* (Oxford: Clarendon Press, 1970), and see Reames 'Origins and affiliations'.

The Office liturgy, whatever the cursus, centred on the singing of psalmody, and ordinarily encompassed all one hundred and fifty psalms in the course of one week. The other components with non-liturgical origins were the readings: either brief (for instance, the chapter at Vespers) or extended (the lessons at Matins) and contributing, especially in the latter case, to the skeletal structure of the Office. A number of textual and musical genres supplemented the psalms and readings, all with distinct functions. The texts of the liturgy, if not drawn from psalmody, were drawn from Scripture, patristic literature and sermons, or some other authoritative source with a reasonably fixed text, except in the case of newly-composed offices where the text was often composed on the basis of a saint's *Vita* or other such text.[9]

The precise contents and structure of some services on certain days were fixed as early as the sixth-century Rule of St Benedict; others by the *Regularis Concordia* of the tenth century, and others by established convention for which there is no written documentation. Billett suggests that the *Regularis Concordia* was 'the first clear evidence for the use of the Benedictine *cursus* in England.'[10] The psalms to be sung on any given day were often determined by referring to a 'liturgical' psalter (as opposed to a Biblical psalter, where psalms 1–150 were arranged sequentially), which provided antiphons and psalms arranged for the days of the week, rather than on a precise pattern peculiar to an individual day. This is particularly true for the days recorded in the Temporale, the part of a liturgical book which details the Christological feasts. Later, newly-composed offices could have a fixed pattern of antiphons, particularly if the antiphons were proper to a saint. The general structure of an Office was variable depending upon the ranking of the observance.[11] The ranking also determined how

---

[9] By newly-composed, we mean compositions of medieval origin dedicated to a saint, and often regional in origin; compare the 'standard' set of offices observed across Christendom. See Andrew Hughes, *Late Medieval Liturgical Offices: Resources for Electronic Research*, Subsidia Medievalia 23–24, 2 vols (Toronto: Pontifical Institute of Mediaeval Studies, 1994–95), I: *Texts*, 105.

[10] Billett, 'The Divine Office in Anglo-Saxon England', p. 145.

[11] Sometimes the classification of a feast can suggest its relative importance in a worshipping community; the saint to which a church is dedicated can be given special prominence. Much has been made of, for instance, the promotion in one manuscript to a 'major duplex' feast of an observance which ordinarily does not hold this classification, but Pfaff warns us that 'discussions of [the classification of feasts] tend to be rather abstract and to imply a sempiternality and permanence which were rarely the case'. Richard W. Pfaff, *The Liturgy in Medieval England: A History* (Cambridge: Cambridge University Press, 2009), p. 434. I henceforth refer to this text as Pfaff, *LME*.

much proper material would be used for a saint on his feastday: sometimes, especially for days where two feasts converged, the Office would be that of the more important saint with the middle nocturn of Matins, or sometimes a simple commemoration, used to observe the less important saint. Where an important saint had limited proper material or none at all, the texts and chants for his service could be taken from the Common of Saints, a selection of generic feasts of saints grouped by class (one or several martyrs, bishops, bishops martyr, confessors, and so on). Details of the convoluted method of ranking and classification, along with the organization of manuscripts to provide the necessary material, can be found elsewhere.[12]

It is necessary to expound upon several liturgical genres to indicate why their patterns were significant. Antiphons were intoned before and sung in full after each psalm, set to a simple, usually syllabic melody. The texts of antiphons were often drawn from the psalm, or from some other suitable text, and thematically reflected upon the psalm or some aspect of the liturgical observance. Responsories, more florid in their musical setting, followed lessons at Matins, and their texts were designed to meditate upon some aspect of the lesson. They were supplemented by verses, which continued or emphasized the sense of the responsory. These verses were sung by a cantor or small group of singers, in contrast to responsories, which were often sung by the full choir. Since antiphons and psalms were often fixed by a source external to the office in question, the patterns of responsories and verses, 'responsory series', have been instrumental in identifying differences among witnesses of the same service. I refer to antiphons, responsories, and verses as 'sungtexts', after Andrew Hughes, in contrast to those items which were sung primarily to a reciting note and those which were spoken.

Adjacent texts were often designed to complement one another. The lesson provided a stimulus for the responsory, whose theme was emphasized or contrasted in the verse, after which a portion of the responsory was often repeated. If desired, a particular image or idea could be very clearly expressed in the confluence of these texts. The consistency of the message conveyed in each Office

---

[12] John Harper, *The Forms and Orders of Western Liturgy from the Tenth to the Eighteenth Century: A Historical Introduction and Guide for Students and Musicians* (Oxford: Clarendon Press, 1991), pp. 53–57. For another introduction to the structures of the Office, see also Lila Collamore, 'Prelude: Charting the Divine Office', in *The Divine Office in the Latin Middle Ages: Methodology and Source Studies, Regional Developments, Hagiography*, ed. by Margot E. Fassler and Rebecca A. Baltzer (Oxford: Oxford University Press, 2000), pp. 3–11. See also Hughes, *Medieval Manuscripts for Mass and Office*.

is clear in the following example, which shows how themes in one genre may be expanded upon in others, and how the principal themes of the service are emphasized.

Vespers of Advent Sunday — Proper Texts from Sarum

Deus in adiutorium	Opening versicles
A. Benedictus Dominus Deus meus. Ps (Ipsum) A. In eternum et in seculum. Ps Exaltabo. A. Laudabo deum meum in vita mea. Ps Lauda anima mea dominum. A. Deo nostro iocunda sit laudacio Ps Laudate domino quoniam bonus A. Lauda Ierusalem Dominum Ps (Ipsum)	Five antiphons
Erit in novissimis diebus preparatus mons domus domini in verticem montium et eleva-bitur super colles et fluent ad eum omnes gentes.	Chapter (Isa 2. 2), the calling of the nations to the house of the Lord
R. Ecce dies veniunt dicit Dominus et suscitabo David germen iustum, et regnabit rex et sapiens erit et faciet iudicium et iusticiam in terra. Et hoc est nomen quod vocabunt eum, Dominus iustus noster. V. In diebus illis salvabitur Iuda: et Israel habitabit confidenter. Et hoc. Gloria. Dominus iustus noster.	Responsory (Jer 23. 5–6): the Lord promises the raising up of a righteous branch to David, and a king shall prosper and execute judgement; with verse (Jer 33. 16): in those days Judah and Jerusalem will be saved
Conditor alme siderum	Hymn to Jesus as redeemer
V. Rorate celi desuper R. Et nubes pluant iustum [...]	Versicle and response (Isa 45. 8): the heavens and earth bring forth salvation
Ecce nomen domini venit de longinquo et claritas eius replet orbem terrarum.	Magnificat antiphon (recalling Isa 30. 27): behold the name of the Lord from afar
Magnificat [...]	Canticle of Mary: her vow of obedience to God
Excita quesumus domine potenciam tuam et veni: ut ab imminentibus peccatorum nostrorum periculis te mereamur protegente eripi: te liberante salvari [...] Qui vivis.	Collect, appealing for the Lord's assistance to free us from sin.

The Structures of Liturgical Books

No attention has yet been given here to the physical aspects of the books themselves. The size and contents of service books for the Office were determined by the intended function of each codex, and by the other service books that might be available. To give an example, a large manuscript for choir use containing sungtexts might not include the lessons, which would need to be furnished from another source (a lectionary or other such book). The physical object may inform us, therefore, about the users and what they did with the book. Small, detailed manuscripts would not be able to be used by groups, and might be suitable particularly for individuals who required a complete volume at their stall in choir, or for travelling purposes. The expense involved in the manufacture of large choir books must have been justified by a need for their existence. Some assessments may also be made, subjectively, based on wear and tear: a well-thumbed book may have seen a good deal of use, while a pristine, illuminated book, despite the expense of its production, may never have been used in practice. Similarly it must be remembered that many sungtexts and indeed actions were performed from memory, not necessarily from the written record. In many cases a manuscript may indicate that some liturgical item is to be performed without giving any further details. The presence or absence of a text or liturgical item does not mean that it was, or was not, part of the rite.[13]

The several types of books studied here are characterized as follows. The *Breviary* contains the complete Office, normally including all sungtexts, rubrics, and often many standard texts such as *Deus in adiutorium*, the opening of each of the canonical Hours from Matins to Compline. A complete Psalter and Kalendar are usually provided. The purpose of the breviary is to be self-sufficient as a resource for saying the Office: *noted Breviaries* also contain the requisite music. The *Antiphonal* contains the sung items, much less frequently any other details. Sometimes antiphons and psalms are given elsewhere and may be absent. Rarely, some incipits of lessons may be present. The *Psalter* contains not only the psalms but often also their antiphons in liturgical order for the days of the week along with a Kalendar. Psalters were sometimes also provided with a copy of the Office of the Dead or other votive material which could be for pri-

---

[13] Richard W. Pfaff, 'Prescription and Reality in the Rubrics of Sarum Rite Service Books', in *Intellectual Life in the Middle Ages: Essays Presented to Margaret Gibson*, ed. by Leslie Smith and Benedicta Ward (London: Hambledon, 1992), pp. 197–205; repr. in Richard W. Pfaff, *Liturgical Calendars, Saints, and Services in Medieval England* (Aldershot: Ashgate, 1998), chapter XII.

vate use. Other books such as *Hymnals* or *Processionals* had specific functions within the liturgy, and contained hymnody or processional sequences; the *Tonary* supplied the melodic formulae by which the chanted lessons, prayers, and dialogues were sung along with didactic material assisting in the teaching of singers.

Supplementing these performers' books were the *Customary* and *Ordinal*, reference works which supplied precise instructions as to the observance and precedence of liturgical observances along with instructions for their performance. Such prescriptive reference works as these are often considered to be conservative as they were probably the last to be altered when a new development arose in performance; they may show which issues were under particular scrutiny, but may not be consistent with the rest of the required volumes.[14] Some of the manuscripts considered in this study do not conform completely to these categories: there are eight breviary-missals and one antiphonal-missal, which contained proper material in varying quantities both for Mass and Office; a diurnal (an Office book containing the day-hours only); and several miscellanies, whose contents are discussed in the Catalogue.

Kalendars and responsory series in Books of Hours have also been considered here to illustrate the widest range of evidence in the observance of saints' days and votive observances. While on the whole these manuscripts were created for private devotion and not for corporate recitation — and consequently have often been excluded from liturgical studies — they do frequently contain texts (and sometimes music) of liturgical votive offices such as the Lady Office and the Office of the Dead, and their evidence may therefore be valuable. It is worth mentioning that the 'Sarum' or 'York' contents of Books of Hours, when so identified, must be a part of any investigation of what ascription to a particular Use might have meant.

The contents of breviaries and antiphonals are divided into a number of sections, not all of which may be present depending on individual circumstances. The Temporale, often found at the beginning of English Office books, contains the proper offices for the Christological year from Advent Sunday to the last Sunday after Pentecost. Miscellaneous or astronomical material may then precede the Kalendar, monthly lists of saints' days, and other principal observances. Normally the Psalter follows, arranged either biblically (psalms 1–150 in order) or liturgically (organized for the days of the week). The Psalter may contain proper antiphons for use with the psalms. The Sanctorale gives proper

---

[14] Pfaff, *LME*, pp. 412–16.

texts for saints' days, normally from Andrew (30 November) to Saturninus (the following 29 November), and the Common of Saints the Office texts for saints who have no 'proper' material; that is, texts and/or chants written specifically in their honour. In English manuscripts the Sanctorale is most commonly followed by the Common of Saints; however, in about half of the manuscripts associated with York, the Common is followed by the Sanctorale.[15]

Organizing Variance and Uniformity

In order to characterize the late medieval Office and its variation Richard Pfaff has proposed four 'dimensions of decreasing degrees of uniformity' which this study will adopt: these are the structure of the books (the basic sections enumerated above); the rubrics; the contents (the account of which saints and observances appear); and the 'actual texts',[16] the sungtexts, lessons, and prayers. The components of any individual book can be assigned to one of these categories, and some potential influences related to the structure of Offices and the books that contain them are summarized here.

The *structure* (understood here as the order of sections of a codex) can vary depending on the intended and actual functions of the book, and on what other books were available or required to be used in tandem with the one in question. The *rubrics* are dependent both on the character of the observance and on authoritative prescription as well as on the local context. The *contents* will be dependent on local cults and their strength; regional observances whether popular or imposed by synodal statute; and pan-provincial mandates, as well as the particular proclivities, to varying degrees, of the copyist and the institutions for which he was working. The texts, and chants used for specific offices (*actual texts*) will depend on the grade of the feast and the extent of its promulgation. The precise choice and order of sungtexts, lessons, prayers, and rubrics are dependent on interactions with each other and with the resources available to the copyist (i.e. what is available or preferable locally; the contents of other books either to be used in association with the new book or as exemplars for text or music). As will be seen in chapter 3, the precise texts can be influenced both by developments in the promulgation of the rite and by subsequent textual branches, and also inevitably by random variation.

---

[15] Andrew Hughes and Matthew Salisbury, 'The Ideal Copy: Fallacies in the Cataloguing of Liturgical Books', *Notes and Queries*, 56 (December 2009), 490–96 (p. 493).

[16] Pfaff, *LME*, p. 429.

The diversity in these categories is studied in the succeeding two chapters. The results are compared with the narrative provided by traditional sources for ecclesiastical history in chapter 4. The complex organization of these sources, influenced as they were by precise circumstances, suggests that they are a perfect vehicle for studying the character of and influences on medieval worship.

Writing about English Liturgy in the Nineteenth and Twentieth Centuries

Motivations for studying the liturgy, a subject of considerable interest for certain constituencies, must be considered carefully. W. H. Frere has summarized the situation: liturgy, as symbolic of other theological and intellectual associations, tends to elicit strong feelings in both academic and pastoral circles.[17] This section attempts to situate the history of liturgical research in the context of wider theological and intellectual developments, and to identify the methodological basis for the present study.

The briefest of conspectuses of the pre-Reformation liturgy in the words of the editor of the Prayer Book, Thomas Cranmer, may have been unsuitably influential for English liturgiology:

> And whereas heretofore there hath been great diversity in saying and singing in Churches within this Realm; some following Salisbury Use, some Hereford Use, and some the Use of Bangor, some of York, some of Lincoln; now from henceforth all the whole Realm shall have but one Use.[18]

This observation of Cranmer's, whose point really seems to be about 'great diversity', seems to have been interpreted as satisfactory proof of existence of five great regional liturgical Uses in England in the late Middle Ages.[19] The statement is the definitive potted history of the liturgy of the medieval Church in England, because the idea of an alternative has never been pursued. Nineteenth-century liturgical historians did not restrict themselves to Cranmer's five Uses (some also tracked the putative development of the less imaginary Uses of Exeter and of St Paul's, London), and the overwhelming

---

[17] W. H. Frere, *The Principles of Religious Ceremonial* (London: Mowbray, 1928), pp. 1–10.

[18] 'Concerning the Service of the Church', preface to *The Book of Common Prayer* (1549 and succeeding editions).

[19] See for instance a letter of E. Cobham Brewer, 'Use', in *Notes and Queries*, series 7 IX (17 May 1890), 389: 'It is said that Osmund compiled the 'Use of Sarum' in 1085 or thereabouts; but can some of the correspondents [...] throw any light upon the other four referred to [in the Prayer Book]?'

picture is of an English liturgy whose witnesses could be sorted into groups associated with particular liturgical Uses, presumably based on the presence of consistent forms of worship in the witnesses of each pattern. Much of the literature concerning the liturgy of medieval England seems to take the five Uses as a methodological premise. This may have served to perpetuate their status as truth.[20] One wonders whether Cranmer's comment is anything more than an elaborate rhetorical construct meant to emphasize the import of the new Prayer Book. It is certainly likely that the preface as a whole owes much to the preface to the revised Roman Catholic breviary of Cardinal Quignon, which was inspired and influenced by Christian humanist thinking.[21]

There has been no lack of scholarly interest in liturgical topics, but it seems increasingly clear that much standard published material needs to be treated with caution, and some of it disregarded. Despite the fact that faults have been reported for some time, few are willing to undertake a task that seems as if it has already been completed. It is in the nature of the way we treat an edited text that once the editorial project has been accomplished, there needs to be a suitable reason for it to be replaced. I argue here, based on a reconsideration of previous scholarship, that while it may provide an attractive proportion of raw data for new analyses, the present state of research into English liturgy has been clouded by preconceptions about the uniformity of liturgical texts and music and also, on a more general level, damaged by the premise, based on this idea of uniformity, that it is possible and indeed highly desirable to produce an *Ur*-version of various versions of the Divine Office. In short, the preconceptions are these:

1. That the English liturgy is, from copy to copy within a given time period, relatively static, particularly since much care was taken to produce apparently careful and conservative copies;

2. That English liturgy is derived from a Roman model which itself derives from antiquity, and that there is a clear line of organic development which shows that later versions are outgrowths and/or revisions of earlier ones;

---

[20] John Harper says that the Use of Bangor, known more or less only from this Preface, 'may have been no more than a general indictment of the backward conditions in the Bangor diocese'. See his chapter, 'Liturgy and Music, 1300–1600', in *Hereford Cathedral: A History*, ed. by Gerald Aylmer and John Tiller (London: Hambledon, 2000), pp. 375–98.

[21] For which see Everard Green, 'Cardinal Quignon's Breviary', *Notes and Queries*, series 7 II (11 December 1886), 464–65, as well as the edition by J. Wickham Legg, *A Second Recension of the Quignon Breviary*, Henry Bradshaw Society, 35, 42, 2 vols (London: [n. publ.], 1908–12).

3. That there were about five liturgical Uses in England at the Reformation, distinct enough to be identifiable, and that they formed the basis of the Prayer Book liturgy that replaced them;

4. That a liturgical text can be successfully edited by transcribing and comparing the texts (and possibly music) of several printed editions (or manuscripts, if any are present);

5. That a comparison of these modern editions can show where and how liturgical patterns differed from region to region or from time to time, and that the modern editions generally represent the majority of medieval liturgical practice in England.

The simplistic and thoughtless acceptance of these principles is also indicative of the predilections of past and more recent scholars with respect to textual criticism. These editions were the fruit of the late nineteenth- and early twentieth-century 'liturgiologists' for whom the establishment of authoritative versions of specific liturgical texts for Mass and Office was the main occupation. These scholars were the inheritors of a substantial tradition of textual scholarship, in which the main objective, as for any text of a literary work, was to sift through the various and possibly erroneous or variant witnesses in order to arrive at the earliest, most common, and therefore most authoritative version. Immense editorial projects such as *Monumenta Germaniae Historica* and the revitalization of the *Acta Sanctorum* were stimulated in the nineteenth century. In Britain one of the first such important societies, whose principles of operation formed the basis for others, was the Surtees Society, founded in 1834 with the objective of 'the publication of inedited Manuscripts, illustrative of the intellectual, the moral, the religious, and the social condition of [...] parts of England and Scotland [...] a region which constituted the Ancient Kingdom of Northumberland', bringing to light the texts of documents and codices, including the 1493 Venice print of the York Breviary, 'which, in these times, few individuals would incur the risk of printing at their own cost'.[22] Similar origins are imagined for the Early English Text Society (founded 1864) for which the establishment of texts for consultation, by individuals as well as by larger-scale projects such as dictionaries, was an important philological obligation. The Henry Bradshaw Society, 'founded in the year of Our Lord 1890 for the editing

---

[22] James Raine, in an 1834 letter of invitation to potential members, quoted in *The Surtees Society 1834–1934*, ed. by A. Hamilton Thompson, Surtees Society, 150 (Durham: [n. publ.], 1939), p. 5.

of rare liturgical texts',[23] was similarly motivated to preserve and disseminate sources of local heritage. Among its key early figures was John Wickham Legg, a retired physician who was able to devote, for some years, his full energies to what had previously been a hobby.[24] The intentions of these societies, among the others which proliferated at the time, were noble and very clear. An issue that is less clear is why their early work to produce widely available editions was never supplemented by research to put those editions in context.

Another group with similar origins is the Plainsong and Medieval Music Society, founded in 1888 'for the advancement of public education in the art and science of music and in particular plainsong and medieval music by the presentation of concerts and other activities', but whose early history is characterized by the number of publications which were released. Much of the Society's early history has been narrated by Dom Anselm Hughes, for many years its Secretary. Hughes paints a picture of a Society with origins in 'the late Victorian world of cultured and prosperous leisure', founded by H. B. Briggs, one of 'that now almost extinct species of Civil Servant with a quasi-sinecure in the India Office' and with Sir John Stainer and Arthur Sullivan as vice-presidents.[25] But Hughes's comments are telling with respect to later developments: there was considerable interest within the Society to recover the liturgical Use of Sarum through the editing and publication of the necessary resources. 'This Sarum cult', wrote Hughes, 'was indeed the common denominator which held together this small group of men'. Later, he continued, 'the attempt to revivify the Sarum Use [...] faded away with the discovery by liturgical scholars that it is not the historic English tradition, but a comparatively late innovation from France.'[26] W. H. Frere's publication of the *Antiphonale Sarisburiense* from 1901 to 1924 for the Society had, of course, been anticipated in 1861 by the publication of a Sarum Missal by F. H. Dickinson.[27] Hughes was aware, in his later years, of growing divisions between parties in the Society who were concerned with the *performance* of liturgy, and those who had only an academic concern. He

---

[23] This legend is still printed in the Society's volumes.

[24] Legg's principal publication other than his edition of the *Sarum Missal* was *A Guide to the Examination of the Urine* (London: H. K. Lewis, 1869).

[25] Dom Anselm Hughes, *Septuagesima: Reminiscences of the Plainsong and Mediaeval Music Society, and of Other Things Personal and Musical* (London: Plainsong and Mediaeval Music Society, 1959), pp. 12–14.

[26] Hughes, *Septuagesima*, pp. 33–34.

[27] *Missale ad usum insignis et praeclarae ecclesiae Sarum*, ed. by F. H. Dickinson (Burntisland, 1861).

died years before the establishment of the Society's *Journal* (1978–), a scholarly vehicle, and before the diminution of the interests of performers on its Council.

A great renewal of interest in early liturgical forms was seen in the later nineteenth and early twentieth centuries, most likely as a descendant of the emphasis on public worship associated with the high church party. A significant proportion of scholars working on English liturgical topics, until quite recently, were antiquarians in holy orders. More recent assertions of the existence, antiquity, and authority of the English liturgy have come from the Anglo-Catholic corner, for allusions to Roman practice in early English sources, a perhaps inevitable result, supply a strong support for the catholicity of the Church of England. Both the early Plainsong and Medieval Music Society and the Henry Bradshaw Society had strong associations with at least the aesthetic of Anglo-Catholicism. Many Anglo-Catholics, like other descendants of the Oxford Movement, maintained a belief in the apostolicity (that is, the unbroken, authoritative descent from the early church) of the doctrine and worship of the Church of England. The liturgical evidence for this standpoint was said to have been cluttered by medieval expansion and confusion of priorities. The uncovering of a rite with apparently ancient origins, based on evidence from several surviving examples of the earliest known English liturgy, would be very advantageous as a proof of the catholicity of the Church itself, and the natural approach to this issue would be an editorial project of the sort that has been described, with its objective the synthesis of the earliest, most authoritative text, and with the act of its creation taking precedence over the collation of several different versions and attention to their diversity. With a view to apostolicity, an ancient and preferably Roman origin for the English liturgy would be highly desirable.

There is another reason why Anglican divines of the high church party were heavily involved in the search for authoritative, ancient liturgical forms. Unassociated with the major figures of the Oxford Movement, the nineteenth century also saw the development of a faction, known at least to their enemies as the 'Ritualists', who were concerned entirely with the symbolic importance of the liturgy, among other outward and visible elements of worship such as vestments and architecture. The Cambridge Camden Society (later the Ecclesiological Society) held that the success of the medieval English church as a virtuous institution could be recalled and perhaps reborn by precise re-enactment of high medieval trappings of church.[28] The physical characteristics of an ideal medieval church were established by the Society through the system-

---

[28] See James F. White, *The Cambridge Movement: The Ecclesiologists and the Gothic Revival* (Cambridge: Cambridge University Press, 1962).

atic survey of the architectural features of thousands of 'unmutilated' churches (that is, churches with no features added subsequent to their erection in the Middle Ages). Adherents argued that 'the only safe way to arrive at any general principles [...] is to observe and describe the details [...] and from a large collection of such observations, if carefully recorded, much advantage may accrue to the science'.[29] Due concern was also accorded to liturgical and musical study: indeed, their publication, the *Ecclesiologist*, held that 'liturgical science indeed ranks far higher than architectural skill and knowledge and [should be] a qualification of the ecclesiologist',[30] probably because the architectural features that were deemed desirable were tied to the practicalities of their favoured liturgical habits. In later years, and with similar motivations, the Society also began to consider music as a 'parallel branch' of ecclesiology. 'In our opinion', wrote the *Ecclesiologist*, 'the Plain Song of the Church is not only the most right, and the most beautiful method, of praising God, but also practically the most easy'.[31] Frere noted in the historical edition of *Hymns Ancient and Modern* that many of the contributions of Society member John Mason Neale to that hymnal and to the *Hymnal Noted* were drawn from medieval English practice and particularly intended to be based on Sarum patterns.[32] The comparative method propounded by the *Ecclesiologist* for the study of church architecture did not, however, extend to liturgical analyses.

The so-called 'Ornaments Rubric' was also a motivator for the Ritualists. This rubric was one of several in the 1559 Elizabethan revision of the Prayer Book which had attempted to re-introduce a catholic understanding of the liturgy and extinguish the ardently Protestant character of the Second Prayer Book of Edward VI, which had attempted to underplay the doctrine of the Real Presence. Its text is printed here:

> The chauncels shall remain, as they have done in tymes past. And here is to be noted, that the Minister at the time of the communion, and at all other tymes in hys ministracion, shall use suche ornamentes in the church, as wer in use by aucthoritie of parliament in the second yere of the reygne of king Edward the VI.[33]

[29] White, *The Cambridge Movement*, p. 50.

[30] White, *The Cambridge Movement*, p. 52.

[31] White, *The Cambridge Movement*, p. 216.

[32] White, *The Cambridge Movement*, p. 216.

[33] From the order for Morning Prayer, in the Book of Common Prayer, 1559. The 'catholic' nature of the Elizabethan prayer book has also been linked to its words of administration at Holy Communion, for which see Duffy, *The Stripping of the Altars*, p. 567.

As a consequence of this rubric (and the doctrine which it implied) being embraced, the late nineteenth century saw the reintroduction of such outward signs of catholic doctrine as the chasuble and vestments more generally, as well as the restoration of what was perceived to be the ancient (and therefore Sarum) ceremonial of the English Church.

The liturgical priorities which were a result of the Oxford Movement were also felt in the Roman Church and elsewhere: the so-called 'Liturgical Movement', perhaps both inspired by and inspiring elements of the continued high church party in the Church of England, evinced a desire to return public worship to a position of centrality within Christian life. This work was undertaken in part as a reaction to the over-prioritization of the practical implications of Christian living (i.e. to the world) and in opposition to the tendency, at least among Roman Catholics, to practice various forms of private devotion in lieu of public worship in the form of the Eucharist.

Among the success stories of the Liturgical Movement was the flourishing of the Abbaye-de-St-Pierre, Solesmes, a Benedictine monastery that had been re-founded in 1837, one of the first monasteries to be established in France after the ravages of the Revolution. Solesmes was a product of the same French Romantic ideals which had encouraged the architect Viollet-le-Duc to desire a restitution of 'the entire human past, almost as one might collect an extensive library as the basis for further labours'.[34] Proponents of the monastery, like the Ecclesiologists, sought a better expression of the present through trappings of the glorious past. Solesmes had been founded by an ex-parish priest, Prosper Guéranger, who, in attempting to recreate the entire existence of a monastic religious community, placed a particular emphasis on the performance of Mass and Office. The practical enactment of this became a concern that soon demanded the full attention of Solesmes's budding liturgical research establishment. The immediate concern, as with the Victorian antiquarians across the Channel, was to produce new, archetypical performing editions based on the most appropriate exemplars. This work was to be done through comparative analysis of ancient sources: 'On possède la phrase gregorienne dans sa pureté', Guéranger wrote, '[si] les exemplaires de plusieurs églises éloignées s'accordent'.[35] In the earliest stages, the new liturgical experts at Solesmes, especially Dom Joseph Pothier, favoured the versions appearing in what seemed to be the earliest man-

---

[34] Eugène-Emmanuel Viollet-le-Duc, *The Foundations of Architecture: Selections from the 'Dictionnaire raisonné'*, trans. by Kenneth D. Whitehead (New York: Braziller, 1990), p. 198.

[35] Prosper Guéranger, *Institutions Liturgiques*, 3 vols (Mans, 1840–51), I (1840), 306.

uscripts. Dom André Mocquereau of Solesmes held that methods for textual criticism were equally applicable to chant.[36] No comparable efforts were taking place: France had next to no monastic communities, and none that were skilled in the editing or performance of chant.

The 1883 Arezzo Congress of Catholic prelates and chant scholars condemned 'the divergent and incorrect choir books being used in the churches [...]' and suggested the importance of 'studies and theoretical works [...] which bring light to bear on the masterworks of the liturgical tradition'.[37] In 1903 Pius X issued the *motu proprio Tra le sollecitudini*, which had many effects on the composition, performance, and promotion of church music in the Roman Catholic Church. In a triumph for Solesmes, the Pope stressed the importance of plainsong (*canto gregoriano*) as the ideal musical expression of the Church. This encyclical was also the origin of the phrase 'active participation' employed, not incidentally, in the Constitution on the Sacred Liturgy, *Sacrosanctum Concilium*, issued as a result of the Second Vatican Council, perhaps the ultimate result of the Liturgical Movement, which served not only to promote but also to reform the liturgy in order to make this more likely.[38] Both papal documents emphasize the central position of the liturgy in Catholic living, and both in their own time expressed a need for the liturgy and its origins to be thoroughly discussed and analysed. The earliest forms of liturgical practice were sought in order to promote not only apostolicity but also, especially in the case of *Sacrosanctum Concilium*, to provide an authoritative basis for the creation of new, modern rites. Two further English scholars whose works have attained some prominence were William Maskell, a Roman Catholic convert, and Edmund Bishop, a Catholic civil servant, who both produced studies dealing with various aspects of the liturgy.[39]

---

[36] André Mocquereau in *Paléographie Musicale* ser. 1, vol. 2 (1891) p. 13, quoted by Hartmut Möller, 'Research on the Antiphoner – Problems and Perspectives', *Journal of the Plainsong and Mediaeval Music Society*, 10 (1987), 1–14 (p. 9).

[37] Resolutions of the Arezzo Congress, 1883, reproduced in Appendix I of Pierre Combe, *The Restoration of Gregorian Chant: Solesmes and the Vatican Edition*, trans. by Theodore N. Marier and William Skinner (Washington DC: CUA Press, 2003), pp. 417–18.

[38] *The Documents of Vatican II*, ed. by Walter M. Abbott (London: Geoffrey Chapman, 1966).

[39] Their key works are, respectively, *The Ancient Liturgy of the Church of England* and *Liturgica Historica: Papers on the Liturgy and Religious Life of the Western Church* (Oxford: Clarendon Press, 1918). For Bishop, see N. J. Abercrombie, *The Life and Work of Edmund Bishop* (London: Longmans, 1959).

After the Second Vatican Council

The need to reform the liturgy as a result of the Second Vatican Council has already been mentioned. In an encouragement of liturgical studies, the document on the liturgy, *Sacrosanctum Concilium*, ordered the setting-up, in each region of the Church, of a

> Liturgical commission, to be assisted by experts in liturgical science, sacred music, art and pastoral practice. So far as possible the commission should be aided by some kind of Institute for Pastoral Liturgy, consisting of persons who are eminent in these matters, and including laymen as circumstances suggest. Under the direction of the above-mentioned territorial ecclesiastical authority the commission is to regulate pastoral-liturgical action throughout the territory, and to promote studies and necessary experiments whenever there is question of adaptations to be proposed to the Apostolic See.[40]

The importance of finding the most ancient and therefore most correct version of the liturgy both for Mass and Office was paramount to certain constituencies as soon as the idea of reform was proposed. At its height of scholarly activity in the later twentieth century, Solesmes was home to sophisticated methods of comparative analysis.

In his introduction to what has become one of the most important resources for liturgical research to come out of the twentieth century, the six-volume *Corpus Antiphonalium Officii* (*CAO*), the Solesmes monk René-Jean Hesbert made it clear that the imminent reform of the Roman liturgy made it necessary to speed along the publication of volumes.[41] Despite the emphatic efforts of liturgical scholars such as Hesbert, motivated by their own piety and by the best of intentions, the priority for the Council was to ensure that 'full and active participation by all the people' could be elicited, and this was evidently the priority of the commissions set up to revise the liturgy.[42] The years since Vatican II have seen a significant shift: the study of historic forms of liturgy has been diminished in favour of 'liturgics', now identified as a branch of pastoral

---

[40] *Sacrosanctum Concilium*, the *Constitution on the Sacred Liturgy* in *The Documents of Vatican II*, ed. by Walter M. Abbott (London: Geoffrey Chapman, 1966), pp. 137–77.

[41] Hesbert, *Corpus Antiphonalium Officii*, I, iii.

[42] While this phrase is most closely associated with *Sacrosanctum Concilium*, 'active participation' or 'la partecipazione attiva' was first used by Pius X in the motu proprio *Tra le sollecitudini*, 22 November 1903. < http://www.vatican.va/holy_father/pius_x/motu_proprio/ documents/hf_p-x_motu-proprio_19031122_sollecitudini_it.html> [accessed 25 June 2013].

theology dealing with worship. This development is no doubt a product of the priorities of Vatican II.

In the twentieth century the English Church has witnessed vociferous comments about liturgy from bodies such as the Anglican descendants of the Ritualist camp (and indeed bodies such as the Latin Mass Society and the Society of St Pius X), all of whom have their own preoccupations. The Prayer Book Society supports an authoritative form of worship just as the Latin Mass Society favours the Tridentine rite. Both of these examples see their preferred liturgy as unerring and descended from authoritative models, and both have done much to influence the popular understanding of the development of liturgical forms.[43] As liturgy does not seem to be seen as the province of scholarly activity, no rethinking of the existing editions, or indeed thoughts about uniformity, have taken place.

While the founders of the societies which financed and endorsed the early publication of liturgical texts may have been well-intentioned and enthusiastic, many were not trained to carry out research in the field, and the results have not aged well as editorial standards have been raised. Anselm Hughes admitted that his first publication for the Plainsong and Medieval Music Society, completed while an undergraduate, was full of errors and not likely to have been edited rigorously.[44] Nevertheless, with no other alternative, modern scholars from all disciplines with entirely different priorities and ideological preoccupations continue to use, unquestioningly, the editions of the liturgy which the societies provided for the first time. The likely users of these editions were, and are, casual users with no substantial knowledge of the medieval liturgy. Specialists in literature, drama, music, and art (among other disciplines), and especially cataloguers of manuscripts, in dealing with the presence of liturgical material, are quite rightly concerned with identifying such material and determining its significance. The modern reprints are nearly their sole means of recourse, and satisfy the need for a context for the liturgical items in question, even if it be negative, i.e., 'Not in *Brev. Sarum*; Different than in *Brev. Ebor.*'[45] For these users, it is undoubtedly preferable to have a single liturgical text, i.e. for the

---

[43] Laszlo Dobszay has ventured into these debates in his contribution to a series on 'fundamental liturgy' with Laurence Paul Hemming, *The Restoration and Organic Development of the Roman Rite* (London: T&T Clark, 2009).

[44] Hughes, *Septuagesima*, p. 24.

[45] See, for instance, the entries in N. R. Ker's *Medieval Manuscripts in British Libraries*, 5 vols (Oxford: Clarendon Press, 1969–2002) for the York breviaries in York Minster library.

third responsory at Matins of the second Sunday after Epiphany, for each of a variety of possible provenances. Pfaff has rightly pointed out that the modern existence of uniform (albeit printed) liturgical books and the employment of fixed forms of service in the present day may imply that such uniformity existed from the beginning, a fair argument if the entirely linear, organic view of liturgical development is subscribed to. All of these influences, of course, have combined to produce an atmosphere in which liturgical research, if it happened at all, was bound by methods of textual criticism which favour an overly representative approach. No one, of course, is to blame. All of the contributing factors to these shortcomings in scholarship have been products of their own times and circumstances. But one cannot help but notice one common theme: a reticence to rethink, or to challenge apparently established, apparently understood 'facts' about the liturgy in medieval England.

Organizing the Evidence

Much recent research has been concerned with the establishment of the evidence. Resources for the liturgical researcher were provided by Falconer Madan and M. R. James who, on the basis of much experience with the manuscripts during the preparation of descriptive catalogues, published methods of assessing the provenance of service books.[46] James's catalogues in particular are representative of the desire to have all such manuscripts described in some level of detail. While a few of his descriptions, some of which date from undergraduate days, contain errors they are, for the most part, still reliable.[47]

Many more lasting contributions were made by Walter Howard Frere, priest of the Community of the Resurrection, an Anglo-Catholic religious order, who later became Bishop of Truro. Frere's early work was based on similar

[46] James published a series of 'Points to be Observed in the Description and Collation of Manuscripts, particularly Books of Hours', in *A Descriptive Catalogue of the Manuscripts in the Fitzwilliam Museum* (Cambridge: Cambridge University Press, 1895), pp. xix–xli, and had completed a draft of a longer document, perhaps titled 'Manuscripts: And How to Describe Them', printed by Richard Pfaff in 'M. R. James on the Cataloguing of Manuscripts: A Draft Essay of 1906', *Scriptorium*, 31 (1977), 103–18. His final publication which treats the subject as to provenance is *The Wanderings and Homes of Manuscripts* (London: SPCK, 1919).

[47] Richard Pfaff notes this in several places in his biography *Montague Rhodes James* (London: Scolar, 1980), particularly at p. 330, where he picks up James's own words on the subject: 'If I have had a part to play, it has been that of making known, with what fulness of description I could, the existence of a mass of material, and assigning dates and provenances which in the main are, I hope, correct.'

methods to those of Henry Bradshaw, a contemporary at Cambridge: he was fond of formulating tables and 'copious [...] abbreviations' which were difficult to interpret but were often the best way to relate the evidence of comparative analysis.[48] Frere also produced the narrative which accompanied the facsimile of 'the *Antiphonale Sarisburiense*' (Camb. UL MS Mm. II. 9). His devotion to the task of describing liturgical books is illustrated by his *Bibliotheca Musico-Liturgica*, a 'Descriptive Handlist of the Musical and Latin-Liturgical MSS of the Middle Ages Preserved in the Libraries of Great Britain and Ireland' and the private 'darling' of the editor, according to Dom Gregory Dix.[49]

More recent research has often relied on abbreviations, databases, and sometimes computer assistance in order to organize and navigate the complexities of the data. The adoption of pseudoscientific principles in liturgical studies was successful on the Continent, and general parameters identified by Anton Baumstark in *Liturgie comparée*, a work which treated liturgical developments as manifestations of a natural organism.[50] In the early twentieth century Dom Gabriel Beyssac (of Solesmes) presented a 'moyen court', a short-cut to the identification of a manuscript's provenance with minimal effort which he hoped would become 'l'oeuf de Colomb de la liturgie'.[51] This method was to compare textual incipits of the Offices for the Annunciation and Assumption of the Blessed Virgin, the Triduum (Thursday–Saturday) of Holy Week, All Saints, the Office for the Dead, and the Office for the Dedication feast. Beyssac's research indicated that observable, consistent regional variation could be identified in witnesses of the Office in the responsories and their verses at Matins on those principal days, as well as on the four Sundays and three Ember Days in Advent. His method was to assign a unique number to every distinct responsory and verse, which allowed each 'responsory series' or sequence of such numbers to represent numerically the choice and order of responsories in any

[48] Sydney Nicholson, J. H. Arnold, and P. A. Browne, 'The Musician', in C. S. Phillips et al., *Walter Howard Frere, Bishop of Truro* (London: Faber and Faber, 1947), pp. 158–74 (p. 165).

[49] Dom Gregory Dix, 'The Liturgist', in Phillips, *Walter Howard Frere*, pp. 121–46 (p. 131).

[50] Anton Baumstark, *Comparative Liturgy*, revised by Bernard Botte, trans. by F. L. Cross (London: A.R. Mowbray, 1958). For a retrospective on Baumstark's work, see Fritz West, 'Baumstark's Tree and Thoughts after Harvest', in *Comparative Liturgy: Fifty Years after Anton Baumstark (1972–1948): Acts of the International Congress, Rome, 25–29 September 1998*, ed. by Robert F. Taft and Gabriele Winkler, Orientalia Christiana Analecta, 265 (Rome: Pontificio Istituto Orientale, 2001), pp. 163–89.

[51] G. M. Beyssac, 'Note sur un graduel-sacramentaire de St-Pierre-St-Denys de Bantz, du XIIᵉ siècle', *Revue Benedictine*, 31 (1921), 190–200 (p. 190).

manuscript. Beyssac used a similar method to catalogue the Alleluia verses in missals for the Sundays after Pentecost, a practice explored at length by David Hiley.[52] In 1968, Dom Jacques Froger published an early guide to 'automated' electronic textual criticism,[53] roughly contemporaneous with the early volumes of Hesbert's masterwork *CAO*.

Computer-aided work to analyse the responsory series of the Office of the Dead, based on existing work by Beyssac, was completed by Knud Ottosen, who like Hesbert was able to associate specific series with regional or local patterns.[54] Responsory series for the Triduum were studied in detail by Dom Raymond le Roux and later by Dom Pierre-Marie Gy.[55]

Among active researchers these 'evidence-based' methods continue to be used: responsory series were important to Cristina Dondi's establishment of the Norman origin of the liturgy of the Holy Sepulchre,[56] and online databases supervised by David Hiley, including lists of Advent and Dead responsory series and post-Pentecost alleluias, permit quick comparisons of the series in any book with the existing body of evidence.[57] Andrew Hughes pioneered the use of computer databases in association with complex analysis routines for large bodies of evidence, requiring the development of machine-readable summaries of liturgical data in the form of alphanumeric abbreviations.[58] CURSUS, a project which used hypertext and XML (extensible markup language, a programming language) to produce complete, cross-referenced transcriptions of English monastic Office books was cut short (and its data made inaccessible) by the death of its creator David Chadd. Apart from these scholarly projects,

---

[52] See his chapter 'Post-Pentecost Alleluias in Medieval British Liturgies', in *Music in the Medieval English Liturgy: Plainsong and Mediaeval Music Society Centennial Essays*, ed. by Susan Rankin and David Hiley (Oxford: Clarendon Press, 1993), pp. 145–74.

[53] Jacques Froger, *La Critique des textes et son automatisation*, Initiation aux nouveautés de la science, 7 (Paris: Dunod, 1968).

[54] Knud Ottosen, *The Responsories and Versicles of the Latin Office of the Dead* (Aarhus: Aarhus University Press, 1993).

[55] Raymond Le Roux, 'Repons du Triduo Sacro et de Pâques', *Etudes grégoriennes*, 18 (1979), 157–76.

[56] Cristina Dondi, *The Liturgy of the Canons Regular of the Holy Sepulchre of Jerusalem: A Study and a Catalogue of the Manuscript Sources*, Bibliotheca Victorina, 16 (Turnhout: Brepols, 2004).

[57] Cantus Planus Database <http://www.uni-regensburg.de/Fakultaeten/phil_Fak_I/Musikwissenschaft/cantus/index.htm> [accessed 25 June 2013].

[58] Hughes, *Late Medieval Liturgical Offices*.

a number of other recent efforts to use technology for the benefit of liturgical research must be questioned, especially for the casual way that contents of manuscripts are abstracted and for the promotion of the view that liturgical texts are editable from existing editions and with only occasional reference to manuscripts.

On a more positive note, Sherry Reames has published a number of detailed articles exploring the provision of lessons at Matins for saints' days in the Sanctorale. She contends that these lessons fall into a score of textual families, including a so-called 'Chichele' group, which derives its name from the association of Henry Chichele (archbishop of Canterbury 1414–43) with one of the best-known examples of the group, a prominent manuscript owned by the archbishop (Lambeth Palace MS 69). This textual tradition seems to standardize and more widely impose the liturgical pattern first associated with Salisbury Cathedral across the entire province of Canterbury. Over the last decade this work has developed into a sophisticated analysis of the subtle variants in Sanctorale lessons, which may help to explain some of the reasons for reform of the breviary.[59]

Most recently a major new work by Richard Pfaff has been published, complementing his other contributions to the literature. *The Liturgy in Medieval England: A History* is the culmination of a career-long concern with evidence in manuscripts, and Pfaff uses such evidence to supply a substantial history of events in the development of the English Mass and Office on the basis of manuscript evidence. Most usefully he has included five *excursus* which deal with matters of method when approaching liturgical sources. The episodic nature of the work helps it avoid the tendency of more teleological histories of liturgy to propose a linear sequence of developments. Pfaff has emphasized the need to avoid the definite article when discussing specific rites: he is reluctant to acknowledge the existence of anything as uniform as '*the* Sarum Missal', meaning an apparently authoritative edition produced from medieval exemplars, sometimes quite limited in number.[60]

In common with many of these projects, the present study attempts to arrive at empirically derived conclusions on the basis of evidence which is sometimes

---

[59] See her 'Late Medieval Efforts at Standardization and Reform', 'Lectionary Revision in Sarum Breviaries', 'Unexpected Texts for Saints', and also '*Mouvance* and Interpretation in Late-Medieval Latin: The Legend of St Cecilia in British Breviaries', in *Medieval Literature: Texts and Interpretation*, ed. by Tim William Machan (Binghamton, NY: Medieval and Renaissance Texts and Studies, 1991), pp. 159–89.

[60] For example, Pfaff, *LME*, p. 428.

overwhelming in its complexity, employing databases and related methods both to organize and to analyse the data. For each manuscript, the information required to produce a descriptive catalogue entry has been added to a searchable and sortable database, created with the software FileMaker Pro. Each kalendar has been transcribed and analysed using a purpose-written, automated computer programme, which also calculated the number of relations with every other kalendar in order to produce the tables of relations presented in chapter 2. Responsory series for Advent, the Triduum, and the Office of the Dead were recorded in another database. The word-by-word collation of twenty-eight witnesses of three offices was done manually, but organized on the computer.

The reasons for the present author's preoccupation with the establishment of the real contents of scores of manuscripts can be inferred from the deficiencies of early liturgical scholarship and editions, and the empirically satisfying methods employed by more recent researchers. The following chapters will outline, often in convoluted detail, most of the principal results which will allow, in the end, the condensation of a clearer picture of the development and transmission of the late medieval English Office. The first stage is to lay out the liturgical evidence: that is, the results of analyses based on the choice and order of feastdays and the liturgical texts proper to them.

LITURGICAL ANALYSIS

> A good deal of attention should be paid to the hagiology of service
> books, as contained in the Kalendar, Litany, Proper of Saints, and
> Memoriae. Here again is matter for a large book.
>
> M. R. James

The principal challenge of using liturgical manuscripts as historical sources is learning to discriminate between various copies of a text that, in theory, possess the same characteristics by virtue of having the same function. Studies of such manuscripts tend to exploit the natural organization of these manuscripts into liturgical categories: seasons, feastdays, and textual genres. Consequently, several methods have been adopted in this chapter in order to analyse such liturgical features as correspond to Pfaff's second dimension of the Office: the 'contents'. On the basis of two types of evidence, two contrasting conclusions about the consistency of manuscripts associated with one Use are reached.

First, a well-established method of summarizing contents of an Office — the collation and comparison of responsory series, briefly presented in chapter 1 — is presented and its efficacy in the present investigation is shown. It is demonstrated that while responsory series in many Western liturgies are often tied to local, institutional, or geographical patterns, so much so that the liturgy of neighbouring cities could use different series, English books associated with the pan-provincial Uses of Sarum and York and to a lesser extent the diocesan Use of Hereford have identifiable, consistent responsory series.

Second, a study of the kalendars of liturgical manuscripts reveals a state of organized diversity far more extensive than the picture given by the responsory series. By virtue of its tabular design, the kalendar must have been one of the easiest components of a manuscript for its users to modify; and similarly by virtue of its prominent placement in most manuscripts and its apparent role as an index of liturgical observances, it is one of the most likely features to be seized upon by the modern researcher. Responsory series, conversely, would have been much more difficult to change. Each series is an amalgam of texts, often canonical, which appear in different, consistent patterns across the Western liturgy. As integral components of an Office and, as will be indicated, members of the genre of text most closely associated with a specific occasion, they were clearly subject to a strong tradition of continuity. Responsory series have been well established as a major identifier among the constitutive criteria of a Use.

But the contents of kalendars supply a dramatically different picture. Kalendars of any given Use do have a common baseline, but more importantly and profitably for the researcher they also possess and were clearly susceptible to regional and local influences which demonstrate both the persistence and openness to local features *under* the aegis of a single unified Use. Such features can help to associate kalendars (and manuscripts) of unknown origin with regional traditions. While this may have been proposed previously, it is possible to make assessments of the character of a number of traditions, and judge the constitutive features of Sarum, York, and monastic kalendars and of local variants thereupon, based on a larger survey of kalendars of those Uses than has yet been undertaken.

Responsory Series

It has long been the practice of liturgical scholars to exploit the natural organization of the Office liturgy into individual genres such as antiphons and responsories (some of the categories Hughes has called sungtexts) and to analyse the choice and order of the material chosen for sungtexts that appear in sequence. This was the principle adopted by M. R. James and Falconer Madan, independently, for the assessment of Books of Hours, where the choice of antiphons in the votive Office of the Blessed Virgin Mary served to identify the Use with which the manuscript was related.[1] Similarly W. H. Frere pointed out that the sequence of Alleluias after Pentecost allowed one to discriminate between Mass books of various liturgical patterns.[2] More pertinent to the present sources

---

[1] Madan, 'The Localization of Manuscripts' and James, 'Points to be Observed', in *A Descriptive Catalogue of the Manuscripts in the Fitzwilliam Museum*.

[2] W. H. Frere, *Graduale Sarisburiense* (London: Bernard Quaritch, 1894), p. 1.

were the investigations of Gabriel Beyssac, whose unpublished notebooks, now in the *Bibliothèque nationale*, give details of the textual patterns in some 10,000 manuscripts and printed books. Responsory series allowed Beyssac to assign unprovenanced books to their liturgical Use; indeed, he contended that it was possible to identify the Use of a manuscript solely from its responsory series for the Office of the Dead.[3] In order to compare the texts of the responsories quickly and without the need to record word-by-word variants, Beyssac assigned numbers to each textual passage he encountered in the form of a responsory so that each series could be represented as a numerical string; the strings could be sorted and grouped more easily than texts or even incipits. This method was also adopted by Victor Leroquais, who supplemented Beyssac's compilations by adding series from manuscripts in French libraries for Advent, the Triduum, and the Office of the Dead: these too are in manuscript form in the *Bibliothèque nationale*.[4]

The most important published study involving responsory series to date is the six-volume *Corpus Antiphonalium Officii* (*CAO*) of Dom René-Jean Hesbert, which was primarily an attempt to produce a 'restitution critique de l'Archetype de la tradition', that is, the earliest and (by his logic) the most authoritative pattern of Matins responsories in Advent. Hesbert collected Advent responsory series from some eight hundred manuscripts from across Western Europe, having first assigned a number to each possible responsory text in order to produce Beyssac-style numerical series for each service of Matins in Advent in each manuscript. The edited responsory texts appeared with their identifying number in volume IV of *CAO*, drawn from transcriptions of six secular antiphonals transcribed in volume I and six monastic antiphonals in volume II. The collected series, expressed in numerical form, appeared in the fifth volume, while the sixth illustrated a complex and not entirely clear statistical method constructed by Hesbert, which relied on comparison by shared variant. On this basis, he extrapolated the 'liste-type', the archetypical order of responsories for each Sunday in Advent. This eventual result of the six volumes is no longer seen as the principal benefit of Hesbert's work, since his critical method

---

[3] Ottosen, *Responsories and Versicles*, p. 3.

[4] France, Paris, Bibliothèque nationale, nouvelles acquisitions latines 3160, 3161, 3163, 3164. Jesse Billett has challenged the strategies of Beyssac and Leroquais, suggesting that it is not prudent 'to assume that the *ordo* found in a breviary of the 15th century is probably identical to what would be found in an antiphoner of the same church copied in the eleventh century'. Billett, 'The Divine Office in Anglo-Saxon England', p. 162.

is now not felt to be valid.[5] But the corpus of data in the first four volumes of *CAO*, namely hundreds of Advent responsory series assigned to specific locales or liturgical Uses, has proved invaluable as a base against which to compare responsory series from manuscripts and printed books of unknown origin.[6]

Following on from Hesbert, Matins responsory series were collected *en masse* for the Triduum by Dom Raymond le Roux,[7] and reorganized by Pierre-Marie Gy. A considerable portion of Beyssac's data was computerized and studied by Knud Ottosen in the early 1990s. The resulting book attempted to provide a reliable method for assessing the Use and origin of unknown manuscripts and additionally to gain insight into medieval Christian ideas of death through a comparison of the contents of the responsories.[8] Ottosen also reorganized Hesbert's series for Advent, adding a new introduction to a newly published volume.[9] More recently Cristina Dondi employed more of Beyssac's unpublished data in order to identify the sources of the liturgy of the Holy Sepulchre in Jerusalem: she compared responsory series taken from the most complete manuscripts known to have been associated with the Holy Sepulchre against Beyssac's corpus of data, checking them for the same patterns. The striking result was the association of the Holy Sepulchre liturgy with patterns normally found in Norman sources, adding a new dimension to the history of the establishment.[10]

The method adopted here is adapted from these existing models. It makes use of Hesbert's published data in order to identify, or prove the uniqueness of, the responsory series collected from every extant, complete English Office manuscript in British libraries. The extensiveness of the endeavour is necessary in order to confirm responsory series as the most valid and reliable identifier of liturgical Use, and to demonstrate the consistency of at least this component of books associated with one Use. Series from a number of sections of a manuscript need to be considered, and as many manuscripts as possible should be consulted, for Dondi reminds us that what is true for a single office, in terms of influences,

[5] Möller, 'Research on the Antiphoner – Problems and Perspectives', p. 9; Billett, 'The Divine Office in Anglo-Saxon England', p. 164.

[6] The benefits of Advent as a paradigm for the rest of the year are discussed in Margot Fassler, 'Sermons, Sacramentaries, and Early Sources for the Office in the Latin West: the Example of Advent', in *The Divine Office in the Latin Middle Ages*, pp. 15–47 (p. 15).

[7] Le Roux, 'Repons du Triduo Sacro et de Pâques'.

[8] Ottosen, *Responsories and Versicles*.

[9] Ottosen, *L'Antiphonaire latin au Moyen-Âge: Réorganisation des séries de répons de l'Avent classés par R.-J. Hesbert* (Rome: Herder, 1986).

[10] Dondi, *The Liturgy of the Canons Regular of the Holy Sepulchre*.

may not hold true for a complete Use — multiple sources are the origin of most Uses.[11] That only a few offices have been examined in any detail, and that most of these studies have only involved consulting a few manuscripts, must underline the importance of manuscript study of a much more substantial nature.

Procedures

For each of one hundred and seventy-seven manuscripts, of which one hundred and fifteen are complete breviaries or antiphonals, Matins responsory series were transcribed from the four Sundays in Advent; the three Ember Days (the Wednesday, Friday, and Saturday following the Third Sunday in Advent); the three days of the Triduum (Maundy Thursday, Good Friday, and Holy Saturday); and from the Office of the Dead or All Souls, as variously titled, for a total of nine series from each complete, legible manuscript (the three responsories on each of the three Ember Days are combined to form one nine-responsory series). A three-word incipit for each responsory in a series and another for the lesson preceding it were copied into a computer database and associated with the relevant serial number, based on Hesbert's numbers for Advent; le Roux's table for the Triduum; and Ottosen's table for the Dead.[12] The following account deals with the conceptual, abstracted texts only, not with copy-specific details. It should be noted that no texts not already edited and given a number by Hesbert were found, and that no responsory text differed meaningfully from the version given by Hesbert.

Analysis

Sarum and York Series

The most direct and meaningful statement that can be made about the series collected from these manuscripts is that over 75% of them (five hundred and thirty-six series out of seven hundred and four collected) conform to the patterns of Sarum (four hundred and forty-nine series) or York (eighty-seven). One hundred and sixty-eight series, therefore (that is, somewhat less than 25%), require more detailed attention; these are examined below. The numbers of complete breviaries and antiphonals assigned to the two principal Uses are slightly

---

[11] Dondi, *The Liturgy of the Canons Regular of the Holy Sepulchre*, p. 53.

[12] The numbers and letters in the right section of each column are indexed to Hesbert, *CAO*, vol. IV; Le Roux, 'Répons du Triduo Sacro'; Ottosen, *Responsories and Versicles*.

different (58% Sarum, 16% York) but the proportion of books neither Sarum nor York is similar to the percentage of series not corresponding to either Use.

The number of responsory series associated with Sarum is slightly inflated as a result of the employment of thirty-two Books of Hours (of which twenty-eight have a Sarum office for the Dead), which are not included in the figures above, from each of which the series for the Office of the Dead (only) has been included. The numbers of books associated with Sarum and York by responsory series for each of the nine days from which data were collected are summarized in the following calculation:

Number of Sarum and York responsory series recorded for each of nine liturgical occasions.

	Adv1	Adv2	Adv3	Ember	Adv4	Thu	Fri	Sat	Dead
Sarum	48	47	46	42	48	48	48	47	75
York	11	8	9	10	11	8	8	8	14

These reported numbers vary because not every manuscript contains each of the nine series: occasionally there is no Office for the Dead (or no Sanctorale at all); leaves may be missing (especially those containing Advent 1, which is found at the beginning of most insular Office books where it is most likely to be defaced), or parts of the manuscript may be illegible. This variance is not, then, tied to the series themselves, but to the individual circumstances of the book.

Nevertheless, as far as each is complete, no manuscript that contains primarily Sarum or York series also contained any other series except one, Camb. UL Dd. X. 66, which possesses an otherwise unknown series for the Saturday Ember Day of Advent 3, beginning with the responsory *Qui venturus es* (most commonly the text is *Emitte agnum*). This anomaly is seemingly without explanation and is, I suspect, probably inadvertent rather than deliberate. Another slight complication is that some non-Sarum books share series with Sarum (notably that for Advent 1), but the majority of their series contain patterns distinct from Sarum. As will be underlined later, this provides a crucial argument for the need to consult more than one series from any given manuscript, so as not to provide a false assessment.

The balance of data appears to confirm that the responsory series contained in books self-identified as Sarum or York and in printed editions of both Uses (purportedly the final textual state of a Use) are identical to the series tentatively assigned to Sarum in earlier studies. The data confirm, with the reservations outlined below, that Sarum and York responsory series can serve as identifiable characteristics of their respective Uses.

Table 2.1: Secular responsory series compared. The columns give series for Sarum, York, and Hereford; along with the text of the responsory, the text of the verse follows V. Here, and in all succeeding tables, the numerical codes assigned to responsories by Hesbert in *CAO* (for Advent), the alphabetic codes of Le Roux for the Triduum, and the numerical codes for the responsories of the Office of the Dead assigned by Ottosen can be consulted at the right of each column.

ADVENT 1

Sarum		York		Hereford	
Aspiciens a longe V. Quique terrigine	11	Aspiciens a longe V. Quique terrigine	11	Aspiciens a longe V. Quique terrigine	11
Aspiciebam in visu V. Potestas eius	12	Aspiciebam in visu V. Potestas eius	12	Aspiciebam in visu V. Potestas eius	12
Missus est gabriel V. Dabit ei	13	Missus est gabriel V. Dabit ei	13	Missus est gabriel V. Dabit ei	13
Ave maria gratia V. Quomodo fiet	14	Ave maria gratia V. Quomodo fiet	14	Ave maria gratia V. Quomodo fiet	14
Suscipe verbum virgo V. Paries quidem	34	Salvatorem expectamus V. Sobrie et	15	Suscipe verbum virgo V. Paries quidem	34
Salvatorem expectamus V. Sobrie et	15	Audite verbum domini V. Annunciate et	16	Salvatorem expectamus V. Sobrie et	15
Audite verbum domini V. Annunciate et	16	Ecce virgo concipiet V. Super solium	17	Audite verbum domini V. Annunciate et	16
Ecce virgo concipiet V. Super solium	17	Obsecro domine V. A solis ortu	18	Ecce virgo concipiet V. Super solium	17
Letentur celi V. Orietur in	19	Letentur celi V. Orietur in	19	Letentur celi V. Orietur in	19

* All five Advent series in Hereford are identical to those in Sarum.

ADVENT 2

Sarum		York		Hereford	
Ierusalem cito veniet V. Israel si	21	Ierusalem cito veniet V. Israel si	21	Ierusalem cito veniet V. Israel si	21
Ecce dominus veniet V. Ecce dominus	22	Alieni non transibunt V. Tunc exaltabant	62	Ecce dominus veniet V. Ecce dominus	22
Civitas ierusalem noli V. Ecce in fortitudine	24	Ecce dominus veniet V. Ecce dominus	22	Civitas ierusalem noli V. Ecce in fortitudine	24
Ecce veniet dominus V. Et dominabitur	25	Civitas ierusalem noli V. Ecce in fortitudine	24	Ecce veniet dominus V. Et dominabitur	25
Sicut mater consolatur V. Dabo in syon	26	Ecce veniet dominus V. Et dominabitur	25	Sicut mater consolatur V. Dabo in syon	26
Ierusalem plantabis V. Exulta Satis	27	Sicut mater consolatur V. Dabo in syon	26	Ierusalem plantabis V. Exulta satis	27
Egredietur dominus V. Et preparabitur	28	Ierusalem plantabis V. Exulta Satis	27	Egredietur dominus V. Et preparabitur	28
Docebit nos dominus V. Venite ascendamus	70	Docebit nos dominus V. Venite ascendamus	70	Docebit nos dominus V. Venite ascendamus	70
Rex noster adveniet V. Ecce agnus dei	29	Rex noster adveniet V. Ecce agnus dei	29	Rex noster adveniet V. Ecce agnus dei	29

ADVENT 3

Sarum		York		Hereford	
Ecce apparebit dominus V. Apparebit in finem	31	Ecce apparebit dominus V. Apparebit in finem	31	Ecce apparebit dominus V. Apparebit in finem	31
Bethleem civitas dei V. Loquetur pacem	32	Bethleem civitas dei V. Loquetur pacem	32	Bethleem civitas dei V. Loquetur pacem	32
Qui venturus es V. Deponet omnes	33	Qui venturus es V. Deponet omnes	33	Qui venturus es V. Deponet omnes	33
Egypte noli flere V. Ecce veniet	35	Suscipe verbum virgo V. Paries quidem	34	Egypte noli flere V. Ecce veniet	35
Prope est ut veniat V. Qui venturus es	36	Egypte noli flere V. Ecce veniet	35	Prope est ut veniat V. Qui venturus es	36
Descendet dominus V. Et adorabunt	37	Prope est ut veniat V. Qui venturus es	36	Descendet dominus V. Et adorabunt	37
Veni domine et noli V. Excita domine	38	Descendet dominus V. Et adorabunt	37	Veni domine et noli V. Excita domine	38
Erumpant montes V. Leva ierusalem	80	Veni domine et noli V. Excita domine	38	Erumpant montes V. Leva ierusalem	80
Ecce radix iesse V. Et erit	39	Montes israel ramos V. Rorate celi	60	Ecce radix iesse V. Et erit	39

ADVENT EMBER DAYS

Sarum		York		Hereford	
Clama in fortitudine V. Super montem	51	Clama in fortitudine V. Super montem	51	Clama in fortitudine V. Super montem	51
Orietur stella V. Et adorabunt	52	Orietur stella V. Et adorabunt	52	Orietur stella V. Et adorabunt	52
Egredietur dominus V. Et elevabitur	54	Modo veniet dominator V. Orietur in diebus	53	Egredietur dominus V. Et elevabitur	54
Precursor pro nobis V. Ipse est rex	55	Egredietur dominus V. Et elevabitur	54	Precursor pro nobis V. Ipse est rex	55
Modo veniet dominator V. Orietur in diebus	53	Precursor pro nobis V. Ipse est rex	55	Modo veniet dominator V. Orietur in diebus	53
Videbunt gentes iustum V. Et eris corona	56	Videbunt gentes iustum V. Et eris corona	56	Videbunt gentes iustum V. Et eris corona	56
Emitte agnum domine V. Rorate celi	57	Emitte agnum domine V. Rorate celi	57	Emitte agnum domine V. Rorate celi	57
Germinaverunt campi V. Ex syon species	58	Germinaverunt campi V. Ex syon species	58	Germinaverunt campi V. Ex syon species	58
Radix iesse qui exurget V. Super quem	59	Paratus esto israel V. Ecce dominator	94	Radix iesse qui exurget V. Super quem	59

ADVENT 4

Sarum		York		Hereford	
Canite tuba in syon V. Annunciate in finibus	41	Canite tuba in syon V. Annunciate in finibus	41	Canite tuba in syon V. Annunciate in finibus	41
Octava decima die V. Ego enim sum	42	Octava decima die V. Ego enim sum	42	Octava decima die V. Ego enim sum	42
Non auferetur sceptrum V. Pulcriores sunt	43	Non auferetur sceptrum V. Pulcriores sunt	43	Non auferetur sceptrum V. Pulcriores sunt	43
Me oportet minui V. Hoc est	44	Me oportet minui V. Hoc est	44	Me oportet minui V. Hoc est	44
Ecce iam veniet V. Propter nimiam	45	Virgo israel revertere V. In caritate	46	Ecce iam veniet V. Propter nimiam	45
Virgo israel revertere V. In caritate	46	Iuravi dicit dominus V. Iuxta est	47	Virgo israel revertere V. In caritate	46
Iuravi dicit dominus V. Iuxta est	47	Non discedimus V. Domine dues	48	Iuravi dicit dominus V. Iuxta est	47
Intuemini quantus sit V. Et dominabitur	49	Intuemini quantus sit V. Et dominabitur	49	Intuemini quantus sit V. Et dominabitur	49
Montes Israel ramos V. Rorate celi	60	Nascetur nobis V. In ipso	91	Montes Israel ramos V. Rorate celi	60

MAUNDY THURSDAY

Sarum		York		Hereford	
In monte oliveti V. Verumptamen	A	In monte oliveti V. Verumptamen	A	In monte oliveti V. Verumptamen	A
Tristis est anima V. Vigilate et orate	B	Tristis est anima V. Vigilate et orate	B	Unus ex discipulis V. Qui intingit	F
Ecce vidimus eum V. Vere languores	C	Ecce vidimus eum V. Vere languores	C	Tristis est anima V. Ecce appropinquabit	B
Unus ex discipulis V. Qui intingit	F	Unus ex discipulis V. Qui intingit	F	Seniores populi V. Congregaverunt	I
Iudas mercator V. Avaricie inebriatus	E	Eram quasi agnus V. Omnes inimici	G	Una hora non V. Dormite iam	H
Una hora non V. Quid dormitis	H	Una hora non V. Quid dormitis	H	Tradiderunt me V. Astiterunt reges	
Seniores populi V. Cogitaverunt	I	Seniores populi V. Cogitaverunt	I	Iudas mercator V. Avaricie inebriatus	E
O iuda qui dereliquisti V. Os tuum	L	Revelabunt celi V. In die perdicionis	J	O iuda qui dereliquisti V. Os tuum	L
Revelabunt celi V. In die perdicionis	J	O iuda qui dereliquisti V. Os tuum	L	Revelabunt celi V. In die perdicionis	J

GOOD FRIDAY

Sarum		York		Hereford	
Omnes amici mei V. Et dederunt	A	Omnes amici mei V. Et dederunt	A	Tanquam ad latronem V. Filius quidem	D
Tradiderunt me V. Astiterunt	H	Velum templi scissum V. Amen dico	B	Iesum tradidit impius V. Et ingressus	I
Caligaverunt V. O vos omnes	J	Vinea mea electa V. Ego quidem	C	Ecce quomodo V. In pace factus	
Vinea mea electa V. Ego quidem	C	Tanquam ad latronem V. Cunque	D	Vinea mea electa V. Ego quidem	C
Tanquam ad latronem V. Filius quidem	D	Barabbas latro V. Ecce turba	G	O vos omnes V. Attendite	E
Iesum tradidit impius V. Et ingressus	I	Tradiderunt me V. Astiterunt	H	Omnes amici mei V. Et dederunt	A
Barabbas latro V. Ecce turba	G	Iesum tradidit impius V. Et ingressus	I	Barabbas latro V. Ecce turba	G
Velum templi scissum V. Amen dico	B	Caligaverunt V. O vos omnes	J	Velum templi scissum V. Amen dico	B
Tenebre facte sunt V. Cum ergo	E	Tenebre facte sunt V. Cum ergo	E	Tenebre facte sunt V. Cum ergo	E

HOLY SATURDAY

Sarum		York		Hereford	
Sepulto domino V. Ne forte	A	Sepulto domino V. Ne forte	A	Sepulto domino V. Ne forte	A
Recessit pastor V. Ante cuius	D	Ierusalem luge V. Deduc	B	Ierusalem luge V. Deduc	B
Agnus dei christus V. Christus factus est	H	Plange quasi virgo V. Ululate	C	Plange quasi virgo V. Ululate	C
Sicut ovis ad occisionem V. Ipse autem	I	Recessit pastor V. Ante cuius	D	Agnus dei christus V. Christus factus est	H
Ecce quomodo moritur V. In pace	F	O vos omnes V. Attendite	E	Sicut ovis ad occisionem V. Ipse autem	I
Ierusalem luge V. Deduc	B	Ecce quomodo moritur V. In pace	F	Ecce vidimus eum V. Vere languores	C
Plange quasi virgo V. Ululate	C	Estimatus sum cum V. Posuerunt	G	Caligaverunt V. O vos omnes	J
Estimatus sum cum V. Posuerunt	G	Agnus dei christus V. Christus factus est	H	Estimatus sum cum V. Posuerunt me	G
O vos omnes V. Attendite	E	Sicut ovis ad occisionem V. In pace	I	Recessit pastor noster V. Ante cuius	D

OFFICE OF THE DEAD

Sarum		York		Hereford	
Credo quod redemptor V. Quem visurus	14	Credo quod redemptor V. Quem visurus	14	Credo quod redemptor V. Quem visurus	14
Qui lazarum resuscitasti V. Qui venturus es	72	Qui lazarum resuscitasti V. Requiem eternam	72	Qui lazarum resuscitasti V. Qui venturus es	72
Domine quando veneris V. Commissa mea	24	Domine quando veneris V. Commissa mea	24	Domine quando veneris V. Commissa mea	24
Heu mihi domine V. Anima mea	32	Heu mihi domine V. Anima mea	32	Heu mihi domine V. Anima mea	32
Ne recorderis V. Dirige domine	57	Ne recorderis V. Dirige domine	57	Ne recorderis V. Dirige domine	57
Domine secundum actum V. Amplius lava	28	Libera me [...] inferni V. Clamantes	50	Domine secundum actum V. Amplius lava	28
Peccante me cotidie V. Deus in nomine	68	Peccante me cotidie V. Deus in nomine	68	Peccante me cotidie V. Deus in nomine	68
Requiem eternam dona V. Qui lazarum	82	Deus eterne V. Qui in cruce	18	Requiem eternam dona V. Qui lazarum	82
Libera me [...] eterna V. Dies illa	38	Libera me [...] eterna V. Dies illa	38	Libera me [...] eterna V. Dies illa	38

* Identical to Sarum.

Hereford: Linked to Sarum

The idea of easily distinguishable secular Uses, strongly supported by Sarum and York series, is also supported by the two complete Hereford Office manuscripts, Hereford Cath. P. IX. 7 (EHC) and Worcester Cath. Q. 86 (EWC), and the printed 1505 Hereford breviary, but there is one anomaly which suggests a more complex origin and development for the Use than might be expected. While EHC and EWC share otherwise unique series for the Triduum, the series in EHC for Advent and for the Office of the Dead (identical to those in the 1505 printed breviary) are exactly the same as the Sarum series, though they do not share several of the associated verses.[13] EWC has no Advent section of the Temporale for the purpose of comparison (it begins imperfectly in the office for the Holy Innocents), but does contain the Sarum series for the Office of the Dead. The kalendars of the two manuscripts are relatively well connected (there are twenty points of similarity by shared variant between their kalen-

---

[13] That is, at MR9 of Advent 1; MV2 of feria 4 of Advent 3; and MV8 of Advent 4.

dars CI and DF),[14] and generally speaking both show low levels of difference
from Sarum kalendars. Despite their identical responsory series, the lessons for
the Triduum in both surviving manuscripts are quite different, with occasional
points of commonality. Based on these observations from a limited number of
sources, it would appear that either Hereford has borrowed the Sarum Advent
and Dead series, or the responsory series for these days in both Uses derive
from an origin shared by both Sarum and Hereford. Given that no other tradition has all the Sarum series for Advent, it may be that the former is more
likely. This dilemma emphasizes the need to survey series from more than one
section of a manuscript: had the Advent series alone been collected — or the
Dead series alone, Beyssac's suggestion[15] — no distinction between Sarum and
Hereford would be possible. Rather than contradicting the previous conclusion about the consistency of Sarum series, the fact that some such series are
shared between Uses suggests that in all cases data from a range of sections of a
manuscript must be considered. Evidently the 'Sarum' series for Advent and the
Dead are, perfectly legitimately if not independently, also the 'Hereford' series.

Monastic, Conventual, and Other Series

While this study is intended primarily to address the English secular liturgy, it
is important to show that unlike the responsory series of secular sources, which
demonstrate a high degree of consistency within each Use regardless of the geographic or temporal disparity among witnesses, the only valuable connexions
by series between monastic sources are between books which can be linked
by other means. The monastic series, if nothing else, highlight the consistency
of the Sarum and York series and demonstrate the considerable variation in
the choice of sungtexts for the same services in books from other traditions,
underlining the likelihood that one or more manuscripts sharing series may be
related. Indeed, among these outliers it has been possible to produce five small
groupings of manuscripts which do share a number of series. For a wider view of
the sources involved the following notes also include observations on the other

---

[14] Similar totals are calculated for every kalendar in relation to the number of points of
similarity between it and every other kalendar: these are noted as '44 points', etc., in the
succeeding sections. A fuller description may be found later in this chapter, and the totals here
are given for reference.

[15] Ottosen, *Responsories and Versicles*, p. 3.

contents of the books and, if known, their places of use. Note that Augustinian liturgy (observed in the Guisborough group below) is secular in form.

Cluniac group (Camb., Fitzwilliam 369; BL Addl 49363; Bodl. Univ. 101)

Table 2.2: Responsory series of the Cluniac group.

ADVENT 1			ADVENT 2		
R. Aspiciens a longe	11	V. Quique	R. Ierusalem cito veniet	21	V. Ego enim
R. Aspiciebam in visu	12	V. Potestas	R. Ecce dominus veniet	22	V. Ecce cum virtute
R. Missus est Gabriel	13	V. Dabit	R. Civitas ierusalem	24	V. Ecce in fort'ne
R. Ave maria gratia	14	V. Quomodo	R. Ecce dominus veniet	25	V. Ecce dominator
R. Salvatorem expectamus	15	V. Sobrie	R. Sicut mater consolator	26	V. Dabo in syon
R. Confortate manus	61	V. Civitas	R. Ecce dominus v c s	72	V. Ecce dominator
R. Audite verbum	16	V. Annun'ate	R. Egredietur dominus	28	V. Et preparabitur
R. Alieni non transibunt	62	V. Ego	R. Ierusalem plantabis	27	V. Exulta satis
R. Ecce virgo concipiet	17	V. Super	R. Ecce ab austro	73	V. Aspiciam vos
R. Obsecro domine	18	V. A solis	R. Festina ne tardaveris	92	V. Veni domine
R. Montes Israel	60	V. Rorate	R. Rex noster adveniet	29	V. Super ipsum
R. Letentur celi	19	V. Orietur	R. Ecce dies veniunt	63	V. In diebus

ADVENT 3			ADVENT 4		
R. Ecce apparebit	31	V. Apparebit	R. Canite tuba in syon	41	V. Annunciate
R. Bethleem civitas	32	V. Loquetur	R. Paratus esto israel	94	V. Ecce dominator
R. Qui venturus est	33	V. Deponet	R. Non auferetur	43	V. Pulcriores sunt
R. Suscipe verbum	34	V. Paries	R. Me oportet minui	44	V. Ego quidem
R. Egypte noli flere	35	V. Ecce	R. Ecce iam veniet	45	V. Propter
R. Prope est ut veniat	36	V. Revertere	R. Virgo israel revertere	46	V. In caritate
R. Veni domine et noli	38	V. Excita	R. Non discedimus	48	V. Memento
R. Descendet dominus	37	V. Et adorabunt	R. Iuravi dicit dominus	47	V. Iuxta est
R. Egredietur virga	81	V. Et requiescet	R. Intuemini quantus	49	V. Precursor
R. Ecce veniet dominus	71	V. Veniens	R. Modo veniet dominus	53	V. Et dominabitur
R. Ecce radix iesse	39	V. Dabit ei	R. Radix iesse qui	59	V. Ecce virgo
R. Docebit nos domine	70	V. Venite	R. Nascetur nobis	91	V. Multiplicabitur

Table 2.2: Responsory series of the Cluniac group *(cont.).*

ADVENT EMBER DAYS			OFFICE OF THE DEAD		
R. Clama in fortitudine	51	V. Super	R. Credo q'd redemptor	14	V. Quem visurus
R. Orietur stella	52	V. De iacob	R. Qui lazarum	72	V. Requiem
R. Egredietur dominus	54	V. Et elevabitur	*F: Domine dum ven […] L: Induta est caro	22 36	V. Commissa mea Dies mei
R. Precursor pro nobis	55	V. Ipse est	R. Subvenite sancti	90	V. Requiem
R. Videbunt gentes	56	V. Et erit	R. Heu mihi domine	32	V. Anima mea
R. Emitte agnum	57	V. Ostende	F: Ne recorderis L: Paucitas dierum	57 67	V. Non intres Ecce nunc
R. Rorate celi	90	V. Emitte	R. Peccante me	68	V. Deus in nomine
R. Germinaverunt	58	V. Ex syon	F: Domine secundum L: Memento mei d's	28 46	V. Amplius Et
R. Ecce dominus veniet	72	V. Ecce	F: Memento mei deus L: Libera me […] morte	46 38	V. Et in revert'm Dies illa

* The manuscripts diverge: F = Fitzwilliam 369; L = London, BL, Addl 49363.

MAUNDY THURSDAY			GOOD FRIDAY		
R. In monte oliveti	A	V. Verumptamen	R. Omnes amici mei	A	V. Et dederunt
R. Tristis est anima	B	V. Vigilate	R. Velum templi	B	V. Amen dico
R. Ecce vidimus eum	C	V. Vere	R. Vinea mea electa	C	V. Ego quidem
R. Unus ex vobis	F	V. Qui intingit	R. Tanquam ad latronem	D	V. Cumque
R. Una hora non	H	V. Quid	R. Tenebre facte sunt	E	V. Cum ergo
R. Eram quasi agnus	G	V. Omnes	R. Barabbas latro	G	V. Verax
R. Seniores populi	I	V. Collegerunt	R. Tradiderunt me	H	V. Astiterunt
R. O iuda qui	L	V. Corpore	R. Iesum tradidit	I	V. Et ingressus
R. Revelabunt celi	J	V. In diem	R. Animam meam	F	V. Omnes inimici

HOLY SATURDAY		
R. Sepulto domino	A	V. Ne forte
R. Ierusalem luge	B	V. Deduc
R. Plange quasi virgo	C	V. Ululate
R. Recessit pastor	D	V. Destruxit
R. O vos omnes	E	V. Attendite
R. Ecce quomodo	F	V. In pace
R. Estimatus sum	G	V. Posuerunt
R. Agnus dei christus	H	V. Christus
R. Sicut ovis ad	I	V. Tradidit

All three are Cluniac books: Fitzwilliam 369 was used at the priory of St Pancras, Lewes; Bodl. Univ. 101 contains the Dedication feast of the priory at Pontefract; and BL Addl 49363, probably a book for use while travelling, has no obvious evidence for place of use. The responsory series agree in these three manuscripts in eight out of nine cases: there is no Office for the Dead in Univ. 101, and the other two have different series, differing at four responsories (MR3, 6, 8, 9). It is quite likely that Matins for the Dead was subject to different influences than the other services from which series were collected, which are all in the Temporale. The kalendars of Fitzwilliam 369 and Univ. 101 (Addl 49363 has none) are among the most closely related of all known kalendars: between the two there are 44 points at which the two share otherwise unique contents. Lessons in all three manuscripts are often entirely different, with Univ. 101 somewhat more likely to be unusual among the three.

Guisborough group (BL Addl 35285; Oxford, Keble College 32; to a lesser extent Douai Abbey 4, Bodl. Laud lat. 5)

Table 2.3: Responsory series of the Guisborough group.

ADVENT 1			ADVENT 2		
R. Aspiciens a longe	11	V. Quique	R. Ierusalem cito	21	V. Israel
R. Aspiciebam in visu	12	V. Potestas	R. Alieni non transibunt	62	V. Ecce ego
R. Missus est Gabriel	13	**V. Ave**	R. Ecce dominus veniet	22	V. Ecce cum
R. Ave maria gratia	14	V. Quomodo	R. Docebit nos dominus	70	V. Venite
R. Suscipe verbum virgo	34	V. Paries	R. Civitas ierusalem	24	V. Ecce in
R. Salvatorem expectamus	15	V. Sobrie	R. Ecce veniet dominus	25	V. Et dominabitur
R. Audite verbum	16	V. Annun'ate	R. Sicut mater consolatur	26	V. Deus
R. Ecce virgo concipiet	17	V. Super	R. Ecce dies veniunt	63	V. In diebus
R. Letentur celi	19	**V. Ecce**	R. Rex noster adveniet	29	V. Ecce agnus

ADVENT 3			ADVENT 4		
R. Ecce apparebit	31	V. Apparebit	R. Canite tuba in syon	41	V. Annunciate
R. Bethleem civitas dei	32	V. Loquetur	R. Octava decima die	42	V. Ego enim
R. Paratus esto	94	V. Ex syon	R. Precursor pro nobis	55	V. Ipse est
R. Qui venturus est	33	V. Deponet	R. Non auferetur	43	V. Pulcriores
R. Egredietur dominus	54	V. Et elevabitur	R. Ecce iam venit	45	V. Propter
R. Egypte noli flere	35	V. Ecce veniet	R. Virgo israel revertere	46	V. In caritate
R. Prope est ut veniat	36	V. Qui venturus	R. Iuravi dicit dominus	47	V. Iuxta
R. Descendet dominus	37	V. Et adorabunt	R Non discedimus	48	V. Domine
R. Ecce radix iesse	39	V. Multiplicab'r	R. Nascetur nobis	91	V. Ecce advenit

Table 2.3: Responsory series of the Guisborough group *(cont.)*.

ADVENT EMBER DAYS			OFFICE OF THE DEAD		
R. Clama in fortitudine	51	V. Super	R. Credo q'd redemptor	14	V. Quem visurus
R. Orietur stella	52	V. De radice	R. Qui lazarum	72	V. Requiem
R. Intuemini quantus	49	V. Precursor	R. Domine quando	24	V. Commissa
R. Modo veniet dominator	53	V. Orietur	R. Heu mihi domine	32	V. Anima
R. Videbunt gentes	56	V. Et eris	R. Ne recorderis	57	V. Dirige
R. Montes israel ramos	60	V. Rorate	R. Libera me [...] inferni	68	V. Clamantes
R. Emitte agnum	57	V. Obsecro	R. Peccantem me	28	V. Deus
R. Germinaverunt	58	V. Paratus	R. Deus eterne	40	V. Qui in cruce
R. Rorate celi desuper	90	V. Emitte	R. Libera me [...] eterna	38	V. Dies illa

MAUNDY THURSDAY			GOOD FRIDAY		
R. In monte oliveti	A	V. Verumptamen	R. Omnes amici mei	A	V. Et dederunt
R. Tristis est anima	B	V. Ecce	R. Vinea mea electa	C	V. Ego quidem
R. Ecce vidimus eum	C	V. Vere	R. Tanquam ad latronem	D	V. Cumque
R. Unus ex discipulis	F	V. Qui intingit	R. Barabbas latro	G	V. Ecce turba
R. Eram quasi agnus	G	V. Adversum	R. Tradiderunt me	H	V. Astiterunt
R. Una hora non	H	V. Dormite	R. Iesum tradidit	I	V. Et ingressus
R. Seniores populi	I	V. Cogitaverunt	R. Caligaverunt	J	V. O vos omnes
R. Revelabunt celi	J	V. In die	R. Velum templi	B	V. Amen dico
R. O iuda qui derelequisti	L	V. Os tuum	R. Tenebre facte sunt	E	V. Cum ergo

HOLY SATURDAY		
R. Sepulto domino	A	V. Ne forte
R. Ierusalem luge	B	V. Deduc
R. Plange quasi	C	V. Ululate
R. Recessit pastor	D	V. Ante cuius
R. O vos omnes	E	V. Attendite
R. Ecce quomodo	F	V. In pace
R. Estimatus sum cum	G	V. Posuerunt
R. Agnus dei christus	H	V. Christus
R. Sicut ovis	I	V. Ipse autem

BL Addl 35285 is associated with Guisborough priory, while the Keble book was used at Walsingham. These manuscripts are associated by Anna Parsons with the 'Guisborough Group Use', and have many other common features.[16] Series in the first two manuscripts again agree in eight out of nine cases; there is no Office of the Dead in Keble 32. The series for Advent 1 is shared with Sarum. However, BL Addl 35285 and Bodl. Laud. lat. 5, a psalter with only the Dead series, share the same pattern for the Dead, and their kalendars are linked at thirty-six points. Douai 4 shares Advent 1–3 and the Ember series with the others, but has a different series for the Dead. Parsons argues that unlike their southern counterparts, the York Augustinians had a consistent programme of liturgical standardization. The consistency of these series suggests that the production of a Guisborough form of the Office may have, consciously or otherwise, standardized the set of responsory series. By contrast it should be noted that responsories shared by both Sarum and non-Sarum series may or may not indicate a common origin. *CAO* may supply the context.

Coldingham/Battle OSB (BL Harley 4664, Camb., Trinity College O. 7. 31)

Table 2.4: Responsory series of the Coldingham/Battle group.

ADVENT 1*			ADVENT 2		
C: Aspiciens a longe	11	Quique terrigine	R. Ierusalem cito veniet	21	V. Israel
C: Aspiciebam	12	Potestas	R. Ecce dominus veniet	22	V. Ecce cum
C: Missus est Gabriel	13	Ave maria	R. Docebit nos dominus	70	V. Venite
C: Ave maria gratia	14	Quomodo	R. Suscipe verbum	34	V. Paries
C: Salvatorem expect'mus	15	Sobrie	R. Civitas ierusalem	24	V. Ecce dominator
C: Audite verbum	16	Annunciate	R. Ecce veniet	25	V. Et dominabitur
C: Annunciatum est	93	Caste parentis	R. Sicut mater	26	V. Deus
C: Alieni non transibunt	62	Egredietur	R. Ecce dies veniunt	63	V. In diebus
C: Ecce virgo concipiet	17	Super solium	R. Ierusalem plantabis	27	V. Exulta
C: Obsecro domine	18	A solis ortu	R. Egredietur dominus	28	V. Et preparabitur
C: Orietur stella	52	Et adorabunt	R. Me oportet minui	44	V. Ego quidem
C: Letentur celi	19	Orietur	R. Rex noster	29	V. Ecce agnus

* Given for Coldingham MS only; the Trinity MS is missing responsories 1–3, and shows 14–15–61–16–62–17–18–52–19 for the remainder of the series.

[16] Anna Parsons, 'The Use of Guisborough: The Liturgy and Chant of the Augustinian Canons of the York Province in the later Middle Ages' (unpublished doctoral thesis, University of Exeter, 2004), esp. chp. 6, pp. 224–52.

Table 2.4: Responsory series of the Coldingham/Battle group *(cont.).*

ADVENT 3

R. Ecce apparebit	31	V. Apparebit
R. Bethleem civitas dei	32	V. Loquetur
R. Paratus esto Israel	94	V. Ex syon
R. Qui venturus est	33	V. Deponet
R. Egredietur dominus	54	V. Et elev'tur
R. Egypte noli flere	35	V. Ecce veniet
R. Prope est ut veniat	36	V. Qui venturus
R. Festina ne tardaveris	92	V. Veni domine
R. Descendit sicut	37	V. Et adorabunt
R. Veni domine et	38	V. Excita d'ne
R. Radix iesse qui	59	V. Super
R. Ecce radix iesse	39	V. Dabit ei

ADVENT 4

R. Canite tuba in syon	41	V. Annunciate
R. Octava decima die	42	V. Ego enim
R. Precursor pro nobis	55	V. Ipse est
R. Non auferetur	43	V. Pulcriores sunt
R. Videbunt gentes	56	V. Et eris
R. Ecce iam venit	45	V. Propter
R. Virgo israel revertere	46	V. In caritate
R. Montes Israel ramos	60	V. Rorate
R. Iuravi dicit dominus	47	V. Iuxta est salus
R. Non discedimus	48	V. Domine
R. Intuemini quantus	49	V. Precursor
R. Nascetur nobis	91	V. Multiplicabitur

ADVENT EMBER DAYS

R. Clama in fortitudine	51	V. Super
R. Orietur stella	52	V. Et adorabunt
R. Modo veniet	53	V. Orietur
R. Egredietur dominus	54	V. Et elev'tur
R. Precursor pro nobis	55	V. Ipse est
R. Videbunt gentes	56	V. Et eris
R. Emitte agnum	57	V. Rorate
R. Germinaverunt	58	V. Ecce d'nator
R. Rorate celi desuper	90	V. Emitte

OFFICE OF THE DEAD

R. In monte oliveti	A	V. Verumptamen
R. Tristis est anima	B	V. Ecce
R. Ecce vidimus eum	C	V. Vere
R. Unus ex discipulis	F	V. Qui intingit
R. Eram quasi agnus	G	V. Omnes inimici
R. Una hora non	H	V. Quid dormitis
R. Seniores populi	I	V. Cogitaverunt
R. Revelabunt celi	J	V. In die
R. O iuda qui [...]	L	V. Verax

GOOD FRIDAY

R. Omnes amici mei	A	V. Et dederunt
R. Vinea mea electa	C	V. Ego quidem
R. Tanquam ad latronem	D	V. Cumque
R. Barabbas latro	G	V. Ecce turba
R. Tradiderunt me	H	V. Astiterunt
R. Iesum tradidit	I	V. Et ingressus
R. Caligaverunt	J	V. O vos omnes
R. Velum temple	B	V. Amen dico
R. Tenebre facte sunt	E	V. Cum ergo

HOLY SATURDAY

R. Sepulto domino	A	V. Ne forte / ait
R. Ierusalem luge	B	V. Deduc
R. Plange quasi	C	V. Ululate
R. Recessit pastor	D	V. Ante cuius
R. O vos omnes	E	V. Attendite
R. Ecce quomodo	F	V. In pace
R. Estimatus sum cum	G	V. Posuerunt / et sicut
R. Agnus dei christus	H	V. Christus
R. Sicut ovis	I	V. Ipse autem

Seven series (all but Advent 1 and the Dead) are shared by these two manuscripts, which are associated with two Benedictine abbeys at opposite ends
of the country (Battle Abbey and Coldingham) and with no obvious links.
Advent 1 is incomplete in Trinity O. 7. 31, and the surviving responsories
MR4–9 are not identical with those in Harley 4664. Neither manuscript
contains an Office for the Dead. Comparison with *CAO* series revealed that
4664 is the sole known representative of most of these series (the Trinity MS
is not in *CAO*). Both share the series for Advent 4 with Worcester Cathedral
F. 160, used in the Cathedral itself; and the Ember series with BL Addl 43405
(Muchelney OSB) and Barlow 41 (Evesham OSB). Trinity O. 7. 31 has no
kalendar, so comparison is not possible. The lessons in the manuscripts are not
at all similar, except for the Ember days where there is only ever minimal variation: there are occasional rearrangements, but mostly new selections of text.

Triduum monastic group

See Table 2.5 on the following page. This group incorporates the Coldingham/
Battle and Guisborough groups, along with Camb., Magdalene College F. 4. 10,
from Peterborough Abbey, and Camb. UL Ii. IV. 20 (Ely OSB). All share the
responsory series for all three days of the Triduum. Magdalene F. 4. 10 and
Camb. UL Ii. IV. 20 also share the series for Advent 2 with the others. The
entire group also shares the Holy Saturday series with the Cluniac group. All of
these manuscripts are for conventual use; perhaps they are linked by this fact.
The shared series may be part of the normative English Benedictine or monastic pattern, one that has not been explored adequately, though Billett believes
that this pattern is largely an inheritance of the late tenth-century monastic
reform and did not exist previously. He argues that any common features of
English Benedictine liturgy from the tenth century onward are either 'borrowed' from a Continental framework or, more rarely, a reorganized secular
exemplar.[17] A succeeding part of this chapter enumerates some of the saints
common to Benedictine kalendars, in homage to Francis Wormald's work for
the Henry Bradshaw Society, but with a somewhat greater number of sources.[18]
The presence of Continental and especially French saints in the 'normative'
Benedictine kalendar below may serve to corroborate this view. Further dis-

---

[17] Billett, 'The Divine Office in Anglo-Saxon England', p. 262.

[18] *English Kalendars before AD 1100*, ed. by Francis Wormald, Henry Bradshaw Society,
72 (London, 1934), and *English Benedictine Kalendars after AD 1100*, ed. by Francis Wormald,
Henry Bradshaw Society, 77, 81 (London, 1939–46).

cussions of specific elements of the Benedictine Office may be found in Sally Harper's treatment of the votive office, and in J. B. L. Tolhurst's introduction to English monastic breviaries.[19]

Table 2.5: Responsory series shared by the Triduum monastic group.

MAUNDY THURSDAY

R. In monte oliveti	A	V. Verumptamen
R. Tristis est anima	B	V. Ecce
R. Ecce vidimus eum	C	V. Vere
R. Unus ex discipulis	F	V. Qui intingit
R. Eram quasi agnus	G	V. Omnes
R. Una hora non	H	V. Quid dormitis
R. Seniores populi	I	V. Cogitaverunt
R. Revelabunt celi	J	V. In die
R. O iuda qui [...]	L	V. Verax

GOOD FRIDAY

R. Omnes amici mei	A	V. Et dederunt
R. Vinea mea electa	C	V. Ego quidem
R. Tanquam ad latronem	D	V. Cumque
R. Barabbas latro	G	V. Ecce turba
R. Tradiderunt me	H	V. Astiterunt
R. Iesum tradidit	I	V. Et ingressus
R. Caligaverunt	J	V. O vos omnes
R. Velum temple	B	V. Amen dico
R. Tenebre facte sunt	E	V. Cum ergo

HOLY SATURDAY

R. Sepulto domino	A	V. Ne forte / ait
R. Ierusalem luge	B	V. Deduc
R. Plange quasi	C	V. Ululate
R. Recessit pastor	D	V. Ante cuius
R. O vos omnes	E	V. Attendite
R. Ecce quomodo	F	V. In pace
R. Estimatus sum cum	G	V. Posuerunt / et sicut
R. Agnus dei christus	H	V. Christus
R. Sicut ovis	I	V. Ipse autem

ADVENT 2

R. Ierusalem cito veniet	21	V. Ego enim
R. Ecce dominus veniet	22	V. Ecce cum virtute
R. Civitas ierusalem	24	V. Ecce in fort'ne
R. Ecce dominus veniet	25	V. Ecce dominator
R. Sicut mater consolator	26	V. Dabo in syon
R. Ecce dominus v c s	72	V. Ecce dominator
R. Egredietur dominus	28	V. Et preparabitur
R. Ierusalem plantabis	27	V. Exulta satis
R. Ecce ab austro	73	V. Aspiciam vos
R. Festina ne tardaveris	92	V. Veni domine
R. Rex noster adveniet	29	V. Super ipsum
R. Ecce dies veniunt	63	V. In diebus

[19] Sally Roper, *Medieval English Benedictine Liturgy: Studies in the Formation, Structure, and Content of the Monastic Votive Office, 950–1540* (London: Garland, 1993); J. B. L. Tolhurst, *Introduction to the English Monastic Breviaries (The Monastic Breviary of Hyde Abbey, Winchester, vol. 6)*, Henry Bradshaw Society, 80 (London, 1942).

Other Anomalous Series

There were several, but not many, other manuscripts whose responsory series did not allow them to be associated with any of these groups. BL Lansdowne 460, an incomplete monastic antiphonal (in German Gothic 'hufnagel' notation,[20] not a characteristic English form), might be associated, by virtue of the arms of the diocese of Norwich, with that region. Its responsory series for Advent 1 and the Ember days are associated by *CAO* with Cistercian practice, and the series for Advent 2–4 are unique and not in *CAO*. Bodl. Barlow 41, the winter part of a monastic breviary, is associated with the Benedictines of Evesham by the presence of both feasts for St Egwin, founder of Evesham, and other Worcestershire features. Its series for Advent 1, 3, 4, and the Dead are associated by *CAO* with Winchcombe (relatively close to Evesham), Jumièges, Conches, and Fécamp; but its Advent 2 series is recorded as unique. BL Harley 5037, a breviary of uncertain origin, has series for Advent 1 and 4, and for the Dead, which are also associated in *CAO* with Rome and with Franciscan practice. Finally, BL Burney 225 has an Advent 2 series that is unique and not in *CAO*; its Advent 4 series appears to be Cistercian. By contrast, its Advent 1 series is shared with the Use of York; its Advent 3 series with Bodl. Univ. Coll. 9 (a Carmelite breviary); and its Ember days' series with BL Lansdowne 460, noted above as Cistercian. While they escape present explanation, these series are not incorrect or 'anomalous': if confidence is assigned to responsory series, they must be seen as representatives of a tradition, perhaps a limited one, of which few witnesses are extant.

These putative and sometimes unclear associations suggest something that has been hinted at elsewhere: that single series should not be treated as incontrovertible proof of Use. Similarly, a meaningful relationship on the basis of responsory series between manuscripts should not rest on their sharing one or two series, and ought to be based on as much evidence as possible. There is no doubt, however, that the unique combination of series found in these manuscripts should be taken seriously, and that if they were found elsewhere, they would by their rarity be grounds for association with the venues with which these manuscripts are associated.

---

[20] Resembling horseshoe nails.

Summary

The dominance and consistency of the Sarum responsory series (and to a lesser extent the York, Benedictine, Augustinian, and Cluniac patterns) seem to suggest that the copying of manuscripts allowed the faithful reproduction of liturgical texts from place to place, although the mechanism by which new sets of series were created is unknown. Almost all of the connexions between books other than Sarum and York are supported by geographical or institutional affiliation. This may confirm one of the means by which responsory series (and, by extension, the entire contents of books) were frequently transmitted. However, the Coldingham and Battle group, and the Triduum monastic group both show that there were patterns in English conventual liturgy that were shared across geographic and institutional affiliations.

The Reliability of Responsory Series

CAO supplies a substantial but imperfect picture of the corpus of responsory series: I have encountered several series never recorded in Hesbert's travels. Nevertheless we must mostly accept the variety of his data as representative of the whole, even if he has only recorded a few examples from each venue. Another problem is that Hesbert's ascription of responsory series to a place of use are presumably based on geographical assignments of the books that contain them: since the justification for these assignments is not given, they must be treated with care. The Wollaton Antiphonal, with Sarum series, was used in the province of York. Perhaps the prevalence of certain series meant a privileged or limited number of exemplars. Certainly the Dominican liturgy was subjected to standardizing efforts by Humbert of Romans, a thirteenth-century Master-General of the order. All textual and musical forms used by medieval Dominicans from his tenure onward concurred with a set of exemplary books and were checked against them.[21] Several manuscripts with series associated with a particular city, for example from Cologne, might have been copies from one another, or from a mutual exemplar.

But the heterogeneity of liturgical books, even at more than first glance, makes comparison very difficult. If responsory series seem to form patterns linked to institutional or liturgical boundaries, or to geographical modes of

---

[21] Rome, Santa Sabina, Dominican Archives MS XIV L 1 is one such exemplary volume, probably used by the Master-General whilst travelling and during visitations. See Hughes, *Medieval Manuscripts for Mass and Office*, 7000.

distribution, using them in such an analysis ought to be mandatory. The objective of the comparison of scores of very similar liturgical books, after all, is the detection of a diagnostic feature, something unique to a Use that permits all instances of a book of that Use to be identified. The comparison of responsory series builds on other modes of broad-brush textual comparison dating back to James and Madan. The present data show very convincingly that the patterns in series are, if not damaged or inaccessible, *always* consistent within books clearly associated by other means with Sarum or York. Neither in previous research nor in my own have there been anomalies.

Are, then, responsory series reliable in an English liturgical context? Yes, as diagnostics of either principal secular Use (though not always for Hereford, as the Sarum series for Advent are borrowed there), and probably more reliable for this purpose than any other method identified to date. But responsory series do not always equate to predictable geographical patterns or guarantee the contents of the rest of a book. Like any other property of an Office book, responsory series should not be seen as a litmus test for Use, but rather as a piece of evidence for a systematic, cumulative diagnosis. Any anomalies, for instance unexpected or unique series, demand investigation, and uniformity with established patterns can make assignments more certain. In this capacity they join certain kalendar entries that are more likely, but not guaranteed, to appear in kalendars of either Use, and certain rubrical patterns that have been associated, by their appearance in books aligned with a Use, to that Use themselves (features that will be expounded below). Responsories are also a factor that can help to compare monastic sources. But they are not reliable as an indicator of place of use: monastic manuscripts vary, and single series, like single unusual saints, can appear to represent things they should not. Responsory series, alone, are also not a sufficient assessment tool for the complete contents of a book. Some manuscripts, like those which contain the Guisborough and Hereford series, share series with Sarum on a few occasions, and diverge at others. Inevitably, the greater the number of series collected from a source, the more reliable the result.

In a few cases it is clear that medieval users of Office books were capable of identifying a particular ordered set of responsories at Matins. The Office of the Dead in Bodl. Rawl. C. 553, a Sarum Book of Hours, appears to have been modified, with its responsories, originally Sarum, to the York order. Its kalendar and litany have also been altered to include a number of the putative York saints, including Paulinus and Wilfrid, along with the feast of relics. It also shows marks of erasure, Scholastica (11 February) being one of the most obvious examples. In such cases care has been taken to ensure that a particular order of responsories was recorded; these examples show that responsory series may have been understood by contemporary users to be *characteristic* of a Use. As integral texts of the Office written in dense columns, it has already been suggested that responsories would be quite difficult to modify without rewriting entire leaves. Far more than kalendars or other types of lists, it is likely that they reflect the original arrangement of a manuscript.

It may be questioned how patterns in responsory series could have been accorded any contemporary concern. Yet the responsory was a critical genre; responsory series reflect the natural divisions of Matins and the lesson-responsory pattern, certainly more so than some of the more ritual-based aspects of liturgy which were necessarily tied to specific venues and performing forces. The choice and order of responsories are evidently subject to different influences than, for instance, the proper antiphons of an office. In the case of versified offices such as that for Thomas Becket (discussed in chapter 3), the antiphons remain the same, but the responsories differ considerably: Sarum and York make different selections of sungtexts from the original monastic office in order to populate the nine-lesson secular pattern. It would be useful to consider whether lessons are ever tied to specific responsories, as they are at first glance in the Office of the Dead, or whether the themes in lessons are actually reflected in the responsories that follow them. At first glance, this seems not to be the case, since different Sarum manuscripts with the same responsory series have a diversity of lessons: in fact, lessons are the part of an office most likely to differ from source to source. And the Office of the Dead has similar readings from Job in both principal secular uses, yet the order of responsories is different. Empirically speaking the link between lessons and responsories, if it ever existed, seems to be broken.

But the order of responsories should be thought of as significant: the ritual implications of the responsory are manifold. Antiphons are often tied expressly to psalms, and they are a kind of adjunct to them. But responsories may be thought to be a more central feature. Indeed, the Office of Matins is centred on readings and responding to them in sungtexts. Hesbert and Ottosen, among others, attempted to find meaning in the changing orders of responsories.[22] The Sarum Ordinal edited by Frere among other sources (not least the transcriptions) gives prescriptions as to what the responsories for a given Office should

---

[22] René-Jean Hesbert, *Le Problème de la transfixion du Christ dans les traditions* (Paris: Société de Saint Jean l'Évangéliste, 1940).

be, and who should intone them.[23] That responsory series are also much longer, more florid, and include a solo verse, and that extra ones are added on particular feasts suggests that responsories' composers and users thought they were particularly important. They are also the most interesting compositionally (in both text and melody) and by their length offer a more extensive means of commenting either on Scripture or on the solemnity in question.

Conclusions

On the basis of the evidence from all surviving, complete English breviaries and antiphonals, it is clear that each secular Use had a characteristic set of responsory series that form one of the most convincing forms of diagnostic for the Use of an unknown manuscript. These series were successfully transmitted, unaltered, but whether this preservation of series was a conscious act or not cannot be known; in other words, it is not clear whether responsory series were understood to be tied to Use by their users and those preparing the manuscripts. I would suggest that the consistency of each series makes it difficult to argue against the contemporary awareness of the order of responsories. However it should be eminently clear, from the fact that the Hereford manuscripts appropriate the Advent and Dead series from Sarum, that single series or series from a single section of a manuscript should not be relied upon too extensively. In any case the assessment of responsory series should serve not as the sole test of Use but as one of a battery of tests, whose other constituents will be outlined in succeeding sections.

The Kalendar

In contrast to the relative consistency of responsory series within each secular Use, irrespective of geographical or administrative boundaries, the kalendars of secular manuscripts demonstrate a surprising capacity for variation.

The contention, in principle, that kalendars may reflect the local character of liturgy, even within witnesses of the same Use, has been well established. Functionally speaking from the viewpoint of a modern user, a kalendar is the most easily observable part of a liturgical manuscript: its tabular format makes for easy comparison, especially in view of the dense text which occupies the

---

[23] Frere, *The Use of Sarum: The Original Texts Edited from the Manuscripts*, 2 vols (Cambridge: Cambridge University Press, 1898–1901).

other sections; moreover, its length (usually six leaves) makes it a more manageable prospect. It is also desirable to think of the kalendars as an index for the rest of the volume, although this is a dangerous assumption, as will be shown below. The kalendar has nevertheless been at the centre of the analysis of liturgical books from an early stage, both as an identifier of the tradition which the book may represent, and as part of the body of evidence for wider hagiographical research. M. R. James in his draft guide to manuscript description gave special attention to hagiographical matters:[24] he proposed the presence or absence of certain characteristic saints, particularly in the Kalendar or the Litany, as evidence that a book had been used in one region or another. He was not the first to have done so but perhaps the clearest in articulating what the presence of a saint might mean: 'The student has to serve', he wrote, 'an apprenticeship in discovering which saints are of universal occurrence', but eventually, 'It is very pleasant to be able to put your finger upon the name of some obscure French bishop or Saxon prioress and to say this must mean Cambrai or Sens or Wherwell or Bury.'[25] Across the range of works that deal with the subject, the most conventional means for assignment to a Use, and indeed to a place of use, is the presence or absence of saints in the kalendar.

The attention of manuscript scholars has been appropriately captured: an accurate conspectus of the Christian year is essential to the interpretation of liturgical activity in the Middle Ages, and the kalendar supplies what appears to be a day-by-day summary of that activity. Someone wishing to know about the particular circumstances of the liturgy of one parish church might be able to infer what special or regional feasts were celebrated from the kalendar of a surviving manuscript, or in the absence of such obvious evidence, from reasoned study of the kalendars of manuscripts from nearby venues or from the diocese in question. A study of many kalendars can illustrate, as this section will show, the complex dialogue between long-established basic contents which show the roots of the English liturgy in the Roman liturgy and the imposition (successful or otherwise) of festal observances by authority; the authoritative picture may also contrast with local or popular observances not condoned officially, or which reflect a chronology that does not correspond exactly to the one that might be drawn from the documentary evidence for the promulgation of feastdays.

---

[24] Pfaff, 'M. R. James on the Cataloguing of Manuscripts'.

[25] Pfaff, 'M. R. James on the Cataloguing of Manuscripts'.

But the picture is not as clear as James intimates. It is clear that, for instance, books associated with the Use of Sarum possessed kalendars that had a great many commonalities. But once a kalendar was imposed for the first time, it was also subject to local modification as a result of the official imposition of some feasts (through provincial and diocesan synodal statutes, or ordinals); and the acquisition of saints through regional or local cults, or, as Pfaff has suggested, simply at the request of 'enthusiasts'.[26]

Sometimes these local variations along with additions of feasts have been used, just as James suggests, to situate a manuscript in a geographical or temporal context. But Pfaff has argued that hagiographical evidence, especially from kalendars or martyrologies, is unreliable for assigning books either to a date or to a place of use. An entry in a kalendar, he wrote as early as 1965, means only 'some degree of recognition' and 'at least an ostensible or theoretical observance'.[27] Unlike canonical texts such as the Canon of the Mass, kalendars were subject to change more or less on a whim, and the intention behind including a particular saint in a kalendar, unless he or she is marked out as a saint of great significance, cannot be clear. In other sections the intention of later scribes may be more obvious. The deliberate insertion of a new feast in an existing manuscript is, if the manuscript is designed for use, surely a prescription that it should be observed, an inference made stronger by the amount of proper material included. A similarly strong indicator of difference may be the modification of Litanies, sometimes by addition alone and sometimes by substitution or even erasure. New or modified contents in either the Sanctorale or Litany would suggest a different result in performance: perhaps a change *in what is done* ought to be the key parameter for determining 'significant' difference.

As this chapter demonstrates, the influences on the contents of a kalendar seem to be numerous and not limited to authority, or to the contents of a book, or indeed in a few cases to the venue for which the book was produced. There is no way, then, to assume the existence of a consistent, unvarying 'Sarum kalendar' across all regions, and no way to tell for certain that a kalendar is from Worcestershire, but this survey will present some of the characteristic features of regional patterns.

[26] Pfaff, *LME*, p. 3.

[27] R. W. Pfaff, 'New Liturgical Observances in later Medieval England' (doctoral thesis, University of Oxford, 1965), p. 1.

Procedures: Points of Shared Variance

Each kalendar in the manuscripts surveyed was transcribed into parallel columns in an Excel database (adopting the method used by Dondi and Rushforth)[28] and assigned an anonymizing two-letter siglum. These sigla are indexed in Handlist 1. One hundred and thirty-two kalendars were transcribed, including a number from Books of Hours in order to investigate their properties in relation to those of kalendars in Office books: in all, seventy were transcribed from books associated with Sarum; twenty-two from York books, with the remainder associated with monastic or other traditions. Scripts, or macros, were programmed for the database software FileMaker Pro which extracted the data for each kalendar from the Excel file. By means of the database, over 43,000 individual kalendar entries could be compared. The initial step was to assess, for each day of the year, which kalendars shared notable entries, either in their initial contents or by insertion or omission.

The normative 'base version' for this analysis, the version against which all other witnesses were compared, was the kalendar in the 1531 printed breviary.[29] This is perhaps unfortunate. Despite the fact that Francis Procter and Christopher Wordsworth chose it as the exemplar for their 'edition' of the Sarum Breviary, the 1531 breviary was printed by Chevallon and Regnault in Paris, and many of its entries betray Continental influence. The kalendar diverges at a significant number of points from any manuscript Sarum breviary (an observation which should immediately underline the problem of relying on a single printed edition); Reames also notes that its Sanctorale includes some unusual proper material, for the translation of Chad (which might be best linked with Lichfield), and the principal and translation Offices of Erkenwald, patron of London.[30] This point illustrates the futility of dealing with a single edition!

It should be made clear that while a high number of shared points may indicate a notable relationship between two kalendars, a low number of shared points may be less helpful. Since the number of points refers only to *shared*

[28] Cristina Dondi, *The Liturgy of the Canons Regular of the Holy Sepulchre*; Rebecca Rushforth, *Saints in English Calendars before A.D. 1100*, Henry Bradshaw Society, 117 (Woodbridge: Boydell for the Henry Bradshaw Society, 2008).

[29] STC 15830, in *A Short-Title Catalogue of Books Printed in England, Scotland, and Ireland and of English Books Printed Abroad 1475–1640*, ed. by Alfred W. Pollard and Gilbert R. Redgrave, 2nd edn revised and enlarged by W. A. Jackson, F. S. Ferguson and Katharine F. Pantzer, 3 vols (London: Bibliographical Society, 1976–91).

[30] Reames, 'Unexpected Texts', p. 164.

variants from 1531, a low number does not mean that the pair are necessarily closer to 1531 or that they contain few unusual feasts, merely that they do not *share* many observances that are *different* from 1531. Despite this, York kalendars dominate the top of the list whilst pairs of Norwich kalendars are near the bottom. This indicates that Norwich (Sarum) manuscripts may have kalendars bearing a greater similarity to the printed Sarum kalendar. In any event it was inevitable that one source or another should be used as an unprivileged 'baseline' against which all other kalendars were to be compared. As in all such comparative analyses 1531 is merely a witness against which to compare all others, and the intention is certainly not to suggest that it is a privileged or authoritative version of the Sarum kalendar. In an ideal analytical model, it might have been suitable to compare all kalendars against one of the artificial 'normative' kalendars discussed later in this chapter, instead of using *any* single witness as a baseline, although comparing real kalendars against an artificial one might be questioned. The choice of one of the manuscripts with very few deviations from the normative kalendar would produce the same complication: that kalendars similar to the baseline would not be flagged as possessing a great many shared points of divergence. The advantage of using 1531 is that it outlines the difficulties of using this particular source as an exemplar.

It is also important to mention that the transcriptions used for this analysis always reflect the final state of kalendars where additions or changes have been made to the contents. The task at hand was not to establish the original textual state of a kalendar; rather, to use the final state as an indicator of practice (or consensus among the various influences on the kalendar's contents), and to consider the evidence for the appearance of feastdays on an equal footing.

For each manuscript kalendar a record was produced of its relations with every other kalendar, and how many points of divergence from 1531 it *shared* with every other kalendar. The average number of points of divergence and the standard deviation were also calculated in order to give context for any particular results. (Together, these figures suggest how a particularly high or low number of points relating two manuscripts might be interpreted.) The total number of pairs of manuscripts with one or more shared points of divergence (hereafter 'points') was 12,751. For this population the mean number of shared points of divergence was six (rounded to the nearest whole number) with a standard deviation of 6.8: the mean will have been affected by the facts that 2303 (18%) of all pairs of kalendars were related by only one point, and that one pair was related at one hundred and fifty points. The mean and standard deviation figures are much more helpful with respect to single manuscripts, illustrating the importance of a relatively high or low number of shared points.

Analysis

The pair of manuscripts with the greatest number of shared points (150) were Sloane 2466 (with kalendar siglum BE)[31], a Sarum breviary, and Gough lit. 3 (AL), a Book of Hours with a Sarum Office of the Dead. Both of their kalendars contain a large number of idiosyncratic saints, some of whom have been associated by W. H. Frere with Roman kalendars of between the fifth and seventh centuries, or with different dates in the preponderance of kalendars; others, like Polychronius (17 February) and Asterius (3 March) do not appear in any other kalendar discussed here.[32] Similarly the second-highest number of points (fifty-seven) was shared by two more Books of Hours, Rawl. lit. g. 3 (AC) and Gough lit. 10 (AJ), both of the fifteenth century and with links to the Continent, though both appear by their Office of the Dead to be associated with Sarum. Both of these extreme examples, however, are anomalies, and possessed obviously non-English kalendars, but strong relations were found in English kalendars as well, particularly those associated with York.

Of the surviving York manuscripts, York Minster Addl 69 has the kalendar that is most similar to the one in the printed York breviary of 1493, with forty-nine shared points of divergence, by a margin of four points. Addl 69 is related to Bodl. Laud misc. 84[33] and Sion[34] by forty-six points, and to York Minster Addl 383 by forty-two points. Kalendars in other York books are related at as few as seventy-seven points. York Minster Addl 68 and Addl 70 are closest to one another, at forty-three points. These groupings may hint at several families of York kalendars. It is also worthwhile to point out that the kalendars of the York Antiphonal (the only surviving example of this genre from York, now at Arundel Castle), used in the chapel of St Mary and the Holy Angels, York Minster, and Bodl. Laud misc. 84 are related at thirty-seven points: there have been unverified suggestions that the Laud misc. book was for use in the Minster as well. The kalendars here would seem to serve as a helpful support for this proposition.

Many East Anglian sources, often identified by means of dedication feasts or with additions based on synodal decisions of which we are aware only from manuscript evidence (see later in this chapter), have similar kalendars: the strongest

---

[31] Kalendar sigla are explained and indexed in Handlist 1.

[32] For Frere's sources, see below, under *Normative kalendars*.

[33] This is the closest relationship between Laud misc. 84 and any other kalendar: it is related to Wood empt. 20 (forty-four points); BL Addl 30511 (forty-three); York Addl 115 (forty-three); York XVI. O. 9 (forty-one); Bodl. Gough lit. 1 (forty).

[34] Sion is equally linked (forty-six points) to Durham Cosin V. I. 2.

of these relationships are noted below in Table 2.7, those of Barnwell and Ely priories and the Ranworth Antiphonal among them. Northern books, whether secular or monastic, are also aligned with one another. Books for Evesham Abbey and Worcester Cathedral (Bodl. Barlow 41 and Worcester Cath. F. 160, kalendars CS-CH) are also closely related with twenty-one shared points.

It is also useful to compare the kalendars of manuscripts which earlier in this chapter were associated with the same groups by their monastic responsory series. Unsurprisingly, manuscripts associated with the same institution or religious order regardless of date also have similar kalendars: two Cluniac books, Fitzwilliam Mus. 369 and Bodl. Univ. Coll. 101 (CA-CP), share forty-four points of difference from the 1531 kalendar; and the two kalendars belonging to Augustinians at Guisborough, BL Addl 35285 and Bodl. Laud lat. 5 (CC-DB), share thirty-six points. Manuscripts from each of the foundations at Peterborough (Bodl. Gough lit. 17, Camb. Magdalen F. 4. 10, CU-CB, thirty-nine points) and also at Gloucester (Bodl. Rawl. lit. f. 1, Bodl. Jesus Coll. 10, CG-DI, thirty points) demonstrate similarly strong local links.

The kalendars of the so-called 'Chichele group' of manuscripts (discussed at length in chapter 3) do not show particularly strong affiliations with one another, with the strongest relation between Camb. UL Addl 4500 and BL Sloane 2466, at fifteen points. Addl 4500 is also linked by eleven points to Camb. UL Dd. X. 66. The explanation for these relatively low numbers is that all seven of the Chichele group kalendars, especially Lambeth Palace 69, are moderately similar to the 1531 kalendar from which the comparisons are taken — all, however, have relatively low numbers of shared variants from it, and it might be suggested that the pairs above are the most divergent from the 'average' Chichele kalendar, if there was one.[35] That these standard Sarum books diverge from 1531 in any substantive way should serve as further proof of the problems with using the 1531 print as a standard exemplar, an attitude adopted here only because 1531 is still frustratingly considered the *de facto* Sarum kalendar.

Table 2.6: **Relations between kalendars of the 'Chichele' group.** In the right column, the number in parentheses indicates the number of shared variants.

Camb., UL, MS Dd. X. 66	Addl 4500 (11), Sloane (8), Ox St John's (7), Lambeth (1)
Camb., UL, Addl 4500	Sloane (15), Dd. X. 66 (11), Lambeth (1)
London, Lambeth Palace 69	all six are close to the 1531 kalendar, esp. Lambeth.
Oxford, St John's College 179	Dd. X. 66 (7), Sloane (6), Lambeth (1)
London, BL Sloane 2466	Addl 4500 (15), Dd. X. 66 (8), Ox St John's (6), Lambeth (1)

[35] In general it might be remembered that the greater the number of points of shared variance, the greater the difference from the 1531 printed edition.

Table 2.7: Kalendars with closest relations. Each kalendar in this study appears once in the left column, indicated by its alphabetic siglum. The kalendar to which it is most closely related (by a stated number of points) is given in the fourth and fifth columns. The sixth column gives a potential explanation for their affinity, if known, or other pertinent information.

	Manuscript	Points		Related to	Notes
AL	Bodl. Gough lit. 3	150	BE	London BL MS Sloane 2466	Two Continental kalendars
AC	Bodl. Rawl. lit. G. 3	57	AJ	Bodl. Gough lit. 10	?
Q	York ML MS Additional 69	49	V	1493.pr	Closest MS to 1493 printed kalendar
AA	Bodl. Rawl. lit. G. 6	48	AC	Bodl. Rawl. lit. g. 3	Both from eastern England?
AD	Bodl. Rawl. lit. G. 1	46	AC	Bodl. Rawl. lit. g. 3	Both Dioc. of Lincoln
E	Bodl. MS Laud misc. 84	46	Q	York ML MS Additional 69	E=York Minster
G	Lambeth Palace MS Sion College 1	46	Q	York ML MS Additional 69	G=Skelton parish
R	Durham UL Cosin V. I. 2	46	G	Lambeth P.MS Sion College 1	R=Rudby parish G=Skelton parish
CA	Camb., Fitzwilliam Museum ms 369	44	CP	Bodl. MS University College 101	Both are Cluniac
U	Bodl. MS Wood empt. 20	44	E	Bodl. MS Laud misc. 84	Province of York
CF	Bodl. Rawl. lit. E. 4	43	AC	Bodl. Rawl. lit. g. 3	?
J	London BL MS Additional 30511	43	E	Bodl. MS Laud misc. 84	E=York Minster
N	Addl 115	43	E	Bodl. MS Laud misc. 84	E=York Minster
O	York ML MS Additional 70	43	P	York ML MS Additional 68	O=Harewood parish
M	York ML MS Additional 383	42	Q	York ML MS Additional 69	Province of York
K	York ML MS XVI. O. 9	41	E	Bodl. MS Laud misc. 84	Province of York
CB	Camb., Magdalene College, F. 4. 10	40	CU	Bodl. Gough lit. 17 = Gough Missals 47	Both Peterborough Abbey
F	Bodl. MS Gough lit. 1	40	E	Bodl. MS Laud misc. 84	Province of York

	Manuscript	Points		Related to	Notes
L	York ML MS XVI. O. 23	37	E	Bodl. MS Laud misc. 84	Province of York
S	Arundel Castle Archives, the York Antiphonal (s.n.)	37	E	Bodl. MS Laud misc. 84	Both from York Minster
AK	Bodl. e Musaeo 226	36	AC	Bodl. Rawl. lit. g. 3	?
CC	London BL Additional 35285	36	DB	Bodl. MS Laud lat. 5	Both Guisborough Augustinians
DP	Bodl. MS Bodley 68	35	AC	Bodl. Rawl. lit. g. 3	?
BY	Bodl. Laud lat. 15	34	AK	Bodl. e Musaeo 226	?
CG	Bodl. Rawl. lit. f. 1	30	DI	Bodl. MS Jesus College 10	Both Gloucester Abbey
CL	London BL MS Harley 4664	30	CU	Bodl. Gough lit. 17 = Gough Missals 47	CL=Coldingham OSB CU=Peterborough
CQ	Bodl. MS University College 9	30	DO	Oxford, Bodl., MS Rawl. D. 1218	?
CT	Bodl. Lat. lit. e. 37, Lat. lit. e. 6, Lat. lit. e. 39, Lat. lit. d. 42 [the Chertsey Abbey breviary]	29	CV	Bodl. MSS Gough lit. 8 (A) and Rawl. lit. e. 1* (B)	CT=Chertsey OSB CV=Hyde OSB
BT	Bodl. MS Wood C. 12	28	AC	Bodl. Rawl. lit. g. 3	?
AM	Bodl. Gough lit. 9	27	AC	Bodl. Rawl. lit. g. 3	?
H	Camb. UL MS Addl 3110	27	Q	York ML MS Additional 69	Province of York
DL	London BL MS Burney 335	25	CP	Bodl. MS University College 101	DL=Cistercian CP=Pontefract/Cluny
CH	Worcester Cathedral Library, MS F. 160	23	CK	London BL MS Additional 43405, 43406	?
DA	Bodl. Douce 293	23	AJ	Bodl. Gough lit. 10	
CD	London BL Additional 33381	22	CV	Bodl. MSS Gough lit. 8 (A) and Rawl. lit. e. 1* (B)	CD=Ely CV=Hyde OSB
CM	London BL MS Royal 2 A X	22	CU	Bodl. Gough lit. 17 = Gough Missals 47	CM=St Albans CU=Peterborough

Table 2.7: Kalendars with closest relations *(cont.)*.

	Manuscript	Points		Related to	Notes
DH	Bodl. Bodley 547	22	CM	London BL MS Royal 2 A X	DH=Beckford OSB CM=St Albans
DT	Bodl. e Mus. 185	22	AL	Bodl. Gough lit. 3	
T	Bodl. MS Rawlinson C. 553	22	Q	York ML MS Additional 69	T=St Mary's York
CS	Bodl. MS Barlow 41	21	CH	Worcester Cathedral Library, MS F. 160	CS=Evesham CH=Worcester Cath
CI	Hereford, Cathedral Library, MS P. IX. 7	20	DF	Worcester, Cathedral Library MS Q. 86	Both for Hereford Cath
I	London BL MS Additional 38624	19	E	Bodl. MS Laud misc. 84	Province of York
CR	Bodl. MS Lat. lit. c. 36	18	CM	London BL MS Royal 2 A X	
DC	Bodl. MS Lat. lit. g. 1	18	CP	Bodl. MS University College 101	DC=St Mary's York CP=Pontefract
CY	London BL MS Lansdowne 431	17	CD	London BL Additional 33381	CY=Barnwell priory CD=Ely priory
AB	Bodl. Rawl. lit. G. 2	16	CF	Bodl. Rawl. lit. e. 4	
DN	Bodl. MS Rawlinson G. 170	16	Q	York ML MS Additional 69	Province of York
AU	Camb. UL MS Addl 4500	15	BE	London BL MS Sloane 2466	
CJ	Oxford Keble MS 32	15	AM	Bodl. Gough lit. 9	
DQ	Oxford, Bodl., MS Rawl. C. 466	15	AC	Bodl. Rawl. lit. g. 3	
BA	Camb. Peterhouse MS 270	14	CZ	London BL MS Addl 59862	East Anglia/Norwich
BS	Bodl. Lat. lit. b. 14	14	AU	Camb. UL MS Addl 4500	BS=Denchworth, Berks
BW	Bodl. MS Laud misc. 299	14	CZ	London BL MS Addl 59862	East Anglia/Norwich
CN	London BL MS Addl 36672	14	AJ	Bodl. Gough lit. 10	Continental

	Manuscript	Points		Related to	Notes
DK	Bodl. MS Lit. 132	13	CF	Bodl. Rawl. lit. e. 4	
W	Ranworth Antiphonal	13	CZ	London BL MS Addl 59862	W=Ranworth CZ=Norwich
Z	Durham, UL Cosin V. I. 3	13	CZ	London BL MS Addl 59862	Both Norwich
AX	Camb. King's MS 30	12	BA	Camb. Peterhouse MS 270	
BU	Camb. UL MS Addl 2602	12	AU	Camb. UL MS Addl 4500	BU=Springfield, Essex
DD	London BL MS Addl 17002	12	CZ	London BL MS Addl 59862	Norwich
AT	Camb. Fitzwilliam Museum MS McClean 65	11	BG	London BL MS Harley 1797	
AY	Camb. SJC MS F. 9 (James 146)	11	BE	London BL MS Sloane 2466	
AZ	Camb. UL MS Dd. X. 66	11	AU	Camb. UL MS Addl 4500	
BC	Camb. Emmanuel MS 64	11	BE	London BL MS Sloane 2466	
BG	London BL MS Harley 1797	11	AT	Camb. Fitzwilliam Museum MS McClean 65	
BH	London BL MS Harley 587	11	AU	Camb. UL MS Addl 4500	
BI	London BL MS Addl 22397	11	AZ	Camb. UL MS Dd. X. 66	
BM	London BL MS Addl 52359	11	BE	London BL MS Sloane 2466	
BN	London BL MS Lansdowne 463	11	BA	Camb. Peterhouse MS 270	Norwich/East Anglia
BX	Bodl. Rawl. lit. f. 2	11	BN	London BL MS Lansdowne 463	BX=Suffolk BN=Norwich
BB	Camb. Clare MS G. 3. 34 (olim, MRJ, Kk. 3. 7)	10	AX	Camb. King's MS 30	
BJ	Bodl. Bodley 948	10	AT	Camb. Fitzwilliam Museum MS McClean 65	
BV	London BL MS Harley 2785	10	BA	Camb. Peterhouse MS 270	

The table on the previous pages gives all pairs of kalendars with at least ten points of shared variance. It provides, for each kalendar in the left column (indicated by its two-letter siglum), the one kalendar to which it is most closely related. The Notes column indicates the relation, if one is clear. In all, forty-one out of seventy-three of these strong pairs can also be related by geographical or institutional ties. Manuscripts may appear more than once in the 'Related to' column, as one manuscript may be the witness with which several others share the greatest number of points of variance.

'Normative' Kalendars for Sarum, York, and Benedictine Manuscripts

The kalendar of an unknown manuscript may often be the principal component to be assessed, and so the establishment of constitutive criteria for each Use is important. While on observation it can be shown that no two kalendars are absolutely alike, there are observable sets of frequently appearing saints for Sarum and York kalendars and, to a lesser extent, for Benedictine witnesses as well. Hereford was not considered here as there were an insufficient number of examples which did not appear to represent the same tradition. All seventy Sarum kalendars, twenty-two York kalendars, and the kalendars of the eleven Benedictine books were surveyed, and all contribute to the results presented below. The shared contents of each Use were expressed in three 'normative' kalendars, artificial constructions, which contain for each day only the saints that appear in the majority (at least 50%) of kalendars of the relevant group.

On three hundred and three out of three hundred and sixty-five days (83% of the year) all three such normative kalendars agree, mostly on days whose observances are linked to the Roman kalendar. It is important to remember that the presence of a saint in the normative kalendar for one Use does not mean that it *never* appears elsewhere in the kalendars of books associated with another Use: the presence or absence of some saint is not sufficient evidence for the 'diagnosis' of the Use of a kalendar or its manuscript. Here as has been stated, observances are meaningful as a group, not as individuals. Similarly, it should be remembered that the appearance of a saint in the succeeding tables means only that it is likely to appear on the basis of its presence in the majority of similar such kalendars.

Feasts in italics in the tables below have been associated with the early Roman kalendar by W. H. Frere, and are not considered further here, since they are common to all Western Roman kalendars.[36] This is not to minimize the fact

---

[36] W. H. Frere, *Studies in Early Roman Liturgy*, 3 vols (London: Oxford University Press, 1930–35), I, 84. He reports his sources as: Philocalian lists from the middle of the fourth century; the Old Roman Martyrology as promulgated in Italy in the fifth century and Gaul in the sixth; the titular and stational church dedications of Rome; service-books (Gelasian and Gregorian lists); and the *'Liber pontificalis'*.

that some of the early-established observances, especially the Christological and Marian ones, are unambiguously prescribed in diocesan lists of feasts. In addition to Frere's early Roman saints, other saints of later date associated with the Roman kalendar also appear, often in all three normative kalendars; these too are not considered further.

Table 2.8: Normative kalendars extrapolated from Sarum, Benedictine (OSB) and York sources. Feasts in roman type appear in all three; those in italics are in Frere's early Roman kalendars. A line in bold type indicates a point of interest. The rightmost columns indicate: (1240) the feasts celebrated as doubles indicated in Walter de Cantilupe's statute for Worcester diocese (W for Worcester, S for Sarum, WS for both); (Ordinal) the feasts mentioned in Frere's text of the Sarum Ordinal; and (c. 15th) the double feasts identified in the kalendar of the fifteenth-century manuscript BL Addl 32427 for Worcester diocese.

	SARUM	OSB	YORK	1240	Ordinal	c.15th
			JANUARY			
1	Circumcision	Circumcision	Circumcision	WS	X	X
2	Oct. Stephen	Oct. Stephen	Oct. Stephen		X	
3	Oct. John	Oct. John	Oct. John		X	
4	Oct. Innocents	Oct. Innocents	Oct. Innocents		X	
5	**Oct Thomas, sometimes Edward the Confessor**		**Edward the Confessor**			
6	*Epiphany*	*Epiphany*	*Epiphany*	WS	X	X
7			**William**			
8	**Lucian**		**(alternative for William)**			
9						
10			Paul			
11						
12						
13	Oct Epiphany, Hilary	Oct Epiphany, Hilary	Oct Epiphany, Hilary, Remigius		Oct Epi X	
14	*Felix in Pincis*	*Felix in pincis*	*Felix in pincis*		X	
15	Maurus	Maurus	Maurus			
16	*Marcellus*	*Marcellus*	*Marcellus*		X	
17	**Sulpicius and/or Antony**	**Antony**	**Antony**		Sulp. X	
18	*Prisca*	*Prisca*	*Prisca*		X	
19	**Wulfstan**	**Wulfstan**	**Germanicus**	W	X	
20	*Fabian&Sebastian*	*Fabian&Sebastian*	*Fabian&Sebastian*		X	

	SARUM	OSB	YORK	1240	Ordinal	c.15th
21	*Agnes*	*Agnes*	*Agnes*		X	
22	*Vincent*	*Vincent*	*Vincent*	*W*	X	
23		*Emerenciana*	*Emerenciana*			
24			Babolenus			
25	*Conv of Paul/ Mem. Preiectus*	*Conv of Paul/Preiectus*	*Conv of Paul*	*W*	X	
26			**Polycarp**			
27	Julian	Julian	Julian		X	
28	*Oct Agnes*	*Oct Agnes*	*Oct Agnes*		X	
29						
30	**Batildis**		**Batildis**		**X**	
31						
		FEBRUARY				
1	Brigid	Brigid	Brigid		X	
2	*Purification*	*Purification*	*Purification*	*WS*	*X*	
3	Blasius	Blasius	Blasius		X	
4			**Gilbert**			
5	*Agatha*	*Agatha*	*Agatha*	*W*	*X*	
6	Vedast and Amand	Vedast and Amand	Vedast and Amand		X	
7						
8						
9						
10	Scholastica	Scholastica	Scholastica		X	
11						
12						
13						
14	*Valentine*	*Valentine*	*Valentine*		X	
15						
16	*Juliana*	*Juliana*	*Juliana*		X	
17						
18						
19						
20						
21						
22	*Cathedra Petri*	*Cathedra Petri*	*Cathedra Petri*	*W*	*X*	

	SARUM	OSB	YORK	1240	Ordinal	c.15th
23						
24	Mathias	Mathias	*Mathias*	*W*	*X*	X
25						
26						
27						
28						
			MARCH			
1	**David added, often**	**David and Chad added or not**	**Albinus**			
2	**Chad added, often**	**David and Chad added or not**				
3						
4						
5						
6						
7	**Perpetua & Felicity**	**Perpetua & Felicity**			X	
8						
9						
10						
11						
12	Gregory	Gregory	Gregory		X	X
13						
14						
15						
16						
17						
18	**Edward, king and martyr**	**Edward, king and martyr**			X	
19						
20	Cuthbert	Cuthbert	Cuthbert		X	
21	Benedict	Benedict	Benedict		X	
22						
23						
24						
25	Annunciation	Annunciation	Annunciation	S	X	X

	SARUM	OSB	YORK	1240	Ordinal	c.15th
26						
27						
28						
29						
30						
31						
			APRIL			
1						
2						
3	**Richard, sometimes added or missing**				X	
4	Ambrose	Ambrose	Ambrose	S	X	
5						
6						
7						
8						
9						
10						
11		**Guthlac**				
12						
13						
14	*Tyburtius & Valerian*	*Tyburtius & Valerian*	*Tyburtius & Valerian*		X	
15						
16						
17						
18						
19	**Alphege**	**Alphege**			X	
20						
21						
22						
23	*George*	*George*	*George*		X	
24			**Tr. Wilfrid**			
25	Mark	Mark	Mark	WS	X	X
26						
27						

	SARUM	OSB	YORK	1240	Ordinal	c.15th
28	*Vitalis*		*Vitalis*		X	
29						
30						
			MAY			
1	*Philip and James*	*Philip and James*	*Philip and James*	WS	X	X
2		**Athanasius**				
3	*Inventio Holy Cross/ Mem. Alexander and Eventius*	*Inventio Holy Cross*	*Inventio Holy Cross*	WS	X	X
4						
5						
6	*John Portlatin*	*John Portlatin*	*John Portlatin*	WS	X	
7	John of Beverley often added	John of Beverley sometimes added	John of Beverley			
8						
9	**Tr.Nicholas sometimes added**					
10	*Gordian & Epimachus*	*Gordian & Epimachus*	*Gordian & Epimachus*		X	
11						
12	*Nereus & Achilleus*	*Nereus & Achilleus*	*Nereus & Achilleus*		X	
13						
14						
15						
16						
17						
18						
19	Dunstan/ Mem. Potentiana	Dunstan	Dunstan	S	X	
20						
21						
22						
23						
24						
25	**Aldelm, often and/or *Urban***	*Urban* **more than Aldelm**	*Urban*	Aldelm S	Aldelm X	
26	Augustine	*Augustine*	Augustine, Bede	S	X	X
27						

	SARUM	OSB	YORK	1240	Ordinal	c.15th
28	**Germanus**		**Germanus**		X	
29						
30						
31	Petronilla	Petronilla	Petronilla		X	
			JUNE			
1	*Nicomedis*		*Nicomedis*		X	
2	*Marcellinus & Peter*	*Marcellinus & Peter*	*Marcellinus & Peter*		X	
3						
4			**Petroc**			
5	Boniface		Boniface		X	
6						
7						
8	**Medard&Gildard**	**Medard, but often blank**	**William**		X	
9	**Tr.Edmund and/or** *Primus & Felician*	*Primus & Felician*	*Primus & Felician*		X	
10						
11	Barnabas	Barnabas	Barnabas	WS	X	
12	*Basilidis*	*Basilidis*	*Basilidis*		X	
13						
14	Basil	Basil	Basil		X	
15	*Vitus & Modestus*	Edburga/ *Vitus & Modestus*	**Oct William**		Vitus, Mod's	
16	**Tr.Richard; Ciricus and Julitta with or without Richard**	**Ciricus and Julitta, or Richard**	**Ciricus and Julitta**		Richard	
17		**Botulph**	**Botulph**			
18	*Mark & Marcellian*	*Mark & Marcellian*	*Mark & Marcellian*		X	
19	*Gervasius & Protasius*	*Gervasius & Protasius*	*Gervasius & Protasius*		X	
20	**Tr.Edward**				Edw.	
21		**Leufrid**	**Leufrid**			
22	Alban	Alban	Alban		X	
23	Etheldreda, often added	Etheldreda	Etheldreda			
24	*Nativity of John the Baptist*	*Nativity of John the Baptist*	*Nativity of John the Baptist*	WS	X	X
25						
26	*John & Paul*	*John & Paul*	*John & Paul*		X	

	SARUM	OSB	YORK	1240	Ordinal	c.15th
27						
28	*Leo*	*Leo*	*Leo*		X	
29	*Peter&Paul*	*Peter&Paul*	*Peter and Paul*	WS	X	X
30	*Commem.Paul*	*Commem.Paul*	*Commem.Paul*		X	
JULY						
1	Oct SJB	Oct SJB	Oct SJB		X	
2	*Processus & Martinian,* Swithun, Visit	**Swithun,** *Processus & Martinian*	**Swithun,** *Processus & Martinian*		X	
3						
4	Tr. Ord. Martin	Tr. Ord. Martin	Tr. Ord. Martin		X	
5						
6	*Oct Peter and Paul*	*Oct Peter and Paul*	*Oct Peter and Paul*	W	X	
7	**Tr.Thomas,** often erased		**Tr. Thomas**		X	X
8			**Grimbald**			
9			**Everild**			
10	*7 Brothers*	*7 Brothers*	*7 Brothers*		X	
11	**Benedict,** some-times absent	**Tr Benedict**			X	
12						
13						
14						
15	**Tr. Swithun**				X	
16	**Osmund** some-times added					
17	**Kenelm**	**Kenelm**			X	
18	**Arnulf**	**Oct. Benedict**			X	
19						
20	Margaret	Margaret	Margaret	W	X	
21	*Praxedis*	*Praxedis*	*Praxedis*		X	
22	Mary Magdalene	Mary Magdalene	Mary Magdalene	W	X	
23	*Apollinaris*	*Apollinaris*	*Apollinaris*		X	
24	Christina	Christina	Christina		X	
25	*James* / Christopher	*James* / Christopher	*James* / Christopher	W	X	X
26	Anne	Anne	Anne			

	SARUM	OSB	YORK	1240	Ordinal	c.15th
27	**7 Sleepers**	**7 Sleepers**	**Martha**		X	
28	Samson	Samson	Samson, Pantaleon		X	
29	*Felix, Faustinus*	*Felix, Faustinus*	*Felix, Faustinus*		X	
30	*Abdon & Sennen*	*Abdon & Sennen*	*Abdon & Sennen*		X	
31	Germanus	Germanus	Germanus		X	
AUGUST						
1	*Peter in chains*	*Peter in chains*	*Peter in chains*	W	X	
2	*Stephen.pope*	*Stephen.pope*	*Stephen.pope*		X	
3	Inv. Stephen	Inv. Stephen	Inv. Stephen		X	
4						
5	Oswald	Oswald	Oswald	W	X	
6	*Sixtus et al*, unless Transfig added	*Sixtus et al*	*Sixtus et al*		X	
7	*Donatus* unless HolyName added	*Donatus*	*Donatus*		X	
8	*Cyriacus*	*Cyriacus*	Oct Petri, *Cyriacus*		X	
9	**Romanus**		**Romanus**		X	
10	*Laurence*	*Laurence*	*Laurence*	W	X	
11	*Tyburcius*	*Tyburcius*	*Tyburcius*		X	
12						
13	*Hypolitus*	*Hypolitus*	*Hypolitus*		X	
14	*Eusebius*	*Eusebius*	*Eusebius*		X	
15	*Assumption.BVM*	*Assumption*	*Assumption*	WS	X	X
16						
17	*Oct Laurence*	*Oct Laurence*	*Oct Laurence*			
18	*Agapitus*	*Agapitus*	*Agapitus*		X	
19	*Magnus*	*Magnus*	*Magnus*		X	
20						
21						
22	*Oct. Assumption; Timothy and Symphorian*	*Oct. Assumption; Timothy and Symphorian*	*Oct. Assumption; Timothy and Symphorian*		X	
23	Timothy & Appolinaris	Timothy & Appolinaris	Timothy & Appolinaris			
24	*Bartholomew /* Mem. Audeonus	*Bartholomew*, Audoenus	*Bartholomew*	W	X	X
25			Hilda			

	SARUM	OSB	YORK	1240	Ordinal	c.15th
26						
27	*Rufus*	*Rufus*	*Rufus*		X	
28	Augustine of Hippo / Mem. Hermes	Augustine, Hermes	Augustine of Hippo		X	X
29	Decollatio John the Baptist; *Sabina*	Decollatio John the Baptist; *Sabina*	Decollatio John the Baptist		**X**	
30	*Felix & Adauctus*	*Felix & Adauctus*	*Felix & Adauctus*		X	
31	**Cuthberga**	**Aidan**	**Cuthberga**		X	
SEPTEMBER						
1	Giles, *Priscus*	Giles, *Priscus*	Giles, *Priscus*		X	
2						
3		**Ord. Gregory**				
4	Tr. Cuthbert	Tr. Cuthbert	Tr. Cuthbert, Birinus		X	
5	Bertin	Bertin	Bertin		X	
6						
7			**Evortius**			
8	*Nativity BVM*	*Nativity BVM; Adrian*	*Nativity BVM*	WS	X	X
9	***Gorgon***		***Gorgon***			
10		**Egwin or Ethelwold**				
11	*Protus & Hyacinth*	*Protus & Hyacinth*	*Protus & Hyacinth*			
12						
13			**Maurilius**			
14	*Exaltatio Holy Cross sometimes Cornelius and Cyprian*	*Exaltatio Holy Cross*	*Exaltatio Holy Cross*	W	X	X
15	Oct BVM or, less frequently, Nicomedes	Oct BVM, Nicomedes	Oct BVM, *Nicomedes*	S	X	
16	*Edith, Eufemia*	*Eufemia*	*Eufemia, Lucy*		X	
17	Lambert	Lambert	Lambert		X	
18						
19						
20						
21	*Matthew*	*Matthew*	*Matthew*	W	X	X
22	*Maurice*	*Maurice*	*Maurice*		X	
23	**Tecla**		**Tecla**		X	
24						

	SARUM	OSB	YORK	1240	Ordinal	c.15th
25	**Firminius**		**Firminius**		X	
26	**Cyprian & Justina**		**Cyprian & Justina**		X	
27	*Cosmas & Damian*	*Cosmas & Damian*	*Cosmas & Damian*		X	
28						
29	*Michael*	*Michael*	*Michael*	WS	X	X
30	Jerome	Jerome	Jerome		X	X
OCTOBER						
1	Remigius	Remigius	Remigius		X	
2	**Leodegar (some-times Thomas of Heref ord added)**	**Leodegar**	**Thomas of Hereford**		X	
3						
4			**Francis**			
5						
6	Faith	Faith	Faith		X	
7	*Mark & Marcellian*	*Mark & Marcellian*	*Mark & Marcellian*		X	
8			**Pelagia**			
9	Dionysius	Dionysius	Dionysius		X	
10	**Gereon**	**Paulinus**	**Paulinus**		X	
11	Nichasius	Nichasius	Nichasius		X	
12		**Wilfrid**	**Wilfrid**			
13	Tr. Edward	Tr. Edward	Tr. Edward		X	
14	*Calixtus*	*Calixtus*	*Calixtus*		X	
15	Wulfran	Wulfran	Wulfran		X	
16	**often Michael in monte tumba**				X	
17	**often Tr. Etheldreda added**					
18	*Luke*, Justus	*Luke*, Justus	*Luke*	W	X	X
19	**either nothing or Frideswide added**		**Relics**			
20			**Austreberta**			
21	11,000 Virgins	11,000 Virgins	11,000 Virgins / Hillarion		X	
22						
23	Romanus	Romanus	Romanus		X	
24						

	SARUM	OSB	YORK	1240	Ordinal	c.15th
25	Crispin & Crispinian, often with Tr. John of Beverley	Crispin & Crispinian	Tr. John of Beverley		X	
26						
27						
28	*Simon & Jude*	*Simon & Jude*	*Simon & Jude*	W	X	X
29						
30			**Germanus**			
31	Quintin	Quintin	Quintin		X	

			NOVEMBER			
1	All Saints	All Saints	All Saints	WS	X	X
2	All Souls	All Souls	All Souls		X	
3	**Eustace, often Winifred added**	**Eustace**	**Eustace**			
4						
5						
6	Leonard	Leonard	Leonard	W	X	
7			**Willebrord**			
8	*4 Crowned Martyrs*	*4 Crowned Martyrs*	*4 Crowned Martyrs*		X	
9	*Theodore*	*Theodore*	*Theodore*		X	
10			**Martin, pope**			
11	Martin, bishop, *Mennas*	Martin, bishop, *Mennas*	Martin, bishop, *Mennas*	W	X	
12						
13	Bricius	Bricius	Bricius		X	
14						
15	**Machutus**		**Machutus**		X	
16	**Edmund, archbishop**		**Edmund, archbishop**		X	
17	**Hugh, Anianus**		**Anianus**		X	
18	Oct. Martin	Oct. Martin	Oct. Martin		X	
19						
20	Edmund, king and martyr	Edmund, king and martyr	Edmund, king and martyr		X	
21						
22	*Cecilia*	*Cecilia*	*Cecilia*		X	
23	*Clement*	*Clement*	*Clement*	W	X	

	SARUM	OSB	YORK	1240	Ordinal	c.15th
24	*Chrysogonius*	*Chrysogonus*	*Chrysogonus*		X	
25	Katherine	Katherine	Katherine	W	X	
26	**Linus**		**Linus**		**X**	
27						
28						
29	*Saturninus & Sisinius*	*Saturninus & Sisinius*	*Saturninus & Sisinius*		X	
30	*Andrew*	*Andrew*	*Andrew*	WS	X	X
DECEMBER						
1			**Chrysanthus & Daria**			
2						
3						
4	**nothing, or Osmund added**					
5						
6	Nicholas	Nicholas	Nicholas	W	X	
7	*Oct. Andrew*	*Oct. Andrew*	*Oct. Andrew*		X	
8	Conception BVM	Conception BVM	Conception BVM			X
9						
10						
11		*Damasus*				
12						
13	*Lucy*	*Lucy*	*Lucy*	W	X	
14						
15						
16						
17						
18						
19						
20						
21	*Thomas*	*Thomas*	*Thomas*	W	X	X
22						
23						
24						
25	Christmas	Christmas	Christmas		X	X
26	Stephen	Stephen	Stephen		X	X

	SARUM	OSB	YORK	1240	Ordinal	c.15th
27	John	John	John		X	X
28	Innocents	Innocents	Innocents		X	X
29	Thomas Becket	Thomas Becket	Thomas Becket		X	X
30						
31	Silvester	sometimes Silvester	Silvester		X	

The table illustrates that some feasts are only observed in one normative calendar; others are in two. The following pages illustrate these divisions.

Sarum Only

Lucian (8 Jan); Richard (3 Apr); Tr. Nicholas (9 May); Tr. Edmund (9 Jun); Tr. Edward (20 Jun); Tr. Swithun (15 Jul); Tr. Osmund (16 Jul); Arnulph (of Metz, 18 Jul); Gereon (10 Oct); Michael in monte tumba (16 Oct); Tr. Etheldreda (17 Oct); Frideswide (19 Oct); Hugh (of Lincoln, 17 Nov); Osmund (4 Dec).

Many of the saints in this category are English. It is notable that Richard, the translations of Nicholas and Edmund, Osmund, Etheldreda, and Frideswide were specifically promulgated in the province of Canterbury (see chapter 4). The appearance of the non-English saints may suggest their presence in the early Salisbury Cathedral kalendar.

York Only

Tr. William (8 Jan); Babolenus (24 Jan); Polycarp (26 Jan); Gilbert (4 Feb); Albinus (1 Mar); Tr. Wilfrid (24 Apr); Bede (26 May); Petroc (4 Jun); William (8 Jun); Grimbald (8 Jul); Everild (9 Jul); Martha (27 Jul); Evortius (7 Sep); Maurilius (13 Sep); Thomas of Hereford (2 Oct); Francis (4 Oct); Pelagia (8 Oct); Austreberta (20 Oct); Tr. John Baptist (25 Oct); Germanus (30 Oct); Willebrord (7 Nov); Martin (10 Nov); Chrysanthus and Daria (1 Dec).

In addition to English saints, several from this group have French associations, perhaps related to the reputed Norman origin of the Use of York.[37] William and Wilfrid are associated with York itself, while Everild was associated with Wilfrid. Willebrord, archbishop of Utrecht, was born in Yorkshire. Gilbert (of Sempringham), Petroc (of Cornwall), and Grimbald, dean of New Minster/

---

[37] See below in chapter 4; also Salisbury, *The Use of York*.

Winchester, are regional saints who are not particularly associated with the Northern province, but seem to have been liturgically commemorated. Maurilius (of Angers) and Evurtius, a little-known bishop of Orléans, along with Austreberta, are both of French origin. Pope St Martin, Pelagia (a fifth-century penitent) and the translation of John the Baptist appear without an obvious cause.

Benedictine

Germanicus (19 Jan); Guthlac (11 Apr); Athanasius (2 May); Edburga (15 Jun); Aidan (31 Aug); Ordination of Gregory (3 Sep); Tr. Egwin (10 Sep); Ethelwold (10 Sep).

Guthlac was a Lincolnshire hermit whose early cult spanned a number of English Benedictine houses. Athanasius was the author of the famous life of St Antony, which was well known in monastic circles. The cult of Egwin, founder of Evesham Abbey, was strengthened by a 'successful fund-raising tour of England' in the eleventh century.[38] Ethelwold, another Benedictine, was a central figure in the tenth-century monastic revival. The appearance of an ancillary feast of Gregory the Great should come as no surprise, though it is interesting that it appears with frequency only in Benedictine kalendars.

Sarum and York

Germanus (of Paris, 28 May); Vitalis (28 April); Nicomedes (1 Jun); Boniface (5 Jun); Tr. Thomas Becket (7 Jul); Romanus (Roman martyr, 9 Aug); Cuthberga (31 Aug); Gorgonius (of Rome, 9 Sep); Tecla (of Iconium, 23 Sep); Firmin (25 Sep); Cyprian and Justina (26 Sep); Machutus (Malo, 15 Nov); Dep. Edmund (of Abingdon, 16 Nov); Anianus (of Orleans, 17 Nov); Linus (26 Nov).

This group, too, demonstrates both English and Continental influences. Boniface, Thomas, Edmund, and Machutus are all bishops with English connexions; Germanus, Firmin, and Anianus are all French bishops; the others are Roman in origin.

---

[38] D. H. Farmer, *Oxford Dictionary of Saints*, 5th edn (Oxford: Oxford University Press, 2004), p. 168.

Sarum and Benedictine

Wulfstan (19 Jan); Batildis (30 Jan); David (1 Mar); Chad (2 Mar); Perpetua and Felicitas (7 Mar); Edward king and martyr (18 Mar); Alphege (19 Apr); Medard (of Vermandois, and Gildard in Sarum) (8 Jun); Tr. Richard (16 Jun); Benedict (11 Jul); Kenelm (17 Jul); 7 Sleepers (27 Jul); Leodegar (2 Oct); Crispin and Crispinian (25 Oct).

It is notable that this group is composed of English saints except for the Roman feast of Perpetua and Felicitas, Medard and Gildard (two French bishops), Benedict, the Seven Sleepers, Leodegar (bishop of Autun), and Crispin and Crispinian. Notably, bishop Wulfstan was a Benedictine. Batildis (Bathilde) was more popular in France than in England.

York and Benedictine

Emerenciana (23 Jan); Botulph (17 Jun); Leufrid (21 Jun); Paulinus (10 Nov); Wilfrid (12 Oct).

Paulinus and Wilfrid are 'York saints' whose feastdays seem also to have been observed by Benedictine houses (making them unhelpful as identifiers of York use, though the translation of Wilfrid appears only in York books). Botulph was the abbot of Icanho (an unidentified site in East Anglia). Emerenciana was a Roman martyr.

In the Sarum and Sarum/Benedictine groups, English saints enjoy some prevalence; the other saints may come in the former case from the early Salisbury kalendar or from a common exemplar. In addition to English regional saints, the York group and Sarum/York groups show some French influence, with French saints perhaps owing their existence to a Norman exemplar at a similarly early stage. The explanation for these saints without an obvious cause is speculative, but certainly plausible. The Benedictine group offers few surprises: all these saints have some reason to appear and three of five have English associations.

The three columns on the right-hand side of Table 2.8 provide an indication of which saints in the Sarum normative kalendar are found in several tables of observances: first, a 1240 statute of the diocese of Worcester indicating which saints were Sarum doubles (marked S) and *festa ferianda* in Worcester diocese.[39]

---

[39] Festa ferianda are dealt with by C. R. Cheney, 'Rules for the Observance of Feast-Days in Medieval England', *Bulletin of the Institute of Historical Research*, 34 (1961), 117–47.

The next column indicates the feastdays in the contents of the Sarum 'Old' Ordinal as synthesized by W. H. Frere in his edition.[40] The rightmost column gives the contents of a table of Sarum feasts in the upper margins of a fifteenth-century kalendar in Salisbury Cathedral MS 152. These three documents provide some corroboration for the list of 'standard' Sarum observances. All feasts prescribed in the Ordinal (Frere dates this to *c.* 1270) are in the Sarum normative kalendar, except the Offices for the Dedication and Relics. Nineteen feasts are in the normative kalendar but not in the Ordinal:

Oct. Thomas Becket; Lucian; Maurus; DAVID; CHAD; JOHN of BEVERLEY; TR. NICHOLAS; ETHELDREDA; Swithun; OSMUND; ANNE; Oct. Laurence; Timothy and Apollinaris; Protus and Hyacinth; Tr.ETHELDREDA; FRIDESWIDE; WINIFRED; OSMUND; Conception.

Eleven of these (in capitals) are saints added from 1383 (the promulgation of Anne) onward, which would not be expected to be accommodated in an early Ordinal. The eighteen saints to appear in all three lists *and* the Sarum normative kalendar are predictable: all are Christological or Marian, or pertain to a Biblical saint.

Circumcision; Epiphany; Purification; Mark; Philip and James; Inventio Holy Cross; Nat. John Baptist; Peter and Paul; Assumption; Nat. BVM; Exaltatio Holy Cross; Matthew; Michael; Luke; Simon & Jude; All Saints; Andrew; Thomas.

All are predictable inclusions, and many are principal feasts of the universal Church.

It is worthwhile pointing out that the York/Benedictine group represents the non-Roman saints which were popular or more prevalent in the North, and that the Sarum/York group represents those non-Roman saints which were popular across England in the secular cursus. Of the Sarum/York group, seven were bishops and commemorated as such, and the translation of Thomas Becket and the feast of Edmund were widely promulgated in England. Otherwise these saints, too, with few other common features, may be ascribed to the common Norman inheritance of the post-Conquest English kalendar; or to pre-existing English patterns not affected by legislation, or to trends in early exemplars shared by both Sarum and York.

[40] W. H. Frere, *The Use of Sarum*.

In four of six groups (Sarum, York, Benedictine, Sarum/Benedictine) the strong presence of English saints is seen, including some saints with regional cults who, like Grimbald and Petroc, seem surprisingly to have been venerated outside the areas with which they are most associated. Perhaps their liturgical veneration was extended beyond obvious borders. The presence of English saints in English kalendars is unsurprising. Yet Sarum/York most of all, and indeed all other groups, also contain a number of Roman and French saints whose presence may be the result either of pre-existent veneration in early English kalendars, or of the influence of Norman ecclesiastical patterns on post-Conquest liturgy. T. A. Heslop noted in a study of manuscripts from before and after the Conquest hailing from Christ Church, Canterbury, that twenty-seven saints had disappeared in the latter, some 'of Anglo-Saxon national importance',[41] but this conventional narrative has been challenged by Richard Pfaff and Susan Ridyard, who suggest that the picture is not as clear.[42]

These observations, of course, represent trends in groups of manuscripts of a single Use, attempting to identify what is most frequently present, and they do not take divergent patterns into account. The presence or absence of one or a few saints cannot, therefore, be said to be diagnostic of Use. Much local variation (sometimes restricted to one or two manuscripts) is discussed later in this chapter. However, the normative kalendars and groups of saints by Use are based on a larger survey of manuscript evidence than has yet been attempted.

Some, but not all, of these saints' days were imposed by statute, and terminal dates for the manuscripts which contain them may be hypothesized on the basis of their dates of institution. The feasts of Edmund of Abingdon (1246) and Richard of Chichester (1260); Anne (1383); David, Chad, Winifred, and the translation of Thomas Becket (1398, re-promulgated with George 1415); John of Beverley (1416); and Osmund, the Translation of Etheldreda, and Frideswide (1481) were ordered to be celebrated by successive convocations of the province of Canterbury, sometimes by the promulgation of the papal document proclaiming their sanctity.[43] Of these, Edmund, Richard, Osmund, Etheldreda, and Frideswide are all in the Sarum group above, and David and

---

[41] T. A. Heslop, 'The Canterbury Calendars and the Norman Conquest', in *Canterbury and the Norman Conquest: Churches, Saints and Scholars 1066–1199*, ed. by Richard Eales and Richard Sharpe (London: Hambledon, 1995), pp. 53–85 (p. 56).

[42] Pfaff, 'Lanfranc's Supposed Purge'; Susan J. Ridyard, '*Condigna veneratio*: Post-Conquest Attitudes to the Saints of the Anglo-Saxons', *Anglo-Norman Studies*, 9 (1986), 179–206.

[43] See chapter 4.

Chad are in the Sarum/Benedictine group, suggesting that their cults were mainly to be found in these constituencies, and that these Canterbury promulgations had little effect in the Northern province. Anne was widely venerated, perhaps even before 1383, and John of Beverley's local cult too seems to have spread before it became a prescribed Sarum observance in 1416. A fuller discussion of the adoption of new feasts is in chapter 4.

On the Basis of which Observances Should the Use of a Kalendar be Assessed?

It seems that the groups of non-Roman saints most likely to appear in kalendars of each English Use (or province) included many English and regional saints, a fact that is not surprising. But these saints should not be seen individually as identifiers of their Use: having served James's 'apprenticeship' in determining the universal saints of all English liturgy, it is not sufficient to say that the presence or absence of one or two local saints proves or negates the identification of a manuscript with a Use. Paulinus of York is found both in York kalendars and Benedictine kalendars of both provinces. Saints common to kalendars from specific regions are outlined later in this chapter.

Nevertheless, these normative kalendars provide a tool for assessment, to be used with caution. The best assessment of Use using data from kalendars ought to include a holistic assessment of the group — the more saints here associated with Sarum appear in a kalendar, the more likely the identification of that kalendar with that Use. This section provides comprehensive and complete diagnostic lists for such a procedure: it should not be forgotten that the lists for each Use include both the main group and groups associated with the Use; that is, the complete register of 'standard Sarum saints' against which a putative Sarum kalendar should be compared includes the list of Sarum-only saints as well as those for Sarum/Benedictine and Sarum/York.

Provincial, Regional, and Local Observances: Dedication and Relics Feasts

In addition to saints' days and the Christological and Marian feasts which enjoyed more or less general observance, many kalendars also included entries for the feast of the Dedication or consecration of a church, and for a general feast of Relics, which was kept on a single day of the year in honour of all saints' relics kept in a church. The Sarum Dedication feast was kept on 30 September, although it seems rarely to be indicated in kalendars; similarly, the York Dedication does not appear with regularity, although in 1489 it was prescribed that all dedications of churches should be observed on the Sunday after the feast of the Commemoration of St Paul (30 January).[44] The manuscripts do, however, supply the dates of a number of monastic, cathedral, and parochial Dedication feasts which can be corroborated by external evidence, and can reliably give an indication of place of use.

Table 2.9: Dedication feasts indicated in kalendars. The venue is noted in column 2, if known. The witnesses are indicated in column 3 by kalendar siglum.

8 Jan	Muchelney	CK
26 Jan	Coltishall, Norfolk	Z
14 Feb	unknown	CE
16 Apr	'eccl S Joh ev'	CP
18 Apr	'Cap Norh'm'	CK
29 Apr	'S Mich in Coldingham'	CL
11 May	Hereford	CI, DI
13 May	Wollaton	DU
4 Jun	Mordiford	CI
7 Jun	Worcester	CH
2 Jul	Harwood	O
30 Jul	'Eccl fr minor no'ta'	AQ
17 Sep	Ely	CD
18 Sep	Gloucester	CG, DI
23 Sep	Norwich (*recte* 24 Sep)	BN
24 Sep	Norwich	AW, BB, CZ, DD
28 Sep	Peterborough	CU
3 Oct	unknown	BW
15 Oct	Coldingham	CL
15 Oct	Therouanne	CN
25 Oct	'eccl Clugn'	CA
9 Nov	'basilice salvatoris'	AQ
13 Nov	'bricii ded huius eccl.'	CS
18 Nov	'basilice petri et pauli'	AQ
9 Dec	Launton	BW
29 Dec	St Albans	CM

[44] *The Records of the Northern Convocation*, Surtees Society, 113 (Durham, 1907), p. 203.

Manuscript evidence for Relics feasts is more consistent in secular books. The York feast of Relics was kept on 19 October, witnessed here in twenty-two York kalendars.[45] The Sarum feast was originally kept on 15 September, but was moved in 1319, under Roger Martival, bishop of Salisbury, to the first Sunday after the translation of Thomas Becket, to avoid convergence with the octave of the Nativity of the Blessed Virgin Mary.[46] Pfaff suggests that an 'awareness' of the change of the date of Sarum Relics may indicate that a manuscript's users were keeping current with the developing Sarum liturgy,[47] whose widespread use of 'usum ecclesie nostre' is hinted at in the document which promulgated the change of date. The early date is present in three kalendars (BZ, CO, CX), whilst the rubric for the celebration of the later movable date is in fourteen kalendars.[48] Further dates of all Relics feasts found in the kalendars studied here are listed below.

Table 2.10: Relics feasts indicated in kalendars. Places of use are noted in column 2, if known. The witnesses are indicated in column 3 by kalendar siglum.

27 Jan	St Albans	CM
12 Jul	Beckford, Gloucs (Aug)	DH
24 Aug	Hyde Abbey (OSB)	CV
31 Aug	Coldingham (OSB)	CL
15 Sep	Sarum (old date)	BZ, CO, CX
18 Sep	Lewes (Cluniac)	CA
11 Oct	Pontefract (Cluniac)	CP
15 Oct	Muchelney (OSB)	CK
15 Oct	Worcester (OSB)	CH

The Relics feasts for Sarum and York should be added to the list of features which indicate an association with either Use; the presence of the 15 September date for Sarum in an original hand, or the presence of the rubric for the July date in a new hand, may suggest the relative antiquity of a kalendar. Likewise the July rubric in an original hand certainly suggests a date of manufacture after 1319.

[45] Kalendars E, F, G, H, I, J, K, L, M, N, O, P, Q, R, S, T, U, V, CC, DB, DN, EB.

[46] *The Registers of Roger Martival, Bishop of Salisbury 1315–1330: The Register of Divers Letters*, ed. by C. R. Elrington, Canterbury and York Society, 57 (Oxford: Oxford University Press, 1963), p. 293.

[47] Pfaff, *LME*, p. 286.

[48] Kalendars W, AW, AZ, BD, BF, BJ, BM, BQ, BR, BU, BV, BX, CW, DE.

No positive indicator can be found with Sarum or York Dedication days, but the dates for a number of cathedrals as well as parish churches should permit the assignment of otherwise unknown books to places of origin. In some cases Dedication dates are the only explicit indication of place of use. In some cases they agree with other data, as for the books with a Norwich dedication which also contain the Norwich synodal feasts (see below). Similarly the Cluniac books have explicit ascriptions of origin.

Both Dedication and Relics feasts are particularly useful because they can be tied to identifiable venues, the best sort of indicator of place of use. Similarly, the generic Sarum and York Relics feasts should be seen to be diagnostic of those Uses, as both were well disseminated and seem to have been consistent.

Provincial, Regional, and Local Observances: Regional Kalendars

The manuscript evidence supports the argument that kalendars associated with the same geographical area can contain a unified group of local saints, a view also held by Reames.[49] Initial assessment was carried out by identifying pairs of kalendars with a high number of points of shared variation, although not all groups of kalendars with geographic affiliations necessarily share variants from the 'base version' in the 1531 breviary. The three manuscripts associated with Gloucester do form a group whose kalendars share a number of notable saints:

Table 2.11: Regional feasts for Gloucester.
The witnesses are indicated in column 3 by kalendar siglum.

9 Feb	Teilo	CG DH DI		25 Jun	Kyneburga	CG DH DI
23 Feb	Milburga	CG DI		25 Aug	Audoenus	CG DI
28 Feb	Oswald	CG DI		3 Sep	Ord. Gregory	CG DH DI
29 Mar	Gwynllyw	CG DI		10 Sep	Tr. Egwin	CG DI
11 Apr	Guthlac	CG DI		18 Sep	Dedication	CG DH DI
15 Apr	Paternus	CG DI		23 Sep	Paternus	CG DI
2 May	Athanasius	CG DI		8 Oct	Tr. Oswald	CG DI
20 May	Ethelbert	CG DH DI		30 Dec	Egwin	CG DI
7 Jun	Tr. Wulfstan	CG DI				

[49] Reames, 'Unexpected Texts for Saints'.

Most of the saints in this list are shared only by books from the cathedral itself. All three have Teilo, probably because of the proximity of Wales; Ethelbert, king of the East Angles and patron of Hereford; Kyneburga of Gloucester; and Gregory's Ordination feast. CG and DI, both associated with Gloucester Abbey itself, are clearly closest, whilst DH, from Beckford Priory, Gloucestershire, is at some distance from them. All have the Benedictine feast of the Ordination of Gregory, and some of the local saints, as well as the cathedral's dedication. But beside DI, CG is closer to CS, from Evesham; CH, from Worcester; and two kalendars of Peterborough (CU and CB, probably because of the Benedictine connexion), than it is to DH. DH itself is closer to a St Albans kalendar, CM, than to CG or DI.

This group of saints includes only three which are not English: these are Athanasius, patriarch of Alexandria and part of the normative Benedictine kalendar; Audoenus (*recte* 24 August), bishop of Rouen, whose relics were claimed by Canterbury; and the Ordination of Gregory, also a Benedictine feast. Otherwise the Gloucester kalendars include six saints whose cults are local or at least from an adjacent region (Milburga, abbess of Wenlock, but common elsewhere; Oswald of Worcester and his translation; Ethelbert; Wulfstan of Worcester; Kyneburga; Egwin and his Translation) as well as three Welsh saints (Teilo, Gwynllyw, and Paternus). The feast of Paternus on 15 April is that of Paternus of Wales, monk and bishop; that on 23 September is Paternus of Avranches, but his feast is sometimes confused with that of the former, probably the reason for its appearance here on the latter date. Guthlac (11 April) is associated with Crowland and Repton, but is also found in the Benedictine normative kalendar.

The two Hereford manuscript kalendars, CI and DF, share a closer bond, with eleven saints shared by both.

Table 2.12: Regional feasts for Hereford.
The witnesses are indicated in column 3 by kalendar siglum.

5 Mar	Piran (of Cornwall)	CI DF
11 Apr	Guthlac	CI DF
20 May	Ethelbert	CI DF
17 Jun	Botulph	CI DF
21 Jun	Leufrid	CI DF
8 Jul	Grimbald	CI DF
12 Jul	Cletus	CI DF
2 Oct	Thomas of Hereford	CI DF
7 Oct	Osith	CI DF
12 Oct	William of York	CI DF

Among these are two saints with local connections: Ethelbert, to whom the cathedral is dedicated; and Thomas de Cantilupe, thirteenth-century bishop of the diocese. Seven other English saints also appear: Piran of Cornwall, possibly of Welsh origin, whose relics were claimed by Exeter; Guthlac; Botulph, an abbot associated more with Suffolk; Grimbald of New Minster (Winchester), a Benedictine observance; Osith, associated with Chich, Essex; and two archbishops of York, William fitzHerbert and Paulinus, who was later bishop of Rochester. No doubt the other English saints are attributable to Benedictine observance, though few appear in the normative kalendar.

The kalendars associated with Worcester and environs (CS is associated with Evesham) share up to ten saints, with CH, a Worcester Cathedral book, sharing Milburga, Guthlac, and Egwin with the Evesham kalendar.

Table 2.13: Regional feasts for Worcester. The witnesses (BH, CH, DE from Worcester; CS from Evesham) are indicated in column 3 by kalendar siglum.

23 Feb	Milburga	CH CS
28 Feb	Oswald	BH CH CS
11 Apr	Guthlac	CH CS
7 Jun	Tr. Wulfstan	BH CH DE
15 Jun	Edburga	BH CH CS DE
10 Sep	Tr. Egwin	CH CS
8 Oct	Tr. Oswald	BH CH CS DE (erased in BH)
10 Oct	Paulinus	CH
12 Oct	Wilfrid	CH
30 Dec	Egwin	BH CH CS DE

This group has five saints with local connexions: Milburga; the translations of Oswald and Wulfstan, bishops of the diocese; Edburga of Winchester, whose relics were at Pershore; Egwin, bishop of Worcester and founder of Evesham. It is notable that Paulinus and Wilfrid, saints who might more reasonably have been transmitted in monastic circles, were still observed in CH, a Sarum book. No non-English saints are in this group.

By contrast, the most unusual saints to be shared between two roughly contemporary Sarum manuscripts from the South East, used at Denchworth, Berkshire (BS), and Ashridge, Buckinghamshire (DW) appear to be those which were officially added to the Sarum liturgy.

Table 2.14: Regional feasts for the South East. The witnesses (BS and DW) are indicated in column 3 by kalendar siglum.

28 Feb	Oswald	BS DW
1 Mar	David	BS DW
2 Mar	Chad	added to BS, blank in DW
7 May	John of Beverley	added to BS, blank in DW
16 Jul	Tr. Osmund	added to both
17 Oct	Tr.Etheldreda	added to BS, blank in DW
19 Oct	Frideswide	added to BS, blank in DW
4 Dec	Osmund	added to both

While the main feastday and the translation of Osmund (canonized 1457) are present in both manuscripts, Chad is only in BS, although David, added to the Sarum kalendar at the same time, does appear in both. The October feasts of Etheldreda and Frideswide, added at the same time as Osmund, appear only in BS. These two Sarum kalendars, from churches less than forty miles apart, do not suggest that official prescriptions to insert these late additions to the kalendar were uniformly followed, even in a limited geographical area.

Similarly, two London manuscripts do not have absolutely consistent contents, and their monastic counterparts in Sussex and Surrey share only sporadically some of the distinctive saints. Erkenwald, bishop of London and the only local saint, is in the London books; Milburga is in both monastic books but neither London kalendar. Thomas Aquinas, Columbanus, and Agricola are in CA (the Cluniac volume from Lewes) and DX, a diurnal from the London Charterhouse.

Table 2.15: Regional feasts for London, Surrey, Sussex.
The witnesses BJ DX (London); CA (Lewes, Cluniac);
CT (Chertsey OSB, Surrey) are indicated in column 3 by kalendar siglum.

23 Feb	Milburga	CA CT
1 Mar	David	BJ DX CA CT
2 Mar	Chad	CT; added in BJ
7 Mar	Thomas Aquinas	CA DX
30 Apr	Erkenwald	CT; added in BJ, DX
21 Nov	Columbanus	CA DX
27 Nov	Agricola	CA DX

East Anglian kalendars, often the subject of discussion, also form an identifiable group. It is interesting to note how many manuscripts that can be associated with East Anglia continue to exist, perhaps more than for any other region. The saints observed in distinct patterns are these:

Table 2.16: Regional feasts for East Anglia.
The witnesses are indicated in column 3 by kalendar siglum.

23 Jan	Emerenciana	BZ CB CD CU
24 Jan	Babolenus	BZ CB CU
30 Jan	Batildis	all except CB CD CJ CU
3 Feb	Werburga	CB CD CU
13 Feb	Ermenilda	BB CB CD CU CZ
1–2 Mar	David and Chad	Not in BB BZ CD CX
3 Mar	Winnol	BB BZ
6 Mar	Kyneburga/Kyneswitha	CB CU
8 Mar	Felix	all but BB BM CB CX
17 Mar	Withburga	BB CD CZ
11 Apr	Guthlac	AV BZ CB CD CJ CU
24 Apr	Yvon	CB CU
29 Apr	Tr. Edmund	all but AV AW BB BM BZ CJ CU CX
2 May	Athanasius	CB CD CU
3 Jun	Erasmus	W BB BM
16 Jul	Tr. Osmund	Z AV AW BA BM BN CZ
5 Aug	Dominic	AP BN CZ; added to W Z AW BA BB
4 Oct	Francis	Z BA BB BM BN BZ CX CZ
10 Oct	Paulinus	CB CD CU
12 Oct	Wilfrid	BZ CB CD CU
17 Oct	Tr.Etheldreda	BN CB CD; added to Z AV AW BA BB BM CZ
19 Oct	Frideswide	BN CB CD; added to Z AV AW BA BB BM CZ
2 Nov	Winifred	W Z AM BN CZ; added to AW BA BB

Notable pairings within this group are CB–CU, both Peterborough Abbey books, with fourteen notable saints shared; CB–CD (Ely) with twelve saints shared; CD–CU (Ely with the other Peterborough kalendar) with eleven; and CJ–CU (Walsingham Augustinians and Peterborough) with six.

There are ten feastdays with local connexions in this group, those of
Werburga, abbess and former nun at Ely; Ermenilda, daughter of Sexburga and
Erconbert, king of Kent; Winnol, a Breton abbot with a cult in East Anglia;
Kyneburga and Kyneswitha, Mercian princesses and abbesses of Castor con-
vent, Northamptonshire; Felix of Dunwich, bishop; Withburga, sister of
Etheldreda and buried at Ely; Ives, a 'Persian bishop'[50] buried at Ramsey Abbey;
the Translation of Edmund king of the East Angles; Botulph, of Suffolk; and
Etheldreda, founder of Ely. Other English saints represented were Guthlac
(hermit of Crowland), Erasmus (who had an altar at Faversham, Kent),
Osmund, Tecla (nun of Wimbourne, Dorset), Paulinus, Wilfrid, Frideswide,
and Winifred, of Welsh origin. The remaining saints which frequently
appeared were Emerenciana, Roman martyr, Babolenus the bishop of Antioch,
Athanasius, Germanus of Paris, Dominic, Cyprian of Carthage, and Francis.

It is worth mentioning that despite the consistency of some of these rarer
observances which were local in nature, these kalendars do not seem to have
added the latterly adopted feasts with consistency: four kalendars (BB BZ CD
CX)[51] do not have David or Chad, while the feasts of John of Beverley, the
Visitation, Transfiguration, and Holy Name are also inconsistently present.
This certainly underlines the fact that local cults had strong followings, and
perhaps that such local observances were more easily sustained (or introduced)
than were the widely promulgated, provincially mandated feasts, a point which
itself indicates the regional character of the Office liturgy, an idea that will be
explored in chapter 4.

Diocesan Feasts: Norwich 'Synodals' and Dublin 'Constitutions'

In at least one case certain notable features of kalendars have illuminated a consistent group of feastdays which were singled out as locally-mandated observances. Sherry Reames has noted these along with some of the regional observances noted above as regional versions of Sarum requiring further investigation.[52] A number of Sarum witnesses of the fourteenth and fifteenth centuries,
associated with the diocese of Norwich, have a set of feasts marked with the
annotations 'non Sar.' or 'non Sar. sed sinodalis'. They refer to *festa synodalia*,

[50] According to Farmer, *Oxford Dictionary of Saints*, p. 266.
[51] Cambridge Clare MS G. 3. 34; BL Stowe 12; BL Addl 33381; Bodl. MS Lyell empt. 4,
all of which are associated with East Anglia.
[52] Reames, 'Unexpected texts for saints', p. 165.

observances which were promulgated by the diocesan bishop or through a synodal statute. Chapter 4 outlines the justification and procedure for synodal statutes, and assesses the relative success of some such observances in the manuscript evidence.

Table 2.17: Manuscripts Containing 'Synodal' Feasts.

Durham Univ. Cosin V. I. 2	R	s.xv	York breviary for Rudby parish church
Ranworth Antiphonal	W	s.xv	Sarum antiphonal (L) for St Helen's, Ranworth
Bodl. e Musaeo 188	AP	s.xv	Sarum book of Hours with Norwich synodals
Camb. Peterhouse 270	BA	s.xiv	Sarum breviary with Norwich synodals
BL Lansdowne 463	BN	s.xv	Sarum antiphonal with Norwich synodals
BL Harley 2785	BV	s.xiv	Sarum breviary with Norwich synodals
Bodl. Laud misc. 299	BW	s.xv	Sarum breviary of East Anglian manufacture? Used at Launton, Oxon.
BL Addl 59862	CZ	s.xv	Sarum breviary with Norwich features including synodals; Cathedral dedication; and commemoration of Etheldreda
BL Addl 17002	DD	s.xv	Sarum breviary with Norwich dedication and synodals
Wollaton Antiphonal	DU	s.xv	Sarum antiphonal for St Leonard's, Wollaton

The most frequent feasts so marked to appear are Felix (of Dunwich, 8 March), the translation of Edmund king and martyr (29 April), and Dominic (5 August), but a number of others are also annotated: these are given in full below. These Norwich 'synodals' are a rare example of a development illustrated in the manuscript evidence, but not attested in any extant record of synodal decisions, and demonstrate that such local decision-making, unreflected in the documentary record, did have a functional impact on service books. In the section 'The adoption of saints and feastdays', chapter 4 presents the evidence from diocesan and provincial statutes for observances adopted from 1246 until the suppression of the Latin liturgy.

The tables below give all feasts marked as 'synodal'. There are two manuscripts which have such annotations which are *not* from Norwich. The first is kalendar R, Durham Univ. Cosin V. I. 2, for Rudby parish church in the diocese of York, which has the following rubric for the Visitation (unusually on 2 Apr): *Festum visitacionis beate marie virginis. Statutum est celebrari ut festum principale pro mandatum sinodale isto die*. The second is kalendar DU, the

Wollaton Antiphonal used in Wollaton, Nottinghamshire. It is argued from physical evidence that this manuscript has an East Anglian origin.[53]

Table 2.18: Synodal observances in Norwich/East Anglia manuscripts organized by feast.

DAVID (1 Mar) (and **CHAD**, 2 Mar)	As a feast marked synodal in: AP
	Added with Chad in X, AQ, AT, AX, BB, BG, BI, BJ, BS, BU, CL, CO, CQ
	Added without Chad in CS, CV
FELIX (8 Mar)	As a feast marked synodal in: W, AP, BN, BV, BW, CZ, DD
	Present in Z, AL, AW, BA, BE, BZ 'non Sar', CD, CE, CJ, DU
	Added in AX, CU
Tr. EDMUND king and martyr (29 Apr)	As a feast marked synodal in: W, AP, BA, BV, BW, CZ, DU
	Present in BN, BX, CD, CE, CQ, CT, CY, DD, DO
	Added in Z, AO, AX
DOMINIC (5 Aug)	As a feast marked synodal in: W, AP, BN, BV, BW, CZ, DD
	Present in BX, CQ, DK, DL, DO
VISITATION of the BVM (2 Apr)	As a feast marked synodal in: R
	Added in G
THOMAS of HEREFORD (2 Oct)	As a feast marked synodal in: W, AP, BN, BV, CZ
	Ordinary in York
	Present in AP, AV, BJ, BL, BQ, BW, BX, DD 'non Sar', DF, DM, DN, DP, DU
	Added in Z, AQ, BA, BB, CH, CI
FRANCIS (4 Oct)	As a feast marked synodal in: W, CZ
	Ordinary in York
	Present in Z, AA, AB, AC, AE, AG, AJ, AK, AL, AM, AQ, AS, BB,. BE, BI, BM, BN, BV, BX, BY, BZ, CC, CE, CF, CK, CQ, CR, CX, DB, DD 'non Sar', DF, DK, DL, DM, DN, DO, DP, DU
	Added in AX, BA, BS, BW, DH

---

[53] See the entry for the Wollaton Antiphonal in the Catalogue of *The Wollaton Medieval Manuscripts: Texts, Owners, and Readers*, ed. by Ralph Hanna and Thorlac Turville-Petre (Woodbridge: York Medieval Press, 2010), pp. 105–08 for a description of the manuscript. The East Anglia ascription is on the basis of art historical evidence and, remarkably, chemical analysis of the pigments.

Table 2.19: Synodal observances in Norwich/East Anglia organized by kalendar.

Kalendar	Feasts designated as 'synodal'
R	Visitation
W	Felix, Tr. Edmund, Dominic, Thomas of Hereford, Francis
AP	David, Felix, Tr. Edmund, Dominic, Thomas of Hereford
BA	Tr. Edmund
BN	Felix, Dominic, Thomas of Hereford
BV	Felix, Tr. Edmund, Dominic, Thomas of Hereford
BW	Felix, Tr. Edmund, Dominic
CZ	Felix, Tr. Edmund, Dominic, Thomas of Hereford, Francis
DD	Felix, Dominic
DU	Tr. Edmund

Francis, as might be likely, occurs frequently in English books not associated with Norwich. The feasts of David and Chad were mandated by synod in 1398 and are the next most frequently occurring, though neither may be indicated in kalendars as a synodal feast.[54] Felix,[55] the Translation of Edmund, and Thomas of Hereford less frequently appear in kalendars, and it might be thought that some justification of their presence would be necessary. The Visitation will be dealt with below, and as it was promulgated more widely does not have the same regional associations, though it is interesting to note its presence in kalendar R, the Durham manuscript whose rubric is mentioned above.

A similar phenomenon can be found in Trinity College Dublin MS 88, a breviary described by Colker as 'of the Irish use of Sarum'.[56] Its contents are perfectly ordinary (with no added feasts) but its kalendar includes a number of entries with local labelling: five are marked 'non Sar' (David, Chad, Finan, Kevin, Maculinus) and five are marked 'per const[itutiones] D[ublinie]' (Aidan, Brigid, Lacerian, the Translation of Sts Patrick, Columba, and Brigid, and Laurence O'Toole). It may be that the latter annotation refers to the number of lessons prescribed for the service for Dublin. It is interesting to consider the possibility that the annotator felt the need to identify the contents not

---

[54] See chapter 4.

[55] Note that Felix never appears without Dominic.

[56] Marvin L. Colker, *Trinity College Library Dublin: Descriptive Catalogue of the Mediaeval and Renaissance Latin Manuscripts*, 2 vols (Aldershot: Ashgate, 1991), I, 156.

understood as part of what he understood as the 'Use of Sarum' and to underline in other cases why the feast was celebrated in a particular way.

Liturgical Analysis: Conclusions

The inferences made from the study of two different types of data are largely different, but some observations are held in common. Extensive collation of responsory series indicate that in books associated with two secular Uses, Sarum and York, series for Advent, the Triduum, and the Office of the Dead are transmitted and appear with great consistency. The Hereford series are equally consistent (though the sample size was much smaller) but all Advent and Dead series are identical to those which appear in the same positions in Sarum books, creating some ambiguity. Monastic manuscripts, for the most part, can be subdivided into groups by virtue of their responsory series. These groups are mainly based on institutional or geographic affiliations; there is some suggestion that English Benedictine responsory series had some common features, although these do not come close to the consistency of the secular patterns. This confirms the earlier suggestion that monastic communities had greater freedom to develop their own liturgical patterns. It is clear from the surviving evidence that the arrangement of responsory series in English secular manuscripts was a feature that was carefully retained and transmitted, and that the series were linked, consciously or otherwise on the part of the editors, with official models.

In terms of kalendars, M. R. James's perception that certain saints evoke certain localities may be defended, but with considerable provisos. There are clear 'normative' kalendars for Sarum, York, and Benedictine books, although over 80% of their contents are shared among all three, illustrating the inheritance of the Roman kalendar by all English books and demonstrating the widespread acceptance of some later English and French saints, the latter probably a result of Norman influence on the post-Conquest liturgy. There are, however, divergences from these normative kalendars. Regional and local variation can be found in the placement of Dedication and Relics feasts, which can help to indicate place of use. The regional kalendars presented here, as well as the analysis of Norwich 'synodal' feastdays, have demonstrated the consistency of diocese-specific groups of saints, but these should be considered constitutive of a regional manuscript only as a group, as the prevalence of unusual saints in unexpected kalendars has been shown to be unsurprising. Finally, kalendars were modified after their initial construction, most frequently to add new observances which were officially promulgated. More abstractly, the system of comparing two kalendars by number of 'points of shared variance' demonstrates that the kalendars with the highest number of shared points are linked by institutional affiliation, evidently facilitating the consistent transmission of local changes and new entries. Sometimes, as in the case of books for York Minster, the pairing of manuscripts by shared variant can support assignment to a place of use. Kalendars and their points also demonstrate external patterns of redaction. In East Anglia and Ireland local patterns were formalized, and the consistency of their kalendars is notable. The Chichele group of manuscripts have common features both in their kalendars *and* in other features.

It should be underlined that in the analyses of both responsory series and kalendars, comparison of a single criterion is never enough to provide a satisfactory assignment: it is no surprise that two manuscripts with identical responsory series can and almost always do have different kalendars. While interesting and revealing results are given by examining certain features, as much data as possible must be considered, from as many sections of a manuscript as possible. Only the study of a great number of English kalendars has permitted the observation of the subtleties of the witnesses, and the sensitivity to permit the alignment of one source with another on the basis of some peculiar variant. To facilitate an even more delicate analysis of the relationships between manuscripts, in chapter 3 the focus shifts to word-by-word comparison of manuscripts. Keeping in mind the assumption that all books of the same Use should transmit roughly the same material, multiple textual families and precise features will be outlined in the analysis of four complete offices.

TEXTUAL ANALYSIS

His ambition [...] was both generous and modest: 'To find one's way through
the chaos of our ancient texts, to group them according to their affinities, to
classify them, to go back for each legend down to the oldest known form [...]'
In all of this, 'one goal: to understand: one method: to observe.'

Translated from Eugene Vinaver, *A la recherche d'une poétique médiévale*

While the preceding chapter has applied methods of analysis that
address the choice and order of liturgical material within several
given services, here the focus is turned to the texts and melodies
themselves. Having examined the *structure* and *contents* of some one hundred
and seventy-seven manuscripts, concluding that while responsory series demonstrate the unity of books of each secular Use, manuscript kalendars can
illustrate the dramatic extent to which these same witnesses may vary in other
parameters, we move to the remaining two members of Pfaff's hierarchy of
'decreasing degrees of uniformity', the rubrics and proper texts, in a necessarily smaller number of witnesses. Previously we have seen that there are certain
aspects of the Offices studied which give the appearance of homogeneity, at
least within each of the secular Uses. By examining the same services at a more
microscopic level of detail, the textual diversity demonstrated by the sources
— even those of a single secular Use — is demonstrated very clearly. For Sarum
sources in particular it is possible to show the influence of a number of textual
traditions which may imply a process of editorial refinement of sungtexts and
rubrics, which, it will be suggested, may provide concrete evidence for the later
medieval amendment and development of the English Office liturgy, to be discussed later in chapter 4.

Four Offices in particular were selected for particular study at the textual level: those for Advent Sunday and for Thomas Becket, and the Office of the Dead, as well as the Office for St William of York. By virtue of its placement at the beginning of the Temporale, Advent Sunday is the first service to appear in most English Office books. It self-consciously presents what appears to be an extensive archetype, and its rubrics include prescriptions such as, among other items, the terminations of prayers, the seasonal changes in common texts, and the implications of different dominical letters.[1] The texts for Advent Sunday provided a guide for the rest of the year. By contrast, Thomas Becket's Office was chosen because, unlike the other two, it was newly composed by one named author (Benedict of Peterborough, *c.* 1174); further, it represents the feastdays in honour of saints; and finally, because it has been studied in considerable detail by a number of scholars of different disciplines, whose research has made trans-regional study possible: Becket's Office was widely distributed throughout Western Europe remarkably quickly. The Office of the Dead exemplifies both the Sanctorale and votive offices, and has special importance accorded by its exposition of the medieval theology of death. Joining these three in the final section of this chapter will be an analysis of the Office of St William of York, based on witnesses in a separate set of manuscripts. His Office is found complete only in manuscripts and printed books associated with York, and is thus roughly representative of local observances and saints' Offices in the Sanctorale, as well as providing slightly more depth to the textual analysis of offices of the Use of York.

Textual Criticism and Liturgical Manuscripts

There are a number of factors uniquely affecting the editing of the texts of liturgical manuscripts that require explanation, namely the nature of the texts as performance records; the selection of textual witnesses, the procedure by which their texts were recorded; and the types of variants which received the closest study.

Rather than a named and identifiable text with a known author for whom authorial intent can be extrapolated or at least its existence assumed, liturgical texts are instructions for, or records of, a living ritual performance which, while ostensibly based on a fixed, authoritative form, was almost certain to have been influenced by local circumstances. They convey perhaps what was intended to be spoken and sung along with the gesture and movement that accompanied and complemented the meaning of the sungtexts and lessons. While it may be

---

[1] See Hughes, *Medieval Manuscripts for Mass and Office*, paragraph 1003.

worthwhile for the sake of completeness to capture in a critical apparatus every hint of textual drift (and this has in fact been done), it was necessary to focus on the variants of greatest relevance: those that would have provoked a noticeably different *performance result*. This is somewhat more challenging than it seems: the use of a synonym or a slightly differing word order may or may not betray a discernible textual tradition, and the absence of a long rubric prescribing a certain action did not necessarily mean that it did not happen, or was forgotten, merely that it was not prescribed explicitly in some given source. This 'missing' rubric may describe an action so common that it was felt unnecessary to include it; other sources that do transmit it may be of a more prescriptive nature. The so-called Chichele pattern and some of its later adaptations certainly provide immense rubrical detail which may not represent substantive change from the *status quo*. The presence or absence of rubrics which serve as signposts for the structure of the liturgy, i.e. *in primo nocturno*, may be meaningless, although in a typical critical edition the omission of three such whole words might be considered significant. In the following analytical sections certain types of variant which do influence the performance result are emphasized. These matters are discussed again in the final section of chapter 4.

The manuscripts selected for full-text analysis are enumerated below in Table 3.1. They are a small proportion of those employed in chapter 2, where the analyses incorporate a much wider range of sources. As the reader can imagine, including many more than this number of witnesses in a critical analysis of the texts would make it even more difficult to produce and interpret. These manuscripts were selected by virtue of the fact that each contains complete versions of each of the three main Offices (Advent Sunday, Thomas, the Dead) under investigation, but this selection does not purport to be 'representative' of the wider population. While it might have been desirable to use a representative group, two issues would complicate their selection: it is impossible to select a few criteria that might characterize representative sources (as we have seen, results based on one observable criterion may not indicate that the remainder of a manuscript's contents adhere to any pattern); further, it would be disingenuous to create a representative subset of the books that existed in the early sixteenth century from the very small number of extant manuscripts. Owain Tudor Edwards has suggested that a minute fraction of the manuscript service books of the English Middle Ages survive, a figure around 0.105% of the total.[2]

---

[2] Owain Tudor Edwards, 'How Many Sarum Antiphonals were there in England and Wales in the Middle of the Sixteenth Century?', *Revue Bénédictine*, 99 (1989), 155–80.

Table 3.1: List of manuscripts from which full texts have been transcribed. Note that the Office of the Dead does not appear in Salisbury Cathedral MS 224; and that the Office for Thomas has been removed from BL Addl 32427. The column at far right indicates Reames's group assignment, if applicable. (S) and (L) indicate the textual family (Short or Long, shortly to be described) to which Advent Sunday corresponds.

Camb. St John's Coll. 146	s.xv	Sarum breviary (S)	
Camb. King's Coll. 30	s.xiv	Sarum breviary (S)	Portable
Camb. UL Addl 3474–5	s.xv	Sarum breviary (L), Norwich	
Camb. UL Addl 4500	s.xiv	Sarum breviary (L)	Chichele
Camb.UL Dd. X. 66	s.xv	Sarum breviary (L)	Chichele – less predictable
Durham Univ. Cosin V. I. 3	s.xvi	Sarum breviary, Coltishall, Norfolk	Folio
Hereford Cath. P. IX. 7	s.xiii	Hereford breviary s.xiii for Hereford cathedral	
BL Addl 32427	s.xv	Sarum breviary (L), diocese of Worcester	
BL Addl 43405–6	s.xiv	Monastic breviary for Muchelney Abbey	
BL Addl 49363	s.xiv	Monastic breviary	
BL Addl 52359	s.xiv	Sarum breviary (S) for Penwortham, Lancs (cell of Evesham)	Folio
BL Addl 59862	s.xv	Sarum breviary (L), Norwich	
BL Harley 2946	s.xv	Sarum breviary(L)	Chichele
BL Royal 2 A XII	s.xv	Sarum breviary of Continental manufacture	
BL Sloane 2466	s.xiv	Sarum breviary (L)	Chichele
Lambeth Palace 69	s.xv	Sarum breviary (L) owned by Henry Chichele	Chichele
Lambeth Palace Sion 1	s.xiv/xv	York breviary, noted, for Skelton, near York	
Oxford St John's Coll. 179	s.xv	Sarum breviary (L)	Chichele
Bodl. Bodley 976	s.xiv	Sarum breviary (L)	
Bodl. Canon lit. 215	s.xv	Sarum breviary (S) with Irish influence	
Bodl. Hatton 63	s.xiv	Sarum breviary (L)	Chichele – less predictable
Bodl. Laud misc. 84	s.xv	York breviary	
Bodl. Univ. Coll. 9	s.xv	Carmelite breviary	
Ranworth, s.n.	s.xv	Sarum antiphonal (L) for St Helen's, Ranworth	
Salisbury Cath. 224	s.xiv	Sarum breviary (L), noted, for Bedwyn, Wilts.	
1531	s.xvi	Sarum breviary (S), printed by Regnault and Chevallon	Folio
1493	s.xv	First printed York breviary	
1505	s.xvi	First printed Hereford breviary	

A conventional method of textual analysis was initially applied, comparing the transcriptions with various exemplars. These exemplars were necessarily chosen not so much as privileged copies as for the convenience of choosing a 'base version' from which to measure the variance in other sources. Nevertheless the base versions are, for each Office or version of each Office, likely to contain the most material shared by all other such sources. The texts of each Office were transcribed into text files, normalizing but retaining the medieval spelling, and expanding all abbreviations. The music was transcribed into an alphanumeric code allowing it to be machine-readable, first by hand, and then entered into an electronic database.

The entire critical edition, convoluted and extensive, has not been included here. Instead, the textual groupings by shared variant which it illuminates will form the basis for discussion. As for other types of comparative data in chapter 2, one of the electronic databases was programmed to create, for every witness, a list of the variants shared with every other witness, and by extension a judgement of the manuscript(s) to which some witness may be most closely related, in some cases producing a separate total for both sungtexts/rubrics and lessons.

An account of each Office in turn is presented below, beginning with the more complicated evidence from books associated with Sarum and moving to the less prolific but equally important versions from York, Hereford, and the monastic sources. In each case, we will discuss the implications of the sungtexts and rubrics first, then address the lessons, and finally, where possible, the music.

The Office for Advent Sunday

As the first series of services in most English Breviaries and Antiphonals, Advent Sunday can be labelled an archetype, not only because its texts overtly attempted to supply some level of detail for the entire year (or at least for Advent) but also because it seems to demonstrate the chief characteristics of the different versions of the English breviary which had developed by the fifteenth century.[3] In broad outline, the Sarum sources for Advent Sunday fall into two distinct textual families, descriptively titled 'Adv-Short' and 'Adv-Long': the difference between them amounts to about six hundred words, mainly owing to a greatly expanded programme of rubrics in Adv-Long. It is important to note that both versions transmit exactly the same sungtexts in the same order.

---

[3] Fassler describes how sermons written in the fifth and sixth centuries can illuminate how theologians 'spun out the materials for the Advent liturgies then developing'. See Margot Fassler, 'Sermons, Sacramentaries, and Early Sources', p. 16.

Sungtexts and Rubrics: *Adv-Short*

Adv-Short is found in five of twenty-eight witnesses, including the 1531 Great Breviary edited by Procter and Wordsworth, with the remainder dating from both fourteenth and fifteenth centuries; no obvious chronological or geographical factor unites the group.

Table 3.2: Manuscripts containing 'Adv-Short'. The column at far right indicates Reames's group assignment, if applicable.

Camb. St John's Coll. 146	s.xv	Sarum breviary (S)	
Camb. King's Coll. 30	s.xiv	Sarum breviary (S)	Portable
BL Addl 52359	s.xiv	Sarum breviary (S) for Penwortham, Lancs (cell of Evesham)	Folio
Bodl. Canon lit. 215	s.xv	Sarum breviary (S) with Irish influence	
1531	s.xvi	Sarum breviary (S), printed by Regnault and Chevallon	Folio

Adv-Short is characterized by a minimal amount of rubrication at the start of Vespers, with particular attention during and after Vespers to the functional particulars of services, including where and when they should occur: for instance the inclusion of *Alleluia* during paschal time (Eastertide). Other concerns are the placement of commemorations and seasonal changes in their use, and the variable terminations of prayers. Adv-Short incorporates two members (the 1531 printed breviary and BL Addl 52359) of Reames's Folio group, which was constructed based on Sanctorale lesson texts: the remainder do not conform to any of her groups.

The most frequent tendency in Adv-Short sources is to omit material found in the majoritarian version Adv-Long, but it should not be considered merely an abbreviated version of a longer form, since the textual formulations are sufficiently different as to warrant their treatment separately; this will be discussed further below.[4] This is relevant particularly for rubrics, unlike texts which are only omitted if they can be implied (for instance, a sequence of psalms accompanying proper antiphons). BL Addl 52359 and Oxford Keble 30 are particularly likely to shorten the rubrics; occasionally they share such an omission. Beyond these observations no particular groupings by shared variant (or shared type of variant) can be described.

---

[4] The tendency to describe something as an 'omission' relative to the base version is unavoidable. It must not be interpreted in terms of an editor 'taking something out'.

Sungtexts and Rubrics: *Adv-Long*

The rubrics of Adv-Long are so distinctive as to be an immediate identifying characteristic of the family: every source begins with the pattern of opening rubrics found in both Frere's Old and New Ordinals, referring to elements of ceremonial along with the recitation of *Pater noster* and *Ave Maria*. This foreshadows a florescence of rubrication throughout the Advent Office. While Long and Short both provide rubrics in order to give structure to the text and directions for the putting together of the Office throughout the year or the season, the text of Adv-Long adds to those directions considerable precision, particularly at Vespers, and indicates which persons present should perform which actions. Many such instructions are also found in the Ordinals.

Table 3.3: Manuscripts containing 'Adv-Long'. The column at far right indicates Reames's group assignment, if applicable.

Camb. UL Addl 3474–5	s.xv	Sarum breviary (L), Norwich	
Camb. UL Addl 4500	s.xiv	Sarum breviary (L)	Chichele
Camb.UL Dd. X. 66	s.xv	Sarum breviary (L)	Chichele – less predictable
BL Addl 32427	s.xv	Sarum breviary (L), diocese of Worcester	
BL Addl 59862	s.xv	Sarum breviary (L), Norwich	
BL Harley 2946	s.xv	Sarum breviary(L)	Chichele
BL Sloane 2466	s.xiv	Sarum breviary (L)	Chichele
Lambeth Palace 69	s.xv	Sarum breviary (L) owned by Henry Chichele	Chichele
Oxford St John's Coll. 179	s.xv	Sarum breviary (L)	Chichele
Bodl. Bodley 976	s.xiv	Sarum breviary (L)	
Bodl. Hatton 63	s.xiv	Sarum breviary (L)	Chichele – less predictable
Ranworth, s.n.	s.xv	Sarum antiphonal (L) for St Helen's, Ranworth	
Salisbury Cath. 224	s.xiv	Sarum breviary (L), noted, for Bedwyn, Wilts.	

The manuscripts of Adv-Long, found in thirteen of the twenty-eight manuscripts studied, seem to have survived in greater numbers than those of Adv-Short: some witnesses are placed securely in the fifteenth century; others appear to have been produced in the fourteenth. (It should be noted that the best manuscripts of the Ordinal to which many of the Long rubrics can be compared — Salisbury Cathedral MS 175 and Oxford, Corpus Christi College MS 44 — also date from the fourteenth century.) Three manuscripts containing Adv-Long are associated elsewhere in their contents with Norwich and East Anglian patterns of saints, as noted in Table 3.3. Seven are associated with Reames's 'Chichele' group.[5] The precision of the Adv-Long rubrics, and their provision for a variety of circumstances, might also be described as helpful to the codification of a rite.

Notwithstanding the precise wording, some rubrics in Long and Short convey the same instructions, although at other points they seem to diverge. At Vespers, Long gives the distinctive rubrics which provide detail, surrounding *Deus in adiutorium*, which deals with the opening of the service, the assignment of Vespers antiphons to cantors, and notes, in all manuscripts, that the differentia (cadences) *sicut in magno tonali plenius intimatur*. After the Vespers collect, Long has a brief rubric *Hoc modo dicantur* [...] regarding collects. Both Long and Short then have *Nulla fiat processio ante crucem*; then a rubric relating to terminations of prayers, except in BL Addl 52359 and Camb. St John's 146 (Short) and Bodl. Bodley 976 and Camb. UL Dd. X. 66 (Long). The two versions have slightly different wording, but the rubrics have the same effect. During the Memorial to the Blessed Virgin Mary both versions have the same rubric, relating to a proper antiphon, in different wording. After the collect Long has a rubric about the start of Vespers of the BVM, and before the memorial to the Holy Spirit there is a rubric in Long for the priest. After this memorial both have a rubric for the commemoration of Relics, with the version in Short *secundum antiquum Ordinale*, a hint that Adv-Short, notwithstanding its brevity, may postdate a widely disseminated Ordinal. The rubrics for the memorial of All Saints and before Compline are identical, until (primarily Short) a rubric explaining the use of particular hymns for certain times of the year. This rubric is also found in Camb. UL Dd. X. 66, Bodl. Hatton 63, and Bodl. University College 9 (amongst the Long manuscripts). Long has a much more elaborate rubric to start the Preces in Compline, followed by instructions for the *excellencior persona* for the confession and following rubrics. Short has a brief note relating to chants being sung *sub eodem tono* [...] After Compline of the day and Compline of the BVM, Short has an extra rubric *Hec oratio dicitur ad simplex* [...] following the singing of *Benedicamus domino*.

---

[5] Those which are not so associated are not in Reames's analysis.

At Matins, Long has slightly more detail at *Deus in adiutorium* while Short has the extra rubric beginning *Officium principalis* [...] The rubric introducing *Pater noster* is in slightly different wording, with Short invoking 'ecclesia Sar'. At the first lesson Long has a more extensive rubric introducing the act of blessing the reader and movement within the quire. Matins continues with few differences. At the end of Matins, Short has a slightly longer rubric proscribing the *Te Deum*. Lauds is, by comparison, very similar in either Use. In general, the two families do not vary from a functional standpoint, but Long has extended rubrics.

Among the manuscripts transmitting Adv-Long in general terms, several have shared features that allow them to be reliably associated with others. The first pairing is between two fourteenth-century manuscripts firmly in Reames's Chichele group but between which there are no other obvious associations. Harley 2785 and Sloane 2466 share ten textual variants, all of which are either trivial additions or minor textual modifications, or omissions of text. This is more than the average number of shared variants, which owing to the number of variants peculiar to a single witness is very low. The character of some of these variants (*terminetur* for *finietur*, omission of a few insubstantial words from a rubric) in conjunction with the fact that they are shared may suggest that they are both members of the same textual pattern of Adv-Long. Both Harley and Sloane have other variants that are shared with other manuscripts, but not to the same extent: however, Salisbury Cathedral MS 224 may be one related witness. Each variant may not provide a very convincing argument for relation, but the *number* of shared variants suggests a close association, particularly as Reames's analyses corroborate this relationship in another section of the manuscript.

Table 3.4: Types of variants shared between Harley and Sloane.

1 sentence omitted
Three implied words omitted: *Chorus respondeat* Amen.
Christum for Iesum
Terminetur for *finietur*
add *dictis*
Three words omitted: *cum nota Versum*:
Five words omitted: *mutetur Hymnis solummodo, et dicatur*
add *solummodo et dicatur* (above)
add *Deinde dicat executor officii in audiencia sed sine nota* (Sloane adds *sub silencio*)
Terminetur for *finietur*

A second, larger grouping of manuscripts incorporates BL Addl 59862, Camb. UL Dd. X. 66 and Addl 3474–5, and Bodl. MS Bodley 976. These manuscripts do not have a large common body of shared variants, but a trio (excluding the Bodleian book) share seven variants, mostly involving the absence of rubrics giving information that is helpful but not necessary.

Table 3.5: Variants shared between BL Addl 59862, Camb. Dd. X. 66, Addl 3474–5, and Bodl. Bodley 976.

add *scilicet*
omit rubric for the manner of singing a versicle
omit rubric describing how to sing versicles throughout the year
omit rubric giving *Dominus vobiscum / Et cum*
simplification of *Benedicamus* rubric
omit rubric for the manner of saying versicles at Vespers of the BVM
modification to rubric indicating a collect

Of the four, only Dd. X. 66 has associations with the Chichele group (it is in Reames's 'less predictable' subcategory). That the other three have no such association suggests that the contents of these volumes were subject to multiple influences, an observation strengthened by the fact that some but not all of their kalendars are related. The kalendar of Addl 3474 (AW) is most closely related to that of 59862, though the closest relative to the latter is in Peterhouse 270, another Chichele book, but not one in this group. Similarly, the kalendar of Dd. X. 66 is related both to Addl 4500 and Peterhouse 270 (both Chichele books not in the group) and Bodley 976 is equally associated with three kalendars, at nine points each, namely Dd. X. 66, Peterhouse 270, and Addl 52359, the last of which is not in the Chichele group and moreover transmits Adv-Short. Each of the four kalendars in this group is associated closely with at least one other member, but these associations are part of a pattern that appears to extend beyond the present group. On balance, however, the nonsubstantive but consistent variation in a variety of venues described above suggests that the manuscripts are related to the same textual family of Adv-Long.

A third group of two has a stronger relation owing to the fact that both contain texts, primarily rubrics, which are not found in any other witnesses of Adv-Long. Bodl. Hatton 63 and Oxford, St John's 179 are both associated with the Chichele group (Hatton, like Dd. X. 66, is in the 'less predictable' category); although Hatton has no kalendar, that of St John's 179 (BO) is closest to the kalendar in Addl 4500 (like Dd. X. 66). The pair have at least fourteen points within Advent Sunday at which they give either additional or different rubrical material, in all totalling about nine hundred words. Primarily these rubrics give additional directions to users, such as where implied items such as antiphons may be found, i.e. '*infra in psalterio*', or specifics as to which individuals should sing or say a particular item, what they should wear, and how they should be positioned. One rubric gives instructions for the movement of choristers; another gives very precise details of the charging of the thurible and censing of the altar, parts of the sanctuary, and clerics. At two points the rubrics appear to come from a text similar to that printed in Frere's New Ordinal; at one further point the text seems to come from the Old Ordinal also as edited by Frere. The relation of Adv-Long and the additional rubrics to the idea of a Sarum Ordinal will be discussed later. The relation of Hatton 63 and Oxford St John's 179 is unambiguous: at the very least they shared an otherwise unknown common source of new material, which was added in exactly the same places.

Another manuscript which should be mentioned at this point is BL Addl 32427, a large choir breviary of the fifteenth century. Its rubrics, like those just described, at twelve points within Advent Sunday give additional prescriptions for action for the rulers of the choir, various persons who are to read or sing specific items. As in Hatton and St John's 179 there is much concern for the censing at the Magnificat. In addition, BL Addl 32427 transmits two prosas with versicles and collects, found in no other source described here: the first, *De cruce deponitur*, after the main Vespers and the votive services, and the second, *Hora completorii*, just after Compline. Both are known in the Hours of the Cross found in Books of Hours at Vespers and Compline respectively. Here, as with many other features, the rubrics and prosas are also found in Salisbury Cathedral 152, a comparable fifteenth-century choir breviary with striking similarities in content and features to BL Addl 32427 but whose complete texts are not discussed in this chapter.

A further two manuscripts deserve mention which have a text which differs from either Long or Short. Durham UL Cosin MS V. I. 3, originaly from Coltishall, Norfolk, does not begin Advent Sunday complete, but its later rubrics suggest some allegiance to Adv-Long, although in most cases the wording of more involved rubrics is different, and sometimes implies a process of redaction: one rubric puts a personal touch on the rubric addressing terminations of prayers: *Videndum est nobis et magna intencione intelligendum* [...] *qualiter orationes* [...] *dicturi sumus*. Three such passages are shared with Bodley 976. Finally, BL Royal 2 A XII, a fifteenth-century breviary *secundum morem et consuetudinem ecclesie sarum anglicane* (f. 1ʳ) in a non-English hand produced for Antony van Gavere (bookbinder, d. 1505) transmits a somewhat differently worded version which could be compared best with Adv-Short, but without most of the rubrics and with abbreviated lessons and a kalendar evidently copied from a much earlier exemplar. Neither manuscript corresponds well with either pattern. It is thought that both might represent individual editorial renderings of Long and Short for particular purposes; Cosin V. I. 3 has been modified and added to in several places in addition to its divergent contents; the Royal book is of very high quality and does not show signs of heavy use or annotation.

Sungtexts, Rubrics, and Lessons for Advent Sunday: York and Hereford

There are few observations to be made from only three sources for York, and only insubstantial differences exist in the sungtexts of each witness, none of which can be used to support groupings. These observations seem to confirm Reames's argument that York is the most textually stable English Use.[6] It is, however, worth presenting this evidence to demonstrate this point, and also to show how some of the extant manuscripts cohere with the printed editions of the York and Hereford Breviaries. A more thorough approach to York manuscripts is in the part of this chapter dealing with the sources of St William's Office.

The texts of the 1493 printed York breviary and Bodl. Laud misc. 84 are extremely close: they differ by only three rubrics at Lauds. Comparison of 1493 and the Skelton breviary (Lambeth Palace, Sion College 1) shows that Sion alone has a full complement of Vespers antiphons; no rubric before Compline; no rubric after the psalms at Compline; no extensive *Confiteor*, which in fuller sources provided texts for both priest and choir to confess to one another; and an incomplete complement of psalms at Matins, with a replacement rubric. All three have different divisions of text for the lessons at Matins, although the lessons are drawn from the same sources. A fuller discussion of the lessons is provided below.

The two Hereford witnesses (the 1505 printed breviary and Hereford Cathedral MS P. IX. 7, one of two known manuscript breviaries) have considerably different rubrics and lessons but identical sungtexts. 1505 has a long preface after the fashion of the Sarum Ordinal, and what appears to be blatant borrowing of Adv-Long rubrics, especially where they are distinctive at the beginning. 1505 is also much fuller at Compline, where it again appropriates Sarum rubrics with *secundum usum Herfordensis* added, as elsewhere

---

[6] Reames, '*Mouvance* and Interpretation', p. 169.

before ML1 and at Lauds. There is another long rubric which is not in any Sarum pattern concerning prayers after Compline.[7] Given the chronological difference between the two (between 1262 and 1268 for Hereford P. IX. 7 and 1505 for the printed volume) these discrepancies are unsurprising, and may represent an as yet undocumented process of development, but the paucity of Hereford sources, especially in the period between these two, is problematic. The other known manuscript Hereford breviary, Worcester Cathedral P. 86 (of the fourteeth century), does not have the extensive borrowed rubrics either (it is otherwise not accounted for in this analysis). I would hypothesize that the appearance of Sarum rubrics with the notice *secundum usum Herfordensis* were an unusual reaction against the imposition of Sarum elsewhere, which may have been reflected in text by the end of the fourteenth or the early fifteenth centuries, when the efforts to impose the Use of Sarum became more serious and, ultimately, successful. By contrast, the liturgy of Exeter Cathedral promulgated by John Grandisson in the fourteenth century (see chapter 4) expected the Sarum rubrics except where they had been changed locally.

The Monastic Pattern

Table 3.6: Monastic manuscripts from which transcriptions were made.

BL Addl 43405–6	s.xiv	Monastic breviary for Muchelney Abbey
BL Addl 49363	s.xiv	Monastic breviary
Bodl. Univ. Coll. 9	s.xv	Carmelite breviary

All that can be learnt from the three witnesses — two Benedictine, one Carmelite — that are complete is that the monastic cursus cannot be tackled effectively in the present investigation, which focuses necessarily on the secular liturgical books from three specific traditions which are by definition comparable. Monastic liturgy followed an entirely different pattern, and breviaries and antiphonals were more frequently supplemented by other books such as ordinals which gave more detail for the liturgy of individual communities. This supposition appears to be reflected in the manuscripts. Still, it is fruitful to present some observations in order to demonstrate this contrast. To express the general impression briefly, both Benedictine books lack the immensity of

---

[7] It begins *Hec predicta oratio scilicet Illumina cum capitulo predicto scilicet Tu in nobis et versu Custodi nos dicuntur per totum annum ad completorium, nisi a cena domini usque ad octavas pasche.*

detail, especially in rubrics of even the shortest secular versions associated with either Adv-Short or York. The detail of Sarum rubrics is notable by contrast. The brevity of the monastic rubrics could be explained by the likely circumstance that customs within an individual monastic house would be codified both by other types of manuscript and, more generally, by established community habits, unlike customs of a transregional Use based on the practices of a particular venue and imposed on others.

For Advent, the two Benedictine sources have different responsories at Vespers (43405: R. Ecce dies; V. In diebus; 49363: R. Missus est; V. Dabit ei). Neither has substantial rubrics at Vespers; Compline is absent; and the two sources have different responsory series.

Table 3.7: Responsory series (in parallel) from BL Addl 49363 and Addl 43405.

BL Addl 49363 – Advent 1			BL Addl 43405 – Advent 1		
R. Aspiciens a longe	11	V. Quique	R. Aspiciens a longe	11	V. Quique
R. Aspiciebam in visu	12	V. Potestas	R. Aspiciebam in visu	12	V. Potestas
R. Missus est gabriel	13	V. Dabit	R. Missus est gabriel	13	V. Ave
R. Ave maria gratia	14	V. Quomodo	R. Ave maria gratia	14	V. Quomodo
R. Salvatorem expectamus	15	V. Sobrie	R. Ecce virgo concipiet	17	V. Super
R. Confortate manus	61	V. Civitas	R. Salvatorem expec'us	15	V. Preoccupemus
R. Audite verbum	16	V. Annun'ate	R. Obsecro domine	18	V. A solis
R. Alieni non transibunt	62	V. Ego	R. Audite verbum	16	V. Annunciate
R. Ecce virgo concipiet	17	V. Super	R. Letentur celi	19	V. Ecce dominator
R. Obsecro domine	18	V. A solis	R. Alieni non transibunt	62	V. Ego veniam
R. Montes Israel	60	V. Rorate	R. Montes israel ramos	60	V. Rorate
R. Letentur celi	19	V. Orietur	R. Ecce dies veniunt	63	V. In diebus

The Carmelite manuscript, University College 9 (shown in the table opposite), also has minimal rubrics and no notable features after Compline. The structure and contents of the rubrics of Matins are very similar to the Benedictine books, but with different responsory series and following the 9-responsory secular cursus.

It is easy to suggest why additional rubrics might be included — uncontroversial is the provision of more rather than fewer instructions for the performance or organization of what were no doubt convoluted services with capricious seasonal changes even for those who knew them well. More ambiguous is the reason why a number of sources appear to omit passages or entire rubrics.

Bodl. Univ. Coll. 9 – Advent 1		
R. Aspiciens a longe	11	V. Quique
R. Aspiciebam in visu	12	V. Potestas
R. Missus est gabriel	13	V. Quomodo
R. Ave maria gratia	14	V. Dabit
R. Salvatorem expectamus	15	V. Sobrie
R. Audite verbum	16	V. Annunciate
R. Ecce virgo concipiet	17	V. Super
R. Obsecro domine	18	V. A solis
R. Letentur celi	19	V. Ecce d'nator

These matters will be taken up later in this chapter, as will the discussion of Adv-Short and Adv-Long as either unrelated or sequential versions of the Sarum office. We now move from the analysis of the sungtexts and rubrics, texts thought of as primarily liturgical and which determined action and controlled performance, to texts which in many cases were abbreviated from relatively fixed, well-known versions for liturgical reading: the lessons.

Lessons for Advent Sunday

Since these texts were drawn from outside the sphere of liturgical composition, the emphasis here, once the text is identified, is to describe how passages have been selectively chosen for reading and comment on the divisions of text between the lessons of Matins which often represent the only substantive variation. The lessons in manuscripts of the same Use are invariably drawn from the same texts, whether Scripture or sermon, but in differing divisions which vary, with no discernible logic. Therefore, while the presence of lessons drawn from a particular text may help to indicate the Use of the manuscript, in other respects the lessons give no answers, except that their precise division does not appear to be something defined by Use, and provide no specific evidence for the grouping of sources. It is worth noting, therefore, that for Advent Sunday the order and division of lessons does not appear to be a productive indicator of Use, unlike the choice and order of other genres of text. A summary of lessons is given on the following page.

The Sarum sources yield one pairing of manuscripts by three shared variants in lessons, the closest relation possible, and as many as are ever shared in lessons of two such manuscripts: King's College 30 and Camb. UL Addl 3474 supply

Table 3.8: Sources of lessons for Advent Sunday in Sarum, York, Hereford, and monastic breviaries.

1–3	**All** use Isaiah 1. 1–1. 15 in varying divisions.

4–6	**Sarum**: Maximus Taurinensis, 'Homilia II in adventu Dominico,[a] *Igitur quoniam post* [...]
	York: Maximus Taurinensis, 'Homilia I ante natale Domini'[b] *Leticia quantus sit*
	Hereford: extended passage from Isaiah ch. 1
	Monastic: much shorter lessons from Isaiah, continuous (not abbreviated) up to lesson 8.
	Univ. 9: Maximus Taurinensis[c] *Fratres dilectissimi iam adveniet dies*

7–9	**Sarum**: 'de diversis tractatibus' *Bethphage* [...]
	York: John Chrysostom[d] *Puto res ipsa*
	Hereford: Bede, 'In Marci evangelium expositio'[e] *Conferendum* [...]
	Monastic: (lessons 7–8) Isaiah, as above.
	Univ. 9: as York

after	**Monastic**: Bede *Conferendum*, as above.

Gosp

[a] Reproduced in *Patrologia Latina* (henceforth PL) 57 col. 0225, accessible at <http://pld.chadwyck.co.uk> [accessed 25 July 2013].

[b] PL 57 col 0221a.

[c] PL 57 col 843.

[d] Reproduced in *Patrologiae cursus completus* [...] *[Patrologia graeca]*, LVI, ed. by Jacques-Paul Migne (Paris, 1859) col. 834.

[e] PL 92, col 133b.

the only example where the divisions of text among lessons provide any help. The most useful comment that can be made for the Sarum books is that while the *origin* of the text for any given lesson is unambiguous, there appears to have been no standardization of the length or content of the lessons, at least for Advent Sunday (the same is not true of the Sanctorale, as Reames has shown).[8] The following sections, which deal with the more limited number of manuscripts of other Uses, suggest the types of variation prevalent in great diversity in Sarum.

The three York manuscripts are witness to a similarly inconsistent situation, and owing to the inclusion of only these three witnesses it is impossible to make meaningful comments about their variants here. Bodl. Laud misc. 84 has longer lessons and more material not present in the others, and 1493 and Sion are slightly more unified.

[8] For instance in Reames, 'Late Medieval Efforts at Standardization'.

Table 3.9: Divisions of lessons from Isaiah in three York breviaries: the printed breviary (1493); Lambeth Palace Sion College MS 1 (Sion); and Bodl. Laud misc. 84 (LM84).

Lesson 1	1493	Visio – spreverunt me
	Sion	(same)
	LM84	Visio – intellexit
Lesson 2	1493	Cognovit – sceleratis
	Sion	Cognovit – (illeg)
	LM84	Ve genti – fota oleo
Lesson 3	1493	Derelinquant – sanitas
	Sion	Terra vestra – cucumerario
	LM84	Terra vestra – essemus
Lesson 4	1493	Leticia – incedere
	Sion	(same)
	LM84	Leticia – incedere + Credunt – ornatum (as for beg. of ML5, Sion)
Lesson 5	1493	Credunt – debemus
	Sion	(same)
	LM84	Hec autem (mid-Sion ML5) – debemus + Qui pro – successorem
Lesson 6	1493	Qui pro – diligentibus se
	Sion	(same)
	LM84	Qualis (mid Sion ML6) – miratur (unique witness from Quibus […])
Lesson 7 (Gosp)	1493	Cum appropinquabit – contra vos est
	Sion	Cum appropinquabit – pullum cum ea
	LM84	(as 1493)
(Homily)	1493	Frequenter quidem – ascendit
	Sion	(same)
	LM84	(different division)
Lesson 8	1493	Ideo ergo – non potuerunt
	Sion	Ideo ergo – ipsum
	LM84	(different division, with additional sentence at end)
Lesson 9	1493	Duos autem discipulos – corrigite illos
	Sion	Invenientis inquit – amaretur
	LM84	(different divisiom, with additional section at end)

Lessons 8 and 9 in particular apply the same material, with slightly different divisions.

Similarly, the two Hereford witnesses use slightly different excerpts from the same texts. The text of lessons 7–9 in 1505 occupy lessons 7–8 in Hereford P. IX. 7, which uses an otherwise unseen text for lesson 9.

Table 3.10: Divisions of lessons from Isaiah in two Hereford breviaries, EHC P. IX. 7 (EHC) and the printed Hereford breviary (1505).

Lesson 1		(same in both witnesses)
Lesson 2	EHC	Cognovit – prevaricacionem
	1505	Cognovit – intellexit
Lesson 3	EHC	Omne – igni
	1505	Ve genti – retrorsum
Lesson 4	EHC	Regionem – essemus
	1505	Super quo – sanitas
Lesson 5	EHC	Audite verbum – nolui
	1505	Vulnus – igni
Lesson 6	EHC	Cum veniretis – vestri
	1505	Regionem – cucumerario
Lessons 7–9		7 begins Conferendum est hoc in both
		Varying divisions; lesson 9 in EHC is Quia nimirum

Advent Sunday: Some Conclusions

Nearly every manuscript in all three secular Uses has a unique pattern of divisions for the lessons of Advent Sunday, but within various witnesses of any given passage there are no notable textual variants. Rather than suggest that these differences are meaningless because they do not allow many sources to be grouped by shared variant or to associate a particular sequence of lessons with a textual tradition, it is important to recall that within each Use the origins of the texts (that is, the portion of Isaiah 1 and the pertinent homilies) *are uniform*. This suggests that the sources of the lessons, rather than the precise contents, were prescribed at some probably early stage, at which point the lessons in all families of the Sarum Breviary (here both Adv-Long and -Short) began to be chosen from the same longer texts. This process seems consistent with the prescriptions in various Ordinals which provide only the number of lessons to be used and often the source of those lessons; or even rubrics in the service books themselves which indicate *medie lecciones de sermone beati Maximi episcopi*.

Indeed the practice is also consistent with the provision of lessons for recently added saints such as John of Beverley, who was often accorded only the three middle lessons of Matins.

Lessons, then, might be viewed not as texts requiring word-by-word comparison, but instead, like responsory series, as parts of the Office where the *choice* and *order* of the texts are the most useful parameters for analysis. It places a greater importance on the selection of material from a range of possibilities, presumably at the time of manufacture.

The Office for Thomas Becket

The martyrdom in 1170 of Thomas Becket, archbishop of Canterbury, requires no introduction. The cult which venerated him as a saint (he was canonized in March 1173) immediately gained popularity in England, thereafter spreading very quickly throughout Western and Central Europe.[9] Numerous liturgical compositions were constructed in his honour, including up to eight complete offices,[10] although one of these, *Studens livor* (codenamed TH21 in Hughes's *Late Medieval Liturgical Offices*), was the most widely used on his feastday, 29 December. Several other Offices, including one based on some of the texts of *Studens livor*, were used for his Translation feast on 7 July. There were other versions as well, including TH22, *Sacrat Thomas primordia*, found in thirteen primarily Continental manuscripts (including one apparently for English use at Ely), which can be divided into at least two textual families. TH22 also borrows several texts from TH21 as well as from the office of St Vincent of Saragossa.[11] This may underline the influential role that TH21 played at the outset of the cult of Thomas.

The texts and chants of Becket's principal feastday office, with which we will be concerned from henceforth, are unusual among proper material for saints in that they have an identifiable author and likely date of composition: they are associated with Benedict, monk of Peterborough, and were likely to have been composed by 1174. Benedict is said by the chronicler Robert of Swaffham

[9] Andrew Hughes, 'Chants in the Rhymed Office of St Thomas of Canterbury', *Early Music*, 16 (1988), 185–201 (p. 185).

[10] See entries for 'Thomas of Canterbury', TH21–TH28, in Andrew Hughes, *Late Medieval Liturgical Offices*, I.

[11] Matthew Cheung Salisbury, 'An Alternative Office for St Thomas Becket and its Implications', *Anaphora*, 2 (2008), 57–68 (p. 61).

to have written the whole office: 'Unde composuit egregium volumen de passione et miraculis sancti Thome et hystoriam *Studens livor* totam fecit: totam dico quia dictamen cantu excellenter insignivit.'[12] This presumably refers to the sungtexts, for as Hughes has pointed out, each poetic passage must have been conceived in relation to its melodic setting. Both Hughes and Bruno Stäblein agree that the music is unusual:[13] indeed, 'far less repetitive and formulaic than many standard tunes'.[14] This is particularly made clear when the tunes are sung. Slocum also suggests, on the basis of style and the unusually strong thematic linkages between sungtexts and lessons, that one person, probably Benedict, was also responsible for the construction of the Office's proper lessons, beginning *Gloriosi martyris Thome*, which are used in many monastic sources as well as in the Sarum and Hereford versions of the Office. Benedict may have used material from the *Vita* for Becket composed by John of Salisbury, to which allusions are made in the lessons.[15] An example serves to illustrate the strong thematic and textual relations between lessons and responsories:

from Lesson 5

Sic itaque granum frumenti oppressit palea, sic vinee custos in vinea, dux in castris, in caulis pastor, cultor in area cesus est.

Responsory 5

Iacet granum oppressum palea | Iustus cesus pravorum framea | Celum domo commutans lutea. V. Cadit custos vitis in vinea | dux in castris, cultor in area.

The pattern in which the texts first appeared, however, is not easily identifiable from the many examples which are extant, although Slocum suggests an early

---

[12] Quoted in R. W. Hunt, 'Notes on the *Distinctiones monasticae et morales*', in *Liber floridus. Mittellateinische Studien: Festschrift Paul Lehmann*, ed. by Bernard Bischoff and Suso Brechter (St Ottilien: Eos Verlag der Erzabtei, 1950), pp. 355–62 (p. 360).

[13] Bruno Stäblein, *Schriftbild der Einstimmigen Musik*, Musikgeschichte in Bildern, 3: Musik des Mittelalters und der Renaissance, 4 (Leipzig: Deutscher Verlag für Musik, 1975), pp. 162–65.

[14] Hughes, 'Chants in the Rhymed Office', pp. 199–201.

[15] Kay Brainerd Slocum, *Liturgies in Honour of Thomas Becket* (Toronto: University of Toronto Press, 2004), p. 145.

version may be in Klosterneuberg monastery MS 574.[16] Typically the antiphons and responsories are ordered in a number of permutations within the monastic witnesses. They also appear to have consistent permutations in each of the three English secular Uses, as illustrated in the table below. Evidently in each secular pattern it was necessary to truncate the longer monastic Office (nine from twelve responsories, for instance). Each such item, however, appears without numerous internal melodic or textual variants, and assumes a relatively fixed form. Similarly, the rubrics in Becket's office are sufficiently uniform (or exist in a very immutable form which would never need to be altered) that they do not provide any particular insights. The most notable rubric gives instructions for a procession to the altar of St Thomas at the beginning of the observance of his feastday at Vespers, during which the antiphon *Pastor cesus* is sung. If there was no altar to Thomas, then a memorial with antiphon, versicle and response, and collect, was said.

The Monastic Version

Slocum suggests that the original layout of the sungtexts of the Office is not retrievable from the surviving sources. She has given incipits for Camb., Fitzwilliam Museum 369, in order to reflect without speculation the pattern in one stated source. Here the pattern of antiphons and responsories is given from BL Addl 43405, identical to Slocum's transcription and the version in most other English monastic sources. The Carmelite manuscript, Bodl. University College 9, has only nine antiphons and responsories, and the sungtexts employed from the full monastic office are indicated below. Near the end of the *Gloriosi martyris Thome* text University College 9 also adds a passage as follows:

> Sic sic martyr Thomas virtute constancie adamantinus, celestis edificii lapis pretiosus, gladiorum conquadratus ictibus angulari lapidi Christo in celis est coniunctus. Itaque Dei sacerdos migrans celis nascitur quarto kalendas ianuarii, anno ab incarnatione Domini millesimo centesimo septuagesimo proximo die post solemnitatem innocentum: ut qui diu innocenter vixerat, post innocentes tempus celebre sortiretur.

As has been suggested, the monastic manuscripts can only illustrate the general tenor of their counterparts, and should not be expected ever to agree with one

---

[16] Slocum, *Liturgies*, p. 121.

another in either general or detailed textual matters. BL Addl 43405 and Bodl. Univ. 9 have lessons from *Gloriosi martyris*, but BL Addl 49363 has a series of short lessons not in any other source. There is minimal rubrication.

Table 3.11: Order of sungtexts for the two monastic breviaries with the monastic cursus (left column) and Bodl. University College 9 (right column). Bold indicates an item that shifts; *italics* an item in the monastic office not used in University College 9.

Genre	Mon: (BL Addl 43405 and Addl 49363)[a]	Genre	University College 9
VA	Pastor cesus	VA	O[b] pastor cesus [...]
MI	Adsunt Thome	MI	Adsunt Thome
MH	Martyr Dei	MH	Deus tuorum militum
MA1	Summo sacerdocio Thomas	MA1	Summo sacerdocio Thomas
MA2	Monachus sub clerico	MA2	Monachus sub clerico
MA3	Cultor agri Domini	MA3	Cultor agri Domini
MA4	**Nec in agnos**		
MA5	**Exulat vir optimus**		
MA6	**Exulantis predia preda**		
MR1	Studens livor Thome	MR1	Studens livor Thome
MR2	Thomas manum mittit	MR2	Thomas manum mittit
MR3	Lapis iste sex	MR3	Lapis iste sex
MR4	**Post sex annos**		
MA7	**Satane satellites**		
MA8	**Strictis Thomas ensibus**	**MA4**	**Nec in agnos**
MA9	**Hosti pandit ostium**	**MA5**	**Exulat vir optimus**
MA10	*Patrem nati perimunt*	**MA6**	**Exulantis predia preda**
MA11	*Sol inclinans radios*		
MA12	*Fusum spargunt cerebrum*	**MR4**	**Post sex annos**
MR5	Iacet granum	MR5	Iacet granum
MR6	Ex summa rerum	MR6	Ex summa rerum
MR7	**Mundi florem**		
MR8	**Christe Iesu per**	**MA7**	**Satane satellites**
ME	*Fragrat virtus*	**MA8**	**Strictis Thomas ensibus**
MR9	*Ferro pressos*	**MA9**	**Hosti pandit ostium**
MR10	*Thome cedunt per*	**MR7**	**Mundi florem**
MR11	*Novis fulget*	**MR8**	**Christe Iesu per**

MR12	Iesu bone	MR9	Iesu bone
LA1	Granum cadit copiam	LA1	Granum cadit copiam
LA2	Totus orbis martyris	LA2	Totus orbis martyris
LA3	Aqua Thome	LA3	Aqua Thome
LA4	Ad Thome memoriam	LA4	Ad Thome memoriam
LA5	Tu per Thome	LA5	Tu per Thome
LE	Opem nobis O Thoma	LE	Opem nobis O Thoma
WE	Felix locus felix	WE	Felix locus felix

ᵃ Also in Slocum's monastic version, from Camb., Fitzwilliam Museum, MS 369.

ᵇ An unusual textual variant.

The version of the Office from University College 9 demonstrates how a monastic version could be condensed into a secular office with nine lessons and nine responsories. The antiphons at Matins in every case remain the same, and in the same order. The responsories are included in order, although they are divided differently across nocturns, with MR4, *Post sex annos*, moving from the monastic first nocturn to the secular second nocturn, but remaining as MR4. Similarly, MR7 and MR8 from the monastic cursus move to the third nocturn, retaining their position, with the monastic MR12, *Iesu bone*, taking the final place, MR9, in the secular version. In all, three consecutive antiphons (monastic MA10–12) and three consecutive responsories (monastic MR9–11) along with the Gospel antiphon (ME) from the monastic version are not used in the secular version.

Secular Re-Interpretations of the Thomas Office: Sarum, York, Hereford

The table on the following page illustrates the invariable orders of sungtexts for Thomas in the three secular Uses, together with the original monastic assignments of the antiphons and responsories which have taken new positions noted in square brackets.

Sarum

In contrast to the Sarum versions of Advent Sunday, which allow few rational conclusions to be made on the basis of divisions in the lessons, the witnesses of Becket's Office in Sarum manuscripts are grouped primarily on the basis of lessons. This evidence, for a rhymed saint's office, stands in opposition to the less obviously helpful divisions of lessons seen above for Advent Sunday.

Table 3.12: Orders of sungtexts for Thomas Becket in the three secular Uses. Bold in the York and Hereford columns indicates difference from Sarum.

Genre	Sarum	York	Hereford
VE	Pastor cesus	Pastor cesus	Pastor cesus
MI	Adsunt Thome	Adsunt Thome	Adsunt Thome
MH	Martyr Dei	**Deus tuorum militum**	Martyr Dei
MA1	Summo sacerdocio Thomas	Summo sacerdocio Thomas	Summo sacerdocio Thomas
MA2	Monachus sub clerico	Monachus sub clerico	Monachus sub clerico
MA3	Cultor agri Domini	Cultor agri Domini	Cultor agri Domini
MR1	Studens livor Thome	Studens livor Thome	Studens livor Thome
MR2	Thomas manum mittit	Thomas manum mittit	Thomas manum mittit
MR3	Iacet granum [Mon MR5]	**Lapis iste [Mon MR3]**	**Lapis iste [Mon MR3]**
MA4	Nec in agnos	Nec in agnos	Nec in agnos
MA5	Exulat vir optimus	Exulat vir optimus	Exulat vir optimus
MA6	Exulantis predia preda	Exulantis predia preda	Exulantis predia preda
MR4	Ex summa rerum [Mon MR6]	**Post sex annos [Mon MR4]**	**Post sex annos [Mon MR4]**
MR5	Mundi florem [Mon MR7]	**Ex summa rerum [Mon MR6]**	**Ex summa rerum [Mon MR6]**
MR6	Christe Iesu per [Mon MR8]	**Iacet granum [Mon MR5]**	**Iacet granum [Mon MR5]**
MA7	Satane satellites	Satane satellites	Satane satellites
MA8	Strictis Thomas ensibus	Strictis Thomas ensibus	Strictis Thomas ensibus
MA9	Felix locus felix [Mon WE]	**Hosti pandit ostium [Mon MA9]**	**Hosti pandit ostium [Mon MA9]**
MR7	Thome cedunt [Mon MR10]	**Mundi florem [Mon MR7]**	**Mundi florem [Mon MR7]**
MR8	Novis fulget [Mon MR11]	**Christe Iesu per [Mon MR8]**	**Christe Iesu per [Mon MR8]**
MR9	Iesu bone [Mon MR12]	**Ferro pressos [Mon MR9]**	Iesu bone [Mon MR12]
LA1	Granum cadit copiam	Granum cadit copiam	Granum cadit copiam
LA2	Totus orbis martyris	Totus orbis martyris	Totus orbis martyris
LA3	Aqua Thome	Aqua Thome	Aqua Thome
LA4	Ad Thome memoriam	Ad Thome memoriam	Ad Thome memoriam
LA5	Tu per Thome	Tu per Thome	Tu per Thome
LE	Opem nobis O Thoma	Opem nobis O Thoma	Opem nobis O Thoma
WE	Salve Thoma virga	Salve Thoma virga	**Felix locus felix**

In addition to a few unique versions of the lessons containing infrequently appearing material, discussed later, it is perhaps most useful to mention a small group of six manuscripts, all of which are associated with the Chichele group: five are in the main group; the other (Hatton) is in Reames's 'less predictable' group. It should be noted that the only other Chichele book to be examined in this chapter, Camb. UL Dd. X. 66, has a different version of the lessons discussed later.

Table 3.13: Six Sarum manuscripts with similar lessons for Thomas.

Camb. UL Addl 4500	s.xiv	Sarum breviary (L)	Chichele
BL Harley 2946	s.xv	Sarum breviary(L)	Chichele
BL Sloane 2466	s.xiv	Sarum breviary (L)	Chichele
Lambeth Palace 69	s.xv	Sarum breviary (L) owned by Henry Chichele	Chichele
Oxford St John's Coll. 179	s.xv	Sarum breviary (L)	Chichele
Bodl. Hatton 63	s.xiv	Sarum breviary (L)	Chichele – less predictable

All of these manuscripts have the Long version of Advent Sunday and (as related below) for the Office of the Dead; two, St John's 179 and Hatton 63, have already been shown to be related at a closer level of detail for Advent. Only a few kalendars confirm the strength and interrelations of this group, but this may be irrelevant: while the St John's kalendar is closest to 4500, Hatton, and Harley have no kalendars, and Sloane has a heavily modified kalendar. Lambeth 69 is very close to the 'normative' kalendar, and so has very few variants of any description to share with the others. These six manuscripts are related to one another by a wealth of variants (up to thirty-five, shared between Lambeth 69, 4500, and Sloane), mostly in their lessons. This table indicates for each manuscript the number of relations by shared variant in Thomas's Office shared with each member of the group.

Addl 4500:	Lambeth 69 (35); Sloane (35); Ox St John (34); Harley (31); Hatton (31)
Harley:	Sloane (33); 4500 (31); Ox St John (30); Lambeth 69 (28); Hatton (21)
Hatton:	4500 (31); Ox St John (25); Sloane (25); Lambeth 69 (24); Harley (21)
Lambeth 69:	4500 (35); Ox St John (34); Sloane (32); Harley (28); Hatton (24)
Ox St John:	4500 (34); Lambeth 69 (34); Sloane (34); Harley (30); Hatton (25)
Sloane:	4500 (35); Ox St John (34); Harley (33); Lambeth 69 (32); Hatton (25)

The divisions of the lesson text *Gloriosi martyris Thome* are identical in all six manuscripts for lessons 1 through 6; lesson 7 of course reflects the Gospel pericope. Harley, St John's, Hatton, and Lambeth begin lesson 8 at the same place, which picks up the narrative; and the first three of these plus Sloane have a common start to lesson 9. The other variants shared by all six differ in their significance. In one case, *enim* is replaced with *igitur*; in another, *ergo* is omitted. However, these six manuscripts also contain more substantial omissions from the *Gloriosi martyris* text which is found in most manuscripts. The following precise passages are selectively omitted:

— [...] *damnis gravioribus attritus* [...]

— *quia causa ecclesie nondum plemne innotuerat, et personalis videbatur persecutio: cedendum censuit esse malicie*

— *et in monasterio Pontiniacensi studiose commendatus* [by the pope]

— *vel compassionis gladio totiens confossus*

— *directis per abbates quosdam Cisterciensis ordinis ad capitulum generale litteris comminatoriis, eum a Pontiniaco perturbare curavit. Timens autem beatus Thomas occasione sui viris sanctis imminere dispendium, sponte recessit. Sed antequam inde progrederetur, divina revelatione confortatus est: ostenso sibi celitus indicio quod ad ecclesiam suam reditorus esset cum gloria, et per palmam martyrii migraturum ad Dominum. Perturbatum a Pontiniaco excepit summo cum honore christianissimus Francorum rex Ludovicus, et eum humanissime donec pax reformaretur exhibuit. Sepius tamen et licet ipse incassum pulsatus est, ne regis Anglorum proditori aliquod humanitatis beneficium impenderet.*

The intention behind the changes is not entirely clear, but the resulting lessons seem to illustrate a desire to downplay the assistance offered Thomas by Louis, king of France; Thomas's exile; and the fury of Henry II of England. The lessons of the Thomas office, like those in other hagiographical offices in manuscripts of the Chichele group, appear to have been unambiguously redacted in order to satisfy a requirement, here perhaps to displace Thomas's exile (and the reasons for that exile) from an otherwise blameless life. This redaction contradicts the fact that one of Thomas's principal characteristics in his earthly life involved the defiance of corrupt and ungodly earthly power as *novus homo* and defender of the Church.[17]

---

[17] Slocum, *Liturgies*, pp. 5, 7.

There are several further textual developments worth mentioning within the Sarum sources. Each of two manuscripts appears to transmit a particularly distinct version of the lessons. Worcester Cathedral Q. 10 (not otherwise discussed here) is characterized by two unique supplements which supply lessons 8 and 9, beginning respectively *Quinto autem nativitatis* and *Revera pro ecclesia*. BL Addl 52359 has a different supplement for lessons 8 and 9, beginning *Bonus pastor pro ovibus suis* and *Postremum vero, si necesse sit*. This pair and the preceding group of six manuscripts associated by their lessons, all of which have an identical choice and order of responsories for Thomas, suggest that, at least in this case, lessons and sungtexts were subject to different influences, and that changes in lessons did not necessitate any change in the order of sungtexts.

Several other issues offer opportunities for variants: the location of memorials for the preceding four days differs without much logic, and the location of the prosa *Clangat pastor* differs: in eight manuscripts it does not appear after the responsory at Vespers, but rather just before the second nocturn of Matins.[18] Dd. X. 66 places the prosa just after the ninth responsory of Matins, the same place that BL Addl 52359 inserts a new prosa. This prosa reflects on Thomas's miracles, and raises him before God. It recalls the ninth Sarum responsory *Jesu bone*, which explores the theme of restoration (of souls) just as *Thomas victor* notes the deficiencies of the disabled whom Thomas cures.

Thomas victor et celesti
   tutus sedet gloria.
Probet deus suo testi
   vera testimonia.
Ceci muti surdi claudi
   leprosi cum mortuis
Hi sunt Thomas quos saluti
   optate restituis.
Thomam laudant cum supernis
   angelorum moduli.

Thome laus est et in terris
   irrascantur populi.
Age age quod cepisti
   gloriose domine.
Et tuere sponsam Christi
   tua sancta pectore.
Ergo laudes deo nostro
   chorus noster concine.

(from BL Addl 52359, f. 52[r–v])

With these exceptions, many of the remaining variants can be attributed to ordinary textual drift, without a distinctly different performance result.

---

[18] BL Addl 52359, BL Addl 59862, Camb. St John's 146, Camb. UL Dd. X. 66, Lambeth Palace 69, Bodl. Hatton 63, Ranworth.

York and Hereford

The three York books have a similar relation to one another for Becket as they do for Advent: 1493 and LM84 are again closely associated, with LM84 containing significantly more material. All of the lessons are drawn from one source which begins *Hodie fratres carissimi merito beato thome* (a sermon of Benedict of Peterborough on the subject of Thomas).[19] All rubrics, including the most complex (concerning memorials), are the same in every source, except where Sion contains slightly more detail than the others in the opening rubrics. The York lessons tend to emphasize Thomas's new and godly character, and lessons 8 and 9 are a much longer account of Thomas's martyrdom than appears in the Sarum sources, where these lessons are used to recount his miracles.[20]

The 1505 printed Hereford breviary and the manuscript source, Hereford Cathedral P. IX. 7, both use lessons from *Gloriosi martyris*, but do not agree in terms of divisions: as a rule, 1505 tends to have shorter lessons in general. The sungtexts and rubrics in both Hereford sources are identical.

It is not possible with this limited number of sources to derive further conclusions from this insubstantial study of the York and Hereford versions of Thomas's Office, as the witnesses consulted are consistent in their sungtexts and rubrics, but indescribably and unhelpfully divergent in their lessons. Not enough sources are discussed here in order to make a satisfactory determination of the character of the Office across all witnesses of either Use, and further work, with more sources, is required here.

Thomas Becket: Conclusions

This brief study of the office for a popular saint affords several conclusions:

1. Even a newly-composed office, produced by a known individual, boasts four different orders of sungtexts across the secular and monastic patterns;

2. The manifold variants in the lessons, even the lessons within witnesses of the same Use, are only moderated by an obvious programme of redaction of lessons (in the Chichele group) for which other evidence exists;

---

[19] Two Sarum sources (as far as I am aware) exceptionally use lessons from this sermon: these are Liverpool University, Radcliffe MS 37, and Longleat MS 10, neither of which appear in this textual analysis though their lesson incipits have been recorded for Thomas's Office.

[20] Noticed by Slocum in *Liturgies*, p. 227.

3. The Thomas Office illustrates the futility of 'reconstructing' an original version of Benedict's composition. Slocum agrees that collation based on disparate witnesses will only produce an artificial, meaningless paradigm,[21] especially if lessons were constructed or chosen at the discretion of individuals from an early stage, and if nine-lesson secular versions and indeed twelve-lesson monastic versions were variously created from the original monastic version.

The Office of the Dead

Most commonly associated in later breviaries with All Souls' Day (2 November), the Office of the Dead had its origins as a separate, votive commemoration before the institution of the *Commendatio animarum* in the eleventh century.[22] Edmund Bishop argued that the Office as a devotion could be attested before 817, as a practice encouraged by Benedict of Aniane, and Knud Ottosen distrusts any Roman origin for the Office before the ninth century.[23] It is a matter of debate whether the Office began as a regularly scheduled monastic observance to pray for the departed souls of a community, as has sometimes been proposed, or whether it was used in place of the daily Office for the vigil of a funeral, the usage which seems to have been the most frequent in the later Middle Ages. There are compelling arguments on both sides: in support of the vigil of a funeral, it ought to be noted that the liturgy has special prayers used in the presence of the corpse; on the contrary, the foundation in the later Middle Ages of chantry chapels which were enjoined *in their statutes* to say the Office of the Dead for specified individuals may hint at origins of the Office in a votive, perpetual observance. Obvious is the relation of the Office to the doctrine of Purgatory and the belief that succour of the souls therein could be obtained by the prayers of the faithful. Purgatory as a distinct place between Paradise and Hell did not become an authoritative doctrine before 1170,[24] but there are numerous Scriptural and patristic references to forgiveness in the world to come (Mt 12. 31–32) and purgation through fire. The Office of the Dead, with its readings inevitably from Job who complains of his torments and waits for deliverance, can be easily interpreted in the light of

[21] Slocum, *Liturgies*, p. 14.

[22] Ottosen, *Responsories and Versicles*, p. 42.

[23] Ottosen, *Responsories and Versicles*, p. 35, quoting Edmund Bishop.

[24] Ottosen, *Responsories and Versicles*, p. 47, and see Jacques Le Goff, *La Naissance du Purgatoire* (Paris: Gallimard, 1981), pp. 177–80.

Table 3.14a: Orders of sungtexts for the Office of the Dead in the three secular Uses.

Genre	Sarum	York	Hereford
VA	Placebo domino	Placebo domino	Placebo domino
	Heu me quia incolatus	Heu me quia incolatus	Heu me quia incolatus
	Si iniquitates	**Dominus custodit te**	Si iniquitates
	Opera manuum tuarum	Opera manuum tuarum	Opera manuum tuarum
VE	Audivi vocem de celo	**Tuam Deus deposcimus**	Audivi vocem de celo
MA1	Dirige Domine Deus	Dirige Domine Deus	Dirige Domine Deus
MA2	Convertere Domine	Convertere Domine	Convertere Domine
MA3	Nequando rapiat	Nequando rapiat	Nequando rapiat
MR1	Credo quod redemptor	Credo quod redemptor	Credo quod redemptor
MR2	Qui Lazarum resuscitasti	Qui Lazarum resuscitasti	Qui Lazarum resuscitasti
MR3	Domine quando veneris	Domine quando veneris	Domine quando veneris
MA4	In loco pascue	In loco pascue	In loco pascue
MA5	Delicta iuventutis mee	Delicta iuventutis mee	Delicta iuventutis mee
MA6	Credo videre bona	Credo videre bona	Credo videre bona
MR4	Heu mihi Domine	Heu mihi Domine	Heu mihi Domine
MR5	Ne recorderis	Ne recorderis	Ne recorderis
MR6	Domine secundum actum	**Libera me Domine [...] inferni**	Dominus secundum actum
MA7	Complaceat tibi Domine	Complaceat tibi Domine	Complaceat tibi Domine
MA8	Sana Domine	Sana Domine	Sana Domine
MA9	Sitivit anima mea	Sitivit anima mea	Sitivit anima mea
MR7	Peccante me cotidie	Peccante me cotidie	Peccante me cotidie
MR8	Requiem eternam dona eis	**Deus eterne**	Requiem eternam dona eis
MR9	Libera me Domine [...] eterna	Libera me Domine [...] eterna	Libera me Domine [...] eterna
LA1	Exultabunt Domino	Exultabunt Domino	Exultabunt Domino
LA2	Exaudi Domine orationem	Exaudi Domine orationem	Exaudi Domine orationem
LA3	Me suscepit	Me suscepit	Me suscepit
LA4	A porta inferi	**Eruisti Domine**	Eruisti Domine
LA5	Omnis spiritus laudet	Omnis spiritus laudet	Omnis spiritus laudet
LE	Ego sum resurrectio	Ego sum resurrectio	Ego sum resurrectio

Purgatory: Job's grievances become those of the souls in the afterlife awaiting deliverance from Christ.[25] Table 3.14a illustrates the secular texts for the Office. Bold indicates a difference in one or more of the Uses.

By the later Middle Ages, the Office was an extremely widely disseminated observance, appearing in service books sometimes as a separate section (for votive use) and frequently in the Sanctorale, for All Souls' Day. Books of Hours and primers, as well as other personal books, often contained the Office of the Dead with the Offices of the BVM and the Cross. The sungtexts for the Dead existed in distinctive forms for Sarum and York in all sources known (and in Hereford, which appropriated the Sarum pattern except at Lauds, where it has the same antiphons as York). The monastic Office used the secular nine-lesson structure. The responsories are drawn from a clear selection, many with Scriptural references; and the overall structure of the Office does not vary.

It is notable that in all cases, the lessons are drawn from Job 7. 16–10. 22, and as a result, the differences in word choice and order are nonsubstantive and tied more to the transmission of Scripture than liturgy.[26] Examples include the appearance of *Responde mihi*, the end of the previous verse, before *quantus habeo iniquitates*; and *Manus tue (domine) fecerunt me* [...]with *domine* present in five sources. In one of these it is an interlineal insertion.[27] The lessons in all secular sources in this study have the following consistent set of incipits, although the length of each lesson is not completely consistent. This set of lessons corresponds to Ottosen's group 1d, by far the most widely employed lessons, especially in France and England. The distinctive ninth lesson beginning *Quare de vulva*, Ottosen reports, became the normative final lesson in the Roman Office of the Dead in the twelfth century (Table 3.14b).[28]

Among the Sarum books there are again two well-defined textual families, descriptively titled Dead-Short and Dead-Long: although the constituent manuscripts include members of Adv-Short and -Long, the groups are not identical: in the table below, assignments different for the Office of the Dead are marked in bold. Dead-Short is found in BL Addl 59862 and the Ranworth

---

[25] Ottosen, *Responsories and Versicles*, p. 47.

[26] John Harper notes that when the Office was used as a votive observance, only one of three nocturns of Matins would be used each day, on a rotation. Harper, *The Forms and Orders of Western Liturgy*, p. 106.

[27] BL Addl 43405–6, Camb. UL Addl 3474–5, Lambeth P. Sion 1 (inserted), Bodl. Laud misc. 84, BL Royal 2 A XII.

[28] Ottosen, *Responsories and Versicles*, p. 62.

Table 3.14b: Divisions of lessons for the Office of the Dead in the three secular Uses.

Lesson 1	Parce mihi Domine: nihil enim sunt dies mei
Lesson 2	Tedet animam meam vite mee
Lesson 3	Manus tue fecerunt me
Lesson 4	(Responde mihi:) Quantas habeo iniquitates
Lesson 5	Homo natus de muliere brevi vivens tempore
Lesson 6	Quis mihi hoc tribuat ut in inferno protegas me
Lesson 7	Spiritus meus attenuabitur; dies mei breviabuntur
Lesson 8	Pelli mee consumptus adhesit os meum
Lesson 9	Quare de vulva

Antiphonal, both of which have the Long version of Advent Sunday. Camb. St John's College 146 and King's College 30 have Dead-Short but also Adv-Long. Durham Cosin V. I. 3, which has a late and complex version of the Advent Sunday office bearing a greater resemblance to Adv-Long than Adv-Short, also has a consistent version of Dead-Long (Table 3.15).

As for Advent, Short and Long incorporate members of Reames's Folio and Chichele groups, as noted above: the Chichele group always has the Long version. Again, there are some outliers: as in Advent, Royal does not correspond uniformly to either pattern and, with King's 30, omits a number of rubrics; a few others, especially the Durham MS, have divergent rubrics. BL Addl 32427 has two sets of the prayers said in the presence of the deceased, one after Vespers, and one after Lauds, with different texts.[29] Here, though, the texts are more difficult to characterize by shared variant, as all copies of the Sarum Dead follow a more or less rigid pattern, particularly as to lessons, whose divisions do not vary.

The Dead-Long group, like its Advent counterpart, is distinguished from the Short group by the inclusion of more, and more substantial, rubrics. Its initial rubric, which begins *Finitis hiis vesperis statim incipiatur Placebo et dicantur festine vespere mortuorum*, is, like its Advent counterpart, indicative of the rest of the contents. The remaining extra rubrics deal principally with the tolling of bells and the division of labour among the choir and cantors. There is no obvious variant of the Office within witnesses of the Chichele group, although all

---

[29] For instance, *pro episcopis*: Deus qui inter apostolicos (after Vespers); Deus cuius misericordie non est numerus (after Lauds).

Table 3.15: Manuscripts from which the Office of the Dead was transcribed. The family (Long or Short) with which they agree is given (and different assignments from Advent are marked in bold type). The column at far right indicates Reames's group assignment, if applicable.

Camb. St John's Coll. 146	s.xv	Sarum breviary (**Dead-Long**)	
Camb. King's Coll. 30	s.xiv	Sarum breviary (**Dead-Long**)	Portable
Camb. UL Addl 3474–5	s.xv	Sarum breviary (Dead-Long), Norwich	
Camb. UL Addl 4500	s.xiv	Sarum breviary (Dead-Long)	Chichele
Camb.UL Dd. X. 66	s.xv	Sarum breviary (Dead-Long)	Chichele – less predictable
Durham Univ. Cosin V. I. 3	s.xvi	Sarum breviary (**Dead-Short**), Coltishall, Norfolk	Folio
Hereford Cath. P. IX. 7	s.xiii	Hereford breviary s.xiii for Hereford cathedral	
BL Addl 32427	s.xv	Sarum breviary (Dead-Long), diocese of Worcester	
BL Addl 43405–6	s.xiv	Monastic breviary for Muchelney Abbey	
BL Addl 49363	s.xiv	Monastic breviary	
BL Addl 52359	s.xiv	Sarum breviary (Dead-Short) for Penwortham, Lancs (cell of Evesham)	Folio
BL Addl 59862	s.xv	Sarum breviary (**Dead-Short**), Norwich	
BL Harley 2946	s.xv	Sarum breviary (Dead-Long)	Chichele
BL Royal 2 A XII	s.xv	Sarum breviary of Continental manufacture	
BL Sloane 2466	s.xiv	Sarum breviary (Dead-Long)	Chichele
Lambeth Palace 69	s.xv	Sarum breviary (Dead-Long) owned by Henry Chichele	Chichele
Lambeth Palace Sion 1	s.xiv/xv	York breviary, noted, for Skelton, near York	
Oxford St John's Coll. 179	s.xv	Sarum breviary (Dead-Long)	Chichele
Bodl. Bodley 976	s.xiv	Sarum breviary (Dead-Long)	
Bodl. Canon lit. 215	s.xv	Sarum breviary (Dead-Short) with Irish influence	
Bodl. Hatton 63	s.xiv	Sarum breviary (Dead-Long)	Chichele – less predictable
Bodl. Laud misc. 84	s.xv	York breviary	
Bodl. Univ. Coll. 9	s.xv	Carmelite breviary	
Ranworth, s.n.	s.xv	Sarum antiphonal (**Dead-Short**) for St Helen's, Ranworth	
1531	s.xvi	Sarum breviary (Dead-Short), printed by Regnault and Chevallon	Folio
1493	s.xv	First printed York breviary	
1505	s.xvi	First printed Hereford breviary	

Chichele group manuscripts follow Dead-Long. It should also be noted that within the Sarum manuscripts, witnesses are related by no more than a few shared variants, if any occur at all, and that these relations are not significant: the character of the variants, too, is considerably more minor than for either Advent or Thomas.

Similarly, the three York sources have an identical Office of the Dead, except for the following notes: Bodl. Laud misc. 84 has the *Nota quod* rubric before lesson 1 and a further rubric at the end of Lauds; Sion has 4 verses at the end of Matins which are not in Laud misc. 84. The two Hereford books are also more or less identical, except that 1505 has prayers *ante laudes* with the prayers before Matins (and not after it) — instead the rubric *ut supra in vesperis mortuorum* appears. The monastic manuscripts give what is by now a jumbled picture: 43405 has prayers *pro defunctis* near the end of Vespers, which are not in 49363. Both have different responsory series (some of the responsories in 43405 have unconventional non-*CAO* verses), and 49363 has ferial responsories and multiple verses. Univ. 9 has no prayers before Matins.

The Office of the Dead: Conclusions

Despite its ambiguous origins, which seem to have involved neither a named author nor even a theological consensus (until a late stage) about the nature of purgative prayer for the souls of the departed, the Office of the Dead had by the later Middle Ages acquired a remarkable fixity, with a selection of responsories complementing a consistent group of lessons drawn from the book of Job. The two Sarum families, Short and Long as for Advent Sunday, can be explained merely by differences in the rubrication, and not by any more substantial or performance differences. This consistency may exist despite, or perhaps because of, the fact that the Office was included in the widest variety of monastic and secular service books, and also in countless books for private use as the devotional nature of the Office became more prevalent. This pervasiveness in manuscript and printed sources can perhaps also explain its importance to contemporary literature (the influence of the liturgy for the Dead on Dante and Petrarch, for example, has already been mentioned) and the intellectual exploration of death and the afterlife: as Ottosen put it, the Office of the Dead is a human response to the 'eternal questions [...] whence do I come, where shall I go?' which 'make [...] each human being a theologian.'[30] The Office was an expression of, and an

---

[30] Ottosen, *Responsories and Versicles*, p. 385.

interaction with, what has been described by Le Goff as the essential medieval theological concept — Purgatory — and by its consistency and frequency of appearance as demonstrated here we are assured of an unusually accurate portrait of medieval thinking on the subject.[31]

A Core Group Emerges

From twenty-eight sources used for textual analysis, there appears to be a group of six Sarum manuscripts which have shared variants in all three offices. For each manuscript the number of relations with every other member of the group, across Advent Sunday, Thomas, and the Dead, is also supplied. To put these figures into context, few other manuscripts in the sample shared more than ten textual variants with any other witness, so the relations between these manuscripts are substantial.

Cambridge, UL, Addl 4500, c15th breviary-missal
   Sloane (38 shared variants); Lambeth 69 (37); Ox St John's (34); Harley (31); Hatton (27)

London, Lambeth Palace 69, c15th breviary
   Addl 4500 (37); Ox St John's (34); Sloane (32); Harley (28); Hatton (27)

Oxford, St John's College 179, c15th breviary
   Addl 4500 (34); Lambeth 69 (34); Sloane (34); Harley (30); Hatton (27)

Oxford, Bodleian, Hatton 63, late c14th breviary
   Addl 4500 (27); Ox St John's (27); Lambeth 69 (27); Sloane (25); Harley (21)

London, British Library Sloane 2466, c15th breviary
   Harley (46); Addl 4500 (38); Ox St John's (34); Lambeth 69 (32); Hatton (25)

London, British Library Harley 2946, breviary written 1405
   Sloane (46); Addl 4500 (31); Ox St John's (30); Lambeth 69 (28); Hatton (21)

All of these manuscripts, which give the Long version of both Advent and the Office of the Dead, are at least associated with the Chichele group (Hatton is in Reames's 'less predictable' category and is the least close to any other of the six). As might be expected (on the basis of the Chichele group's typical amendment of lessons) the great majority of these shared variants are in the lessons for Thomas Becket, part of a feast of medieval origin and no great antiquity. Only two pairs

---

[31] Jacques Le Goff, *La Naissance du Purgatoire*.

of manuscripts are related substantially in other areas: Harley and Sloane, the pair with the greatest number of shared variants, share some minor changes to rubrics in Advent. Interestingly, however, their kalendars are dramatically different. Hatton and Oxford St John's 179 are similarly aligned based on substantial additions to the rubrics.

It should be recalled that Dd. X. 66, also a 'less predictable' Chichele group member, does not appear here, and in fact is part of another textual group (BL Addl 59862, Camb. UL Dd. X. 66 and Addl 3474–5, and Bodl. MS Bodley 976), centred on omissions from the rubrics. This is a confusing state of affairs made more ambiguous by the fact that their texts, other than for the shared variants, do not necessarily appear to resemble one another. Nevertheless, several in the group have related kalendars as well. But Becket's lessons, by far the most important area linking the six manuscripts in the 'core group' above, do not appear in the Chichele form in Dd. X. 66. They do, however, share 6 variants with Lambeth and Addl 4500, and 5 with Hatton 63 and Oxford St John's 179.

The Office for Thomas Becket, rather more uniform in broad outline, provides us with further evidence for the core group, an internally consistent set of lessons. That the core group is united by rubrical matters on Advent Sunday (and less so for the Office of the Dead) and particularly by lessons for Thomas may appear surprising, and might suggest that lesson texts were subject either to editing or some form of standardization consistent with the reputed origin of the Chichele group. The Office of the Dead provides a further witness: as they do for Advent, the sources with the Long version of the text provide slightly more detail.

Conclusions

To summarize the principal characteristics of the texts, then, the identical words of sungtexts within each Use are the most consistent feature. Each Use also has an unambiguous pattern of sungtexts for each Office, the responsory series at Matins, which can serve as an identifier. The rubrics, unlike the sungtexts, are notable for their consistency in the Long and Short groups for Advent Sunday and the Office of the Dead. The lessons, however, prove more confusing: those for Advent Sunday and the Dead are of no help in grouping sources, as the innumerable variants in the former are rarely consistent between any two witnesses. Singleton offshoots with additional features, such as BL Addl 32427, are more distinctive. The Office of the Dead has unambiguous selections from Job in unvarying divisions. Despite these facts, a core group of manuscripts with many shared textual variants across all three Offices is strengthened particularly by numerous shared variants in the lessons for Thomas, non-Scriptural selections from a set of such lessons probably constructed specially for the Office, but not one which could be divided according to an original or even conventional pattern. All three Offices were widely distributed, and the existence of variation may be attributed simply to that fact. The next section discusses similar variation in an office of much more limited distribution.

A Further Case Study: The Office of St William of York

The preceding examination of three Offices in all three secular liturgical Uses necessarily treated Sarum, without question the most important of the three, with an inevitably greater precision, in part owing to the number of extant witnesses. It will be useful now to examine the complete text of an Office which does not appear in Sarum books at all and which provides an example of a hagiographical feastday in the Sanctorale, another newly-composed saint's office, and an observance very clearly restricted to a limited geographical region. The case of William's Office is an ideal, self-contained, isolated, and complete paradigm for complete liturgical analysis.

The liturgical material for the feast of William of York comprises the only complete rhymed office for a 'York saint'.[32] Commemorations on the feastdays of Wilfrid and John of Beverley are far more common, but neither saint is able to boast a complete set of proper texts and chants for the Office. The usual provision for the former, present in the York office manuscripts and increasingly added to breviaries and antiphonals outside the province as his cult spread, allows, at most, for three lessons and a prayer. The composition of a complete Office for William is perhaps surprising. His cult was never widespread nor particularly successful; indeed, except for the votive antiphon *O Willelme pastor bone* in a few manuscripts, no proper texts to William exist in any surviving sources other than those used in the province of York. Any amount of William's Office greater than this antiphon ought, I have suggested, to be indicative of York Use, one of the few accurate diagnostics that have been found. William's canonization by Honorius III on 18 March 1226 was the high point of his cult, according to Christopher Norton, whose recent work comprises the best account of William's life, death, and sainthood.[33] Norton suggests that William's tomb in the Minster had been the focal point of a Yorkshire-centred cult from the late 1170s.

---

[32] For the constitutive saints of York, see *supra*, chapter 2; and Salisbury, *The Use of York*.

[33] Christopher Norton, *St William of York* (Woodbridge: York Medieval Press, 2006), p. 202. R. B. Dobson suggests the cult 'may have been unduly discounted' as Margery Kempe

The existence of a substantial rhymed office for this seemingly unremarkable saint may be a result of an effort to promote William's sainthood throughout the province. As Thomas French notes, the extant physical evidence for veneration seems to be limited to York itself,[34] and while local appreciation of the indigenous archbishop may have been on the whole successful, an attempt to expand the cult to the rest of the province and beyond may have been inspired by the fact that the metropolitan church did not yet have a saintly patron whose earthly remains were present, unlike, for instance, the major ecclesiastical centres at Durham, Beverley, and Ripon. A liturgical office intended for propagation, in large part an exposition of William's life and miracles, was surely a suitable if ultimately unsuccessful means of publicizing his sanctity.

The non-presence of evidence for the veneration of William is notable. There exists no evidence of any dedications to him, despite the proliferation of commemorative material 'on roods, screens, and stained glass', notably the 'St William window' in the Minster, which was erected *c.* 1414 and which has been the subject of considerable iconographic and historical attention, and may be the means by which William is best known.[35] Relics of St William were recorded at Durham (a tooth); Lichfield (clothing, hair); and the royal chapel at Windsor (arm or hand).[36] The date of the emergence of any local veneration of William can be traced to perhaps the later 1170s on the basis of several documents. The writings of John of Hexham and Reginald of Durham (1160s–70s) on William did not refer to him as a saint; the first reference to William as saintly is in a charter, 1177–1186. While the particular transaction of business is not relevant, it refers to the festival of '*beati Petri ad Vincula post revelationem miraculorum beati Willelmi* [...] *que facta fuit in pentecosten*'.[37]

and others were said to have visited his relics, and his shrine was rebuilt in 1472: see Dobson, *Church and Society in the Medieval North of England* (London: Hambledon, 1996), p. 24. William's translation as a 'grand "state occasion"' attended by Edward I who helped to carry the reliquary, although he 'was a somewhat prosaic saint', pp. 174–75.

[34] Thomas French, *York Minster: The St William Window* (Oxford: Oxford University Press for the British Academy, 1999), p. 9.

[35] In *York Minster*, French notes, p. 19, that 1414, calculated on the balance of evidence, is slightly earlier than previous estimates. For the dedications, see Francis Bond, *Dedications and Patron Saints of English Churches: Ecclesiastical Symbolism: Saints and their Emblems* (London: Oxford University Press, 1914), p. 138.

[36] Summarized in Islwyn Thomas, 'The Cult of Saints' Relics in Medieval England' (unpublished doctoral thesis, University of London, 1975).

[37] Norton, *St William*, pp. 150, 164.

There exist two documents which might have been used to give an account of the sanctity of William. These were a set of miracles attributed to William which occurred in the week of Pentecost, 1177, and a *Vita*, 'notable for its sobriety and restraint, and the modesty of its invention',[38] which corresponded to the typical pattern, surely a helpful document to prove the cause of sainthood, which decision was, by the time of the enquiries into William, by now entirely the purview of the Roman bureaucracy. The miracles were recorded on a wooden 'table' or panel kept in the Minster, now lost; their existence as independent from the *Vita* is witnessed by a transcription completed from the table in the seventeenth century.[39] The *Vita* itself was in two parts: the first was an account of his life after the usual pattern; the second a record of his miracles. Norton thinks it possible that the *Vita* was used as evidence during the process of canonization; several miracles were noted in a bull of 1226 for which the only other source is the *Vita*; such a suggestion would put the date of its composition somewhere between 1210 and 1225, although Norton also suggests that it might otherwise have been compiled either to celebrate the official canonization, which would set its date at 1226 or later, or to support the early cult, which would probably increase its antiquity.

The author of the principal Office to William was, at a minimum, aware of the *Vita*, although no new evidence for its date can be extrapolated here, since it was not unknown for an office to have been composed prior to canonization. The Office for the Translation, which we will consider separately, must have been compiled some time after William's translation itself in 1283/84 when Anthony Bek, upon his consecration as bishop of Durham, paid for it to be done. The lessons for this Office contain references to events which happened in the Minster on the day of translation itself. The principal office, too, must surely have existed by this time.

As for the author of the *Vita*, Norton does make a proposal: Elias, son of Bernard and canon of York, was involved in William's canonization; later, he established a chantry at the Minster altar of St William which he had also founded. Elias, says Norton, may have been not only the author of the *Vita*, whose text seems to have been written by an educated cleric, but also perhaps the figure who adapted components of the *Vita* for use as lessons in the Office, and who wrote the liturgical material for the feast.[40] It does seem clear that the

---

[38] Norton, *St William*, p. 192.

[39] Norton, *St William*, p. 192.

[40] Norton, *St William*, p. 201.

author of the liturgical material was aware of the lessons, and that the two were meant to be used in conjunction. Elias had studied theology at Paris; the first mention of his canonry is in curial correspondence dated April 1224; later, the bull was issued in 1226. Finally, he established the chantry at William's altar in about 1230.[41]

William's Feast in Manuscript and Printed Sources

An entry on 9th June for St William, *archiepiscopus Ebor. et confessor*, appears in the kalendar of every book for the Office which has been identified as pertaining to the Use of York, as well as the kalendars of books which follow other patterns. The complete rhymed office for William appears in twelve of these, enumerated below. Elsewhere, the feast is in the kalendars of York psalters, Books of Hours, and two different sets of three lessons for commemorations can be found in Bodl. Wood empt. 20, what appears to be a priest's notebook; and BL Addl 35285, an antiphonal-missal for the Augustinian priory at Guisborough. Brief material for William, consisting of a single antiphon and probably meant for commemorative purposes, appears in two further sources. These are MS 25 in Aberdeen University Library, a psalter which M. R. James suggested might be localized to Ely, and which contains a Sarum Office of the Dead; and Manchester, John Rylands Library MS Lat. 127, a Sarum Book of Hours. Both contain only the antiphon in question, *O Willelme pastor bone*, without its music. Eight Southern manuscripts contain an entry for William in their kalendars, but contain no proper material or directions for the observance of his feast.[42] These entries, and all entries in liturgical kalendars, must be understood to imply, in Richard Pfaff's words, 'some degree of recognition',[43] not necessarily that the feast was observed. To emphasize, in the eleven Southern Office manuscripts known to me that contain William's name at all, only the two named contain the antiphon, and that alone. Where William's feast in kalendars is given a class, it is with few exceptions a *duplum festum principale*, and William is ordinarily identified as an archbishop in York sources.

[41] *Fasti Ecclesiae Anglicanae 1066–1300*, ed. by Diana Greenway, 12 vols (London: Institute of Historical Research, 1968–2006), vi (1999), 120.

[42] BQ, BU (Springfield, Essex), CT (Chertsey Abbey, Surrey), DK, DL, DP, DQ, DU (the Wollaton Antiphonal).

[43] Pfaff, 'New Liturgical Observances in Later Medieval England', p. 1.

Table 3.16: Sources from which the proper Office for William has been transcribed. The sigla used in the following textual analysis are at far left. References to the sigla in the main text are enclosed within square brackets thus [AB], to avoid confusion with the kalendar sigla used elsewhere.

A	Bodl. Laud misc. 84	15ᵗʰ c. breviary, perhaps for York Minster
B	BL Addl 30511	14ᵗʰ c. breviary in use before 1502, province of York
D	Durham Cosin V. I. 2	15ᵗʰ c. noted breviary, for Rudby parish church
E	Arundel Castle, s.n	15ᵗʰ c. antiphonal, for Minster chapel of St Mary & Holy Angels
F	Dublin, Trinity College MS 85	15ᵗʰ c. breviary-missal, province of York
G	Bodl. Gough lit. 1	15ᵗʰ c. Sanctorale of a noted breviary, province of York
L	Lambeth P. Sion Coll. 1	14ᵗʰ/15ᵗʰ c. noted breviary, for Skelton parish church
P	BL Addl 35285	14ᵗʰ c. breviary (Augustinian), Guisborough
Q	Bodl. Wood empt. 20	1471–72 priest's note-book or miscellany
R	BL Addl 38624	15ᵗʰ c. breviary, province of York
S	1493 pr.	1493 breviary pr. by Hamman, Venice, for York (Bodleian copy)
V	York Minster Addl 68	14ᵗʰ c. breviary, province of York
W	York Minster Addl 115	15ᵗʰ c. breviary, province of York
X	York Minster Addl 383	15ᵗʰ c. breviary, province of York
Y	York Minster XVI. O. 9	14ᵗʰ c. breviary-missal, province of York
Z	York Minster XVI. O. 23	15ᵗʰ c. breviary, summer volume only, province of York

The complete rhymed office for William can also be found in the printed York breviary, whose first edition was produced in 1493, and antiphons for him are in the printed processionals of 1516 and 1530. One of the two modern printings of the text of the Office, in the Surtees Society York Breviary (1880, 1883) is a transcription of the 1493 edition, with apparatus indicating reference to the later editions, mostly by Regnault, of 1526, 1533, and *c.* 1555. The second modern appearance, which excludes the texts of the lessons, is in volume 13 of *Analecta Hymnica*, which lists as its sources one of the two York breviaries at Trinity College Dublin (MS 85) and BL Addl 30511, along with the 1533 printed edition.

There are three manuscript sources that contain the music, complete: these are the York breviary formerly of Sion College and now at Lambeth Palace, which seems to have been used at Skelton parish church; Durham UL Cosin V. I. 2, used at Rudby parish church, about fifteen miles from Skelton; and the Sanctorale of a York noted breviary, now Bodl. Gough lit. 1. The Gough breviary's Office for William is strongly related, by its lessons at least, to the copy in the Rudby book; the chants in these two manuscripts share fourteen unique points of correspondence not in Skelton or elsewhere. The sole surviving York Antiphonal, now at Arundel Castle in Sussex, has only first Vespers for William; the rest of his Office was to be celebrated according to the Common of Saints, although this is curious since the book was written for the Chapel of the Blessed Virgin and the Holy Angels, next door to York Minster, apparently the absolute centre of William's cult! There is another witness for first Vespers, on a verso in another part of the Sion book. Sion appears to be three fragmentary manuscripts bound together, with the psalter, canticles, and litany forming 1 of 3 parts. Vespers for William is on the verso of the last leaf of the litany and is probably present because the compiler of the volume needed the contents of the recto, discarding whatever followed.

Numerous other sources contain the texts of the office. The tradition in the printed breviaries, all of which contain William's office, is represented by the 1493 edition. Bodl. Laud misc. 84 may have been used at York Minster. Five further manuscripts now in York Minster Library also contain the Office; none of these have a specific known provenance but all contain York responsory series. Finally, William's Office appears in two breviaries containing York responsory series now held in the British Library. All of these sources are mentioned in Table 3.16 on the previous page.

Little has been published on the texts and even less on the plainsong, and so the William Office remains a largely unexplored liturgical occasion. Beyond the transcriptions already mentioned, Christopher Norton has supplied a useful discussion of the date and components of the *Vita*; and entries for the Office appear in Andrew Hughes's *Late Medieval Liturgical Offices*; in a brief note Hughes remarks that the Office 'seems extremely conventional, although on several occasions the phrases of text and chant seem dislocated'.[44] The sung-texts, which are printed here without their lessons, are textually stable.

---

[44] Andrew Hughes, 'British Rhymed Offices: A Catalogue and Commentary', in *Music in the Medieval English Liturgy*, pp. 239–84 (p. 279).

Sancti Willelmi Archiepiscopi et Confessoris

Vespers

VA1	In willelmi laudibus laxet clerus lora: sit in hympnis canticis concio canora.[a]
	[*Psalmi feriales*]
VA2	Pius pater hodie ex hac valle fletus: ad supernum solium syon transit letus.
VA3	Quondam thesaurarius[b] iam thesaurus cleri: dedit opes medici: nunc dat opem veri.
VA4[c]	Celum solum siciens gazas Christi miles: ne scandentem retrahant calcat ut res viles.
VA5[3]	In doctrina solidum cibum dat provectis:[d] et lactis dulcedinem miscet imperfectis.
Cap.	Ecce sacerdos.
VR[e]	Plebs occurrit.
VH	Iste confessor.
VV	Amavit eum[f]
VE	Nostri patris in natalicio letas laudes dictet devocio: celi regem lactet oracio: ut iungamur eius consorcio.
Ps	Magnificat.
Or.[g]	Deus qui nos beati willelmi confessoris tui atque pontificis meritis et intercessione letificas: concede propicius ut qui eius beneficia poscimus dono tue gracie consequamur. Per Dominum.

[*Memorial to Medard and Gildard.*]

[a] *decora*, B.

[b] *thesaurus*, D.

[c] VA4 and VA5 exchanged, Z.

[d] *preventis*, B.

[e] om., Y.

[f] om., L.

[g] om., Y.

Matins

MI	Iubilemus regum regi: qui concedit nos hic regi per willelmi merita [^a].
Ps	Venite.
MH	Iste confessor.

First Nocturn

MA1	Ortus clari germinis hunc nobilitavit: et mentis nobilitas genus geminavit.
Ps	Beatus vir. (Ps 1)
MA2	In agendis strenuus fidus in commissis: ad censuram rigidus firmus in promissis.
Ps	Quare fremuerunt (Ps 2)
MA3	Mitis in consorciis in loquela rarus: in responsis providus in sensu preclarus.
Ps	Domine quid multiplicati. (Ps 3)
V.[b]	Amavit eum.
MR1	Voluntatis trutina non legis cassatus: virum novum induit celitus mutatus.
MV1	Iuventutis ianuas claudit[c] cassacio: sic malum sepius boni fit occasio.
MR2	Vir ad sui gloriam redit inglorius: ut unguenti vasculum mundetur in[d] melius.
MV2	Lacrimarum lavacro purgatis[e] personis confertur divinitus munus unctionis.
MR3	Laceratum exulem morsibus malignis: nec fax frangit odii nec livoris ignis.
MV3	Probat hunc exilium sicut hiemps laurum: <u>in fornace ponitur purum</u>[f] exit aurum. Nec. Gloria Patri. Nec.

Second Nocturn

MA4	Ne sampsonem dalida[g] faciat perire: hic carnem spiritui[h] cogit obedire.
Ps	Cum invocarem. (Ps 4)
MA5	Agrum mentis seminat sementis virtutum: et mundi delicias spernit[i] velud lutum.
Ps	Verba mea. (Ps 5)
MA6	Ne recentes flosculi virtutum marcescant: hos scripture rivulis irrigat ut crescant.
Ps	Domine dominus noster. (Ps 8)
V.[j]	Iustum deduxit dominus.

---

[a] *alleluya*, DGL. [d] om., ADGLRZ. [g] *dalidam*, R. [j] om., DG.
[b] om., R. [e] *purgatus*, DG. [h] *spiritum*, DZ.
[c] *claudis*, R. [f] Text underlined added in R. [i] *sprevit*, ABGR.

Second Nocturn *(cont.)*

MR4 Factus iacob vigilat extra[k] supra gregem: nec minus interius regum sapit regem.

MV4 Marthe ministerio copulat mariam: rachelis amplexibus fruitur post lyam. Nec.

MR5 Fragrat odor presulis roma[l] venientis: occurit fragrancie [^m] plebs unius mentis.

MV5 Ex[n] longinquis veniunt[o] nec[p] sunt fatigati: longa via visa est curta caritati. Occurit.

MR6 Plebs occurit presuli cadit pons dissutus: sed a casu populus ruens redit tutus.[q]

MV6 Unda ruens populum recipit ruentem: et se pontem efficit per omnipotentem. Sed.

Third Nocturn

MA7 Ne cursus[r] ad superos animo claudatur: mens dei dulcedini tota[s] copulatur.

Ps Domine quis habitabit. (Ps 15, Vulgate 14)

MA8 Servit elemosinis manus insopita quibus se dat funditus vir israelita.

Ps Domine in virtute. (Ps 21, Vulgate 20)

MA9 In sublime levat ut palma comam[t] spei: et imputrescibilis vivit cedrus dei.

Ps Domini est terra. (Ps 24, Vulgate 23)

V. Magnificavit.

MR7 Fide fuit finees: ut iob [^u] mansuetus: paciens ut israel ut noe discretus.

MV7 Fidelis ut abraham ut loth hospitalis: sagax ut samuel ut ioseph liberalis. Ut.

MR8 Vivum Christus[v] oleo tam large linivit: quod adhuc in mortuo olei fons vivit.

MV8 Ut sit nomen presulis oleum effusum: corpus fundit oleum ad egrorum usum. Quod.

MR9 Adit sancti tumulum languidorum cetus: et qui plangens venerat plaudens[w] redit letus

MV9 Presulis antidotum[x] presens est egenis: quo[y] devotos liberat pluribus a poenis. Et. Gloria. Et.

Ps Te deum.

V. Ora pro nobis beate willelme.

---

[k] om., D.

[l] *romane*, L.

[m] *e*, D.

[n] *et*, ABR.

[o] *venientis*, L.

[p] *ne*, DG.

[q] *tuus*, R.

[r] *cursos*, G.

[s] *totu*, ABR.

[t] *romam*, L.

[u] *in*, R.

[v] *Christum*, R.

[w] *pludens* AR; correction to *plaudens* in Y.

[x] *antitodum* XYZ; *antidodum* DV.

[y] *qui*, LSVWXY.

Lauds

LA1	Claudi recti redeunt furor effugatur: epilepsis passio sanitati datur.
Ps	Dominus regnavit.
LA2	Purgantur ydropici laudes fantus muti: datur paraliticis suis membris uti.
Ps	Iubilate.
LA3	Lepre tergit maculas membra[a] dat castratis: lumen donat pluribus sine[b] luce natis.
Ps	Deus deus meus.
LA4	Rapiunt a pugile lex et hostis lumen: quod per sanctum reparat[c] ceco celi numen.
Ps	Benedicite.
LA5	Ab abyssi faucibus biduo[d] submersum: mater natum recipit a morte reversum.
Ps	Laudate.
Cap.	Benedictionem.
LH	Iesu redemptor.
V.	Iustus germinabit.
LE	O willelme pastor bone cleri pater et patrone mundi nobis in agone confer opem et depone vite sordes et corone celestis da gaudia.
Ps	Benedictus
Or.	*ut supra*

Ad horas antiphone de laudibus. Ceteri de communi cum oracione propria.
Ad vesperas antiphone de laudibus cum psalmis ferialibus.

WE	Iesu noster[e] fiducia: honor noster et gloria: amor virtus leticia: vita[f] veritas et via[g]; iustorum pax et patria: tua nos clemencia willelmi per suffragia: de mundi miseria transfer ad celestia.
Ps	Magnificat.

Oratio ut supra.

[a] *membras*, L.
[b] *sive*, G.
[c] *recipit*, R.
[d] *viduo*, G.
[e] *nostra* ABDGRZ.
[f] *via*, Z.
[g] *una*, AB; *vita* GLR.

The Texts

The normal complement of texts, that found in all of the sources above except [E], which has Vespers alone, and [P] and [Q] (both containing three commemorative lessons), allows for a three-nocturn *duplum festum*, the class of feast normally prescribed in the kalendars that supply more than the minimum of information about William. It seems likely that this form, which would have called for nine lessons, and hence nine antiphons and responsories, at Matins, was the original form of the Office, owing to the distribution of the lesson texts across all nine lessons in a number of the sources containing the most of the first part of the *Vita* [ADGRS]; moreover, all nine lessons in any other sources reach only William's election or his death. No monastic version, which would call for twelve lessons, is extant. In a number of the sources, preceding the Office texts is a substantial rubric which addresses the possibility of William's feastday corresponding with the important feasts of the Ascension, Pentecost, Trinity, or Corpus Christi.[45] In some cases the observance of his octave was to be changed to a three-lesson commemoration with the antiphons and psalms of the first nocturn; three lessons, the first from the Gospel and the remaining two from William's life; and three responsories, the first, second, and ninth of his office.

The antiphons, responsories, and verses of the William Office appear to be newly-composed texts.[46] The accompanying material, namely the psalms, hymns, verses, and chapters, is invariably drawn from the Common of one bishop confessor. These items are identical in the modern printings of the Sarum and York breviaries. At Vespers, the ferial psalms are specified. At Matins and Lauds, all nine psalms, drawn from the Common, are specified by incipit.

The newly-composed material, however, does not rely on the structure or themes of the Common of one bishop confessor, nor does it demonstrate any understanding or sensitivity towards it. It might be expected for a new office built around the Common to have been written with some of this framework material in mind, but this does not seem to have been the case. The texts of the Matins antiphons which precede and follow the proper psalms do not contain any explicit references to William or his activities; nor do they appear to

---

[45] The presence of Corpus Christi suggests that this rubric was added after 1320, the year after which this feast was increasingly celebrated in England. See Miri Rubin, *Corpus Christi: The Eucharist in late Medieval Culture* (Cambridge: Cambridge University Press, 1991).

[46] 'Verse' refers to the subgenre which accompanies the responsory; not to be confused with 'versicle [and response]'. These terms are used casually and interchangeably in some modern liturgical studies.

meditate on the subjects of their corresponding psalms. The closest similarity between a William antiphon and its psalms, in which both MA1 and its psalm contain references to a man and the growth of vegetation, is at best coincidental. Neither does the seventh responsory reflect particularly on the themes of the Gospel reading (*Homo quidam nobilis*, the parable of the ten talents/the good and wicked servants, Lk 19. 12ff) or the related homily that precedes it, both of which are also prescribed in the Common. The lesson is, at least, Biblical, and the responsory notes the virtues of Old Testament patriarchs and prophets.

As mentioned, the antiphons do not appear to be tied to the specific case of William; they would, in fact, be applicable in honour of any virtuous male. Neither are they similar at all to the corresponding antiphons at Matins in the Common, which are appropriately even more general; some of these are drawn from the Psalms. The William responsories, however, bring out a number of the principal *topoi* of William's life in roughly sequential order. MRV1 describe the casting-off of youth in favour of the New Man; RV2 the ideas of ointment and anointing, perhaps anticipating his posthumous miracles; and RV3 the notion of exile. By contrast MRV4 deal with a somewhat more complex typological account of Jacob, Leah, and Rachel; and Christ, Martha, and Mary. The allusion seems to be to the preferment of Henry Murdach over William, and to William's eventual success. Responsory 5 and its verse mention the '*odor presulis*' and the enthusiasm of the people. The latter is emphasized in the relatively explicit brief account of the Ouse Bridge miracle in MRV6, a key moment where upon William's return to York the bridge collapses, but all are saved. The seventh responsory is unrelated to William and follows the lesson from the Gospel. MRV8 again focus on oil and anointing, and RV9 on the curative power of the prelate's tomb.

The order of the antiphons and responsories is identical in each source as far as it is complete, and there is nothing to suggest that the order of either set of texts ever varied, or was designed to vary. Another means of assessing whether items appear in their original order is to evaluate the modal order of the melodies to which they are set. Antiphons and responsories are often set to the musical modes in ascending order, from one to eight. The modal order of the musical settings of the antiphons is 123 456 787. Although the modal order of the responsories is 826 717 711, an unusual order, the sequential and chronological order of the texts themselves seems to suggest that no alternative pattern would be suitable.[47] Comparing the texts of the antiphons and respon-

---

[47] With the possible exception of MRV2, which deals with the vessel of ointment? Or is this perhaps a symbolic reference to William himself as a vessel?

sories themselves among the sources of the Office reveals substantial uniformity. The text-variants are restricted to alternative spellings (hardly true variants in medieval Latin) or the employment of synonyms, often vaguely homonymic (*spernit* ~ *sprevit*) and each of the divergences from the majoritarian version of the text appears in no more than four sources.

The Life and Lessons

The lessons are taken, with exceptions no greater in size than the occasional synonymic word or phrase, from the anonymous *Vita*. The text of the *Vita* survives in only one manuscript, BL Harley MS 2, a thirteenth-century collection of materials known to have been at the Augustinian abbey in Thornton, Lincolnshire. In addition to William's *Vita* (ff. 76–87), a Life and other materials for Thomas Becket also appear (ff. 1–75), and materials for Edmund of Abingdon (ff. 88–97) also appear. The text was transcribed by James Raine,[48] and corrections appear in Norton who notes that some of the *Vita* texts have been corrected from the William lessons in 1493 as it is reflected in the Surtees edition.

Despite their common source, the selection of lesson texts varies in each manuscript of the William Office, and even where similar portions are copied, the *Vita* texts may be differently divided among the nine lessons. All but one of the William manuscripts draw lessons from the first part of the *Vita* alone — the account of his life — and omit the account of miracles found thereafter. The exception is manuscript [Q], one of the two commemorations, which has three lessons which detail the conflagration after which William's tomb was discovered unharmed, with text taken directly and sequentially from the relevant part of the *Miracula*. In every case the *Vita* texts appear in their original order, although varying portions of the text are usually omitted.

As mentioned previously, the sungtexts do not always appear to correspond to the thematic contents of the lessons, and this tendency is particularly obvious with respect to the responsories which, theoretically, ought to 'respond' to the lessons that precede them. MRV8 address the restorative oil, and RV9 the results of the oil and the tomb on the faithful. The only mention of oil in the lessons is in sources [GR], where it appears in lesson 9.

---

[48] In *The Historians of the Church of York and its Archbishops*, ed. by James Raine, Rerum Britannicum Medii Aevi Scriptores, 71, 3 vols (London: Longman, 1879–94), ii.

But convenient correspondence between lessons and responsories is not the case. MRV4, as described above, seem particularly attuned to the preferment of Henry Murdach over William. They ought to appear at a point in the narration of William's story in the lessons where he has been rejected. While six sources [ADGLRS] narrate the Murdach debacle in lesson 3, the four others that make any mention of Murdach [BWXZ] do so in lesson 5.

Similarly, MRV6 deal with the miracle of Ouse Bridge. This is related in the *Vita*, and also in the lessons of all but one of the sources; the lessons in [Y] do not proceed to this point in William's chronology. In all but two cases [AR], however, the account of the miracle in the lessons occurs after the appearance of the responsory, in lesson 8 [BDGLSWXZ]. On the strength of their unusual modal order, it might be argued that the responsories are out of the sequence for which they were designed. Does this suggest, then, that the correspondence between the responsories and the division of the *Vita* into lessons is best in sources [AR]? These two sources are, as will be discussed, otherwise unrelated!

It has been stated that some sections of the *Vita* appear only in certain manuscripts. Two striking examples are the third lesson of [Y], beginning 'verum ne sola [...]', and all three lessons in [Q]. Since the missing excerpts are not always continuous and texts preceding and following them may be present, it might be suggested that the lessons in these William Office manuscripts were drawn from fragmentary or erroneous exemplary sources of the *Vita*, now unknown, that contained incomplete texts. The presence of such passages in a minority of sources does not necessarily mean that they were unknown by the compilers of the others, merely that they could have been omitted, or that they did not exist in one particular exemplar. All it is possible to say, if this is the case, is that the texts were not simply copied from *Vita* exemplar to liturgical book, something which should be obvious.

Transcription and close comparison of all of the sources of the William Office suggest that their lessons fall into three broad groupings. Groups 1 [ADGLRS] and 2 [BWXZ] are based on roughly the same set of texts; the difference being that those in group 2 are significantly shorter and divided differently. Whether the additional material in group 1 has been condensed or omitted in group 1, or whether group 1 is a later, augmented version of a mutual text, is unclear. Group 3, consisting of only two sources [VY], excerpts a number of different points of the *Vita*, and each of its lessons is perhaps one or two sentences in length. [P] and [Q], the two commemorations, do not fit in any group.

It should be pointed out that the kalendars (where they exist) of the manuscripts within each of the three groups do not seem to have particular similarities. Group 1 kalendars have a high number of points of similarity with the kalendar of [A], and with that of York Minster Addl 69, a manuscript from which William's office has been cut out. The kalendar of A is also the manuscript to which every kalendar in group 2 is most closely related.

The Lessons: Group 1

Sections of the *Vita*, in their correct order but omitting certain sections, form the basis for the lessons of group 1, whose sources vary in length. [S], the text of the 1493 printed breviary, contains some of the shorter versions of lessons and is used as a 'base text' against which to compare other copies. Very little in [S] does not appear in the other members of the group, though [L] does not contain as much additional material as the others, and material in [L] that is not in [S] is also found in both [A] and [D]. Group 1 omits the text '*verum ne sola* [...] *geminavit*', which occurs in the *Vita* just after the description of William's parents. This passage appears only in the third lesson of [Y], one of two sources in group 3.

The most prominent textual variants are 'additions' to the text of [S]; 27 such additions are found in four sources [ADGR]; nine are found in every other text [ADGLR]. [G] has the longest lessons, and the greatest amount of additional material.

Among the group 1 sources, [D] and [G] are most strongly related: they share forty-eight points of correspondence; that is to say, they have forty-eight identical variants with respect to [S]. However, thirty-six of these are shared with [A], and thirty of the thirty-six variants shared by [ADG] also include [R]. [A] shares no variants with [R] alone, only those also shared with [D], [G], or both.

It is however interesting that [A] (Bodl. Laud misc. 84, probably a York Minster book) and [R] (BL Addl 38624) are linked, and that [L] (for Lambeth, Sion, for Skelton parish church) is related to [D] (Rudby parish church). Skelton and Rudby are about fifteen miles apart, and both contain notation. So does [G] (Bodl. Gough liturg 1), strongly linked to [D]. [R], however, has no notation. [A] has has no music but is linked to three manuscripts that do: what of its probable existence at the Minster? Are there any correspondences between [A] and the Arundel antiphonal (which has only Vespers for William, and thus no lessons)? Some of the kalendars of group 1 manuscripts are aligned: the kalendar of [A] has close relations to those of [D], its second closest relation, and [S], its third closest relation.

The Lessons: Group 2

In contrast to the texts found only in group 1 (especially lessons 4 and 5, complete), which are supplementary passages from the *Vita*, texts found only in the lessons of the manuscripts in this group [BWXZ] do not appear to convey any additional detail about the life of the saint. Texts in group 2 alone are synonymic rather than additional and, especially in the case of '*Quo defuncto* [...] *consecratur*' in lesson 6, are sometimes condensations. *Quo defuncto* [...] summarizes the action in the passage beginning *Mors enim*, the second part of lesson 5 or 6 in group 1 [DG].

But the sources of group 2 are consistent in the ways these rules are applied; while there are numerous minor variants from the *Vita*/group 1 text, they are consistent, as are the selection and order of the texts. A common feature appears to be the size and portability of the four manuscripts in the group; all are about average height for duodecimos. Perhaps the lessons in group 2, shorter than their counterparts, suggest the existence of reduced-size lessons for portable books, or the copying of portable books from other portable books. This proposal would certainly cohere with Reames's observations that length of lessons may be linked to the physical size of volumes.[49] By contrast, all of the notated and other large books are part of group 1.

Among the internal variants between group 2 sources, [WZ] seem most closely connected, with three shared textual variants. [BX] and [XZ] are related by one shared variant each. There is nothing of the extent to which certain sources of group 1 appear to be related to one another, but there are also fewer and less complicated variants.

If the lessons of group 2 are compared with those of group 1, the greatest similarities are with those in the sources [ADGR]. At six points [ADGR] and group 2 share texts not found in the other group 1 manuscripts; similarly one text is shared with [ADGLR] and one with [ADG]; two further group 2 texts are found elsewhere only in [DG]. None of the kalendars of these manuscripts are particularly closely aligned.

The Lessons: Group 3

The two sources comprising group 3, [VY], are linked primarily on the strength of their first two lessons, which are more or less the same, and are the only two manuscripts to begin *Beatus willelmus* [...] rather than *Gloriosi presulis*. They

---

[49] Reames, 'Late Medieval Efforts at Standardisation'.

are notable for their sparsity and selection of texts from the *Vita*, and so it is worth detailing where they appear elsewhere. At lesson 3 they diverge: here, [V] has the text of lesson 4 in [Y], where [Y] has the unique *'verum ne sola'* excerpt from an early episode in the *Vita*, mentioned above. Lesson 4 in [V] is a text found elsewhere only in group 1 [DG]. Lesson 5 in [V] begins *Hiis et aliis* [...] *effectus* [...] *publica bona* (as in [ADG]) [...] *coegit*. [Y] gives the same text, but preceded by *et ut litterarum laurea* [...] *disciplinis*, a text which follows [...] *pedibus est addictus* where this appears in [ABDGRWXZ]. Lesson 6 in [V] begins *Et si aliquando* [...] (usually found after 'subvenire' or 'coegit') [...] *evacuabat* whereas [Y] gives *Proprias opes* [...] *coegit*, which follows the end of the preceding lesson's text where it appears in [LS], then *nullum thesaurum* [...] *subvenire*, the text that follows *coegit* in [ABDGLRSWXZ]. There is no lesson 7 in [Y], where presumably a Gospel lesson would ordinarily be read, but [V] supplies *inter hec archipresule*, the text which follows that of the preceding lesson where it appears in [AGLR]. Lesson 8 in [V] continues the text as it appears in ADR; [Y] gives *Mors enim* [...] *abrupit*, a text found in [ADLRS] but never following *subvenire* as it does here. Finally, lesson 9 in [V] begins *Sed livor edax*, a text found in [ABDGRWXZ]; [Y] begins *que quidem spiritu*, which follows from the preceding lesson text, ending *abrupit*, in [ADGLRS].

It is clear that both [V] and [Y] contain texts found in group 2, but these are also found in group 1. No text only in group 2 can be identified, and so it should be suggested that only sources corresponding to group 1 were known to the compilers of the group 3 text. These sources may be associated with the same tradition as [ADGR], for the beginning of lesson 1 in group 3 takes the version which appears in those four: [...] *preclarus natalium* [...] *erat enim* [...] Likewise, group 3 has the [ADGR] text *'ignobilitatis turpitudinem'*. Yet neither group 3 nor group 2 uses *viri secundum* [...], another text found in the same four sources. Another potential relation can perhaps be made with sources [DGR], as the text in lesson 4 in [V], *'Delectabatur* [...]', is found elsewhere only in these three manuscripts.

The rest of the texts in the group 3 lessons can be identified as rearrangements of some of the most frequently occurring and important texts of group 1, in the order in which they appear both in that group and in the *Vita*. Another point worth mentioning is that neither source deals with much of William's activity after his successful election. Both sets are of a similar length, and it is therefore worth pointing out that both [V] and [Y], like the sources of group 2, are portable books. Perhaps the group 3 lessons represent another realization of an attempt to summarize an original, considerably longer set found in the choir books and presumably in other sources of the *Vita*.

An attempt to isolate the sources of either of the two group 3 sources is inconclusive. Lessons 6–9 in [V] seem to be drawn from the [DR] version of lesson 2, almost complete and including the passage *'et si aliquando'* found in [DR] only; but the passage in [DR] following *'sed livor'* is not present. Lesson 8 of [Y], conversely, contains the [GR]-only variant *'ut fertur'* (note 53); elsewhere it applies the main text as found generally in [ADGLRS], but more specifically the version found in [AGR]. Both [V] and [Y] seem to be related to [R], but each is related either to [D] or [G], sources which are themselves otherwise strongly related.

Elements of William's Office Borrowed: Richard of Chichester

The main conclusions derived from the analysis of variant texts and melodies are that the (extant) notated sources of William's Office were quite stable and, by extension, that a uniform version of the music did exist. Although the music is unremarkable, there seems nothing to suggest that this was not an office where there was a stable, reasonable relation between text and chant, and it would appear that the whole was associated, at least in the province of York where it was known, securely with St William.

But here a complication arises. A *near-exact* copy of the music appears, as first identified by David Hiley, in the office for another saint entirely, Richard of Chichester.[50] Richard's Office is in the same goliardic metre as William's, with diversions from metre at the same points as William's (that is, the antiphons to the canticles). It uses essentially the same melodies in essentially the same order, albeit with a different underlay and slightly different syllabification to suit the text.

For instance, Matins verse 2 in Richard's office is a slightly longer text than its counterpart in William's. Roughly the same number of pitches (forty-three in William, forty-six in Richard) are therefore spread more thinly, set to a higher number of words, and the setting is less melismatic. For the melody at Matins antiphon 4 (of both Offices), the text is again longer in Richard, and five consecutive pitches, as a little phrase, are repeated immediately after their first appearance, perhaps to accommodate a slightly longer text.

Given the general statement that the music of the two Offices is very similar, we ought of course to be curious as to how extensively the melodies vary, other than in their setting to the texts. I simplified the chants of William's office and

---

[50] First reported by Andrew Hughes, who gives the credit to Hiley, in 'British Rhymed Offices', p. 262.

those of Richard's into two strings of pitches. These diverge at one hundred and thirteen points (here, not discriminating for length). Twenty-two of these involved no change in the number of pitches; sometimes a result of the error of transposition by a third; at other points an exchange of adjacent pitches; and occasionally a new melody altogether, of exactly the same length. Far more numerous, though, were instances where a pitch or string of pitches would appear only in Richard's office (forty-seven instances) or only in William's (forty-four instances). These numbers might seem to be of similar magnitude but I also noted that of the forty-four pitches of William's chant absent from Richard's, eleven (25%) were repeated pitches, repercussions. By contrast Richard's office had only two repeated pitches not in William. The significance of repeated pitches is explained below.

I mentioned that the chants were in the same order in both offices. However only Richard's office has a proper responsory at first Vespers (*Regis in accubitu | nardus dat odorem* [...]). The melody here is not a new composition but the melody of William's Matins antiphon 6, *Plebs occurrit*, omitting the settings of the fourth, antepenultimate, and penultimate words. An incipit of the text of this responsory, with no melody, appears at Richard's antiphon 6 as well, suggesting the same item would be repeated. (Given that *Plebs occurrit* is used for a procession for William in Bodleian e Mus 126, it may have been one of the more prominent or recognizable melodies of the Office.)

There is another significant difference: the Magnificat antiphon at first Vespers of Richard is set to a version of the familiar melody of the Marian antiphon *Ave regina celorum*, and bears some textual similarities to that text: it begins *Ave* coheres *celorum*.

There are similarities in the remainder of the texts of the two Offices as well. The second antiphon at Vespers begins '*Pius pater*' in both cases. *Ex hac valle luctus*, VA3 in Richard, evokes *de hac valle fletus* (VA2) in William; both evoke '*in hac lacrimarum valle*' and Ps 84. 6 the '*valle lacrimarum*'. Similarly, both Matins invitatories exhort the praise of God, the agent of great acts through the intercession of the honoured saint. A Matins antiphon in both offices (A5 in Richard, A4 in William) refers to Samson and Delilah. The verse following both fourth Matins responsories has the second word '*ministerio*'. MV7 of Richard recalls William's antiphon 8, either *studet* or *servit elemosinis*. In both offices the first word of MV9 is '*presulis*'.

Some of these textual allusions appear in the same place in the same item in both Offices. At the three points where this is not the case, it is worth noting that the connection between chant and text has not been preserved; that is, the melodies are largely intact and sequential in both offices, while the text setting varies.

Naturally, of course, we are interested in determining which Office borrowed from which. Perhaps some of the details already reported can be helpful in this matter. Firstly I wonder whether the apparent repetition of the setting of a word (a five-word motive in MA4) suggests that the longer of the two melodies may be a later version of an earlier, shorter one, an efficient adaptation of the melody to suit a longer text. Similarly, I wonder whether the addition of the *Ave regina celorum* melody suggests that generic material (both familiar and accessible) needed to be used in the construction of Richard's Office for liturgical items where its principal source, perhaps William's Office, had no equivalent. Repeated pitches in William's Office omitted in Richard's, as noted, account for a quarter of instances where the chants differ. Perhaps fewer such repetitions was the 'house style', or perhaps they were tedious or difficult to copy accurately. If the William melodies were being written into the new Office without the aid of an exemplar, perhaps repeated pitches seem likely to have been one of the first things to go — and so some of the points of difference are points at which the contour of the melody does not actually vary.

These thoughts are naturally speculative but the inferences seem relatively logical, and no other variants appear to suggest the opposite descent.

What, for instance, of the time-frame? William was canonized thirty-five years before Richard, but this may not necessarily mean that an Office was immediately composed for him. It could have been written for his translation, in 1284. I think it is reasonable to suggest that complete offices were not ordinarily constructed prior to the canonization of their subject. We are aware that the best-known *Vita* for Richard was completed between 1268 and 1272. If any allusions to the text of the Life were found in the lessons in Richard's Office, we could have said that the Office postdated the Life, but no such hints are discernible, other than that similar events are touched upon, and that is hardly remarkable. There is certainly no discernible textual allusion. So we are left with incertitude here, other than that William's cult, in general, was the earlier of the two.

In assembling an office, it should go without saying that a borrower of chants must use a musical source or sources of one office to produce the musical version of the other. We have three complete copies of the notated Office for William, and in all probability there were more in the province of York. At present I am aware of only one extant source of this music for Richard, MS 120 at the Biblioteca Universitaria Alessandrina in Rome. Although we must not be tempted into thinking that no other notated sources of this Office ever existed, another point seems to suggest this process of borrowing.

Alessandrina MS 120 is essentially a non-liturgical book of the fourteenth century whose other contents are wide-ranging. Copies of papal, royal, and ecclesiastical correspondence lie amongst other documentation, some of it relating to the Lives and canonization of saints, especially Thomas Becket. Following the Office for Richard at f. 239, the manuscript gives an Office for St Edmund of Abingdon (f. 243), who as Archbishop of Canterbury was served by Richard as chancellor.[51] The music, and indeed the text for this office, as Andrew Hughes has reported, are 'almost the same as the main office to Thomas of Canterbury'.[52] These two Offices are the only liturgical material, and the only notated material, in the volume. Perhaps the scribe (or the author, if these are not the same person) of these Offices borrowed material from William for Richard, and borrowed from Becket, a fellow archbishop of Canterbury, for Edmund. This of course assumes that these otherwise unknown musical versions of the Offices for Richard and Edmund were compiled by the same author. It may not be the case, but it would be fascinating if these two adjacent offices for English bishops in a non-liturgical volume, which both borrow wholesale from the office for two other somewhat more prominent English bishops, were not in some way related. Both were late additions to the kalendar, added consecutively (see chapter 4), and added together to service books. It might be proposed, though not without considerable doubt, given the circumstances (both otherwise unknown notated offices, adjacent in the same MS, by the same hand) that they might have been composed (or compiled, really), and perhaps written down by the same author.

Let us hypothetically assume that William's Office served as the model for Richard's. We must ask how the appropriation of this material occurred. Re-use obviously demands awareness. In the case of shorter borrowings or allusions, it would seem necessary to consult an exemplar, combing it for some suitable gesture, or, if the text or chant fragment was selected for some didactic, ideological, or otherwise deliberate purpose, it would seem necessary for it to be memorable, or to have a memorable connotation, though not one that would preclude its reuse.

Why William's Office? The choice of a Northern saint is curious. There is no obvious reason for the choice of an archbishop of York, and we must again question how material which was, in its entirety at least, restricted to the Northern province found its way into an Office for the bishop of Chichester. Both, it is clear, were confessors and bishops. That both William and Richard had difficul-

[51] See C. H. Lawrence, *The Life of St Edmund by Matthew Paris* (Stroud: Alan Sutton, 1996), p. 63.

[52] Hughes, 'British Rhymed Offices'.

ties being confirmed to their bishoprics may be another reason. Perhaps the reputation of one bishop might have been used to enhance the standing of another, as seems to have been the case at Cardinal College, Oxford, where the votive antiphon to William (*O willelme pastor bone*) composed by John Taverner was sung with a second verse dedicated to Wolsey, another archbishop of York.

Conclusions

The existence of this complete and extensive Office for William might be surprising if his cult was uncontroversial, but William was not a spectacularly popular saint and as such would be unlikely to warrant a complete set of proper texts. The present Office, then, might be best understood as an employment of liturgy to demonstrate his sanctity and the validity of his cult. It is full-featured and newly-composed, and rather than being based on the Common of Saints has a firm basis in William's *Vita*. A similar ideological motive might be seen in the appropriation of material for William in an Office for Richard of Chichester, where the earlier saint's reputation may have been used to support Richard's liturgical observance, a key feature in the development of his cult. In both cases — the creation of William's Office to promote his own cult, and its subsequent appropriation for Richard — it may be observed that the proper office for a saint might reflect the furtherance of non-liturgical aims through the privileged domain of liturgy.

The case-study of William's Office also confirms some observations about genres of liturgical text. Antiphons, linked to psalmody, may have little bearing on any given observance. Responsories, however, can be seen as a consistent and identifying feature of an office, perhaps, as in William's case, because they can be used as a means of expounding a particular message about the saint in question — here presenting features of his story in roughly sequential order. The lessons, drawn from other texts devoted to William, form another account of his life and sanctity. Each group of lessons is also illustrative of the development of an Office: group 2 illustrates how group 1 lessons have been summarized or truncated, perhaps for use in portable books; group 3 illustrates a second attempt to reduce the longer set. Lessons in general were more subject to projects of redaction, a strong support for the argument that responsory series must be understood as the key (or perhaps only) identifying feature of an Office. William's office, then, also illustrates how the content and focus of an Office could change based on practical concerns. It also demonstrates how even a poorly disseminated office for a local saint could be subject to variability.

In a wider study of the English Office liturgy it is worth underlining the conclusion of this analysis of the limited witnesses of the Office of a local saint: even in these circumstances there exists substantial variation between copies which were produced over a short time span and within a defined geographical area. As with the other Offices, William's sungtexts are consistent, and as much rubrication as is present is consistent, but the witnesses are capable of being grouped into three categories on the basis of their lessons. Variation in lessons, then, ought not to be thought of as a result of inconsistency brought on by wide transmission for long periods; perhaps consistency in the lessons for some Offices was never attempted.

Redaction of Office Liturgy: Evidence and Inferences

On the basis of this textual analysis of four Offices, Richard Pfaff's model of uniformity in the Office liturgy may be in want of a minor revision. The fourth division, 'texts', ought to be subdivided into sungtexts and lessons, for even in the case of a newly added saint (Thomas or William, for instance), sungtexts may have been subject to different influences from lessons, which were much more variable. Lessons are not always globally prescribed like sungtexts, and it is therefore unsurprising that a wider range of variants should be present. The content of lessons must necessarily have been influenced by:

1. The degree to which they were established in the Roman and indeed Western liturgy, and their function within that context (whether didactic, hagiographical, or otherwise), and the histories of the texts from which they were drawn and any textual families in those original texts. These factors are probably most important for texts at the extremities, both those which were extremely well-known, and those which were obscure;

2. The governing authority (whether exemplar, lectionary, editor, ecclesiastical ordinance) that determined and supplied lessons in the context in which any individual manuscript was produced;

3. The priorities of the redactors: the inclusion of specific episodes in the Life or miracles, for instance; or the standardization or reduction of Sanctorale contents, as proposed by Reames and also witnessed here in the group 2 and 3 lessons for William;

4. Scribes' familiarity with (some version of) the text from which the lesson was drawn;

5. An ordinary amount of textual 'drift'.

Sungtexts and especially newly-composed medieval sungtexts, by contrast, had key associations with the Office of which they formed a part. Their copying and transmission were probably influenced by:

1. The fact that it was probably more difficult to change music that was sung, unless provision was made to amend the music suitably;

2. The ubiquity of their Office, and the degree to which it was accurately transmitted;

3. The same editorial processes during selection of material and copying related to the production of a new manuscript.

There is no doubt that many manuscript breviaries were not copied wholesale. There was a healthy attitude to surveying and assessing the correctness of existing service books, and enough of a constant scheme of amendment and correction that specific decisions taken at the same time may be only partially reflected in a contemporary witness. This attention, though, seems to have been restricted to lessons and, to a lesser extent, rubrics. The present evidence entirely supports the argument that within any English Use the sungtexts of both ancient and newly composed offices were not substantially modified, a point that underpins the employment of responsory series as identifiers of Use, itself a confirmation of this belief in a certain amount of fixity. Uncertainty lies more in *why* the specific sungtexts for Advent, Thomas, or the Dead came to be accepted as standard in each Use. To give an example, in the case of Advent and the Dead there are a great many responsories in Western liturgy, nine of which became normal constituents of the Sarum offices, but it is not clear why these were chosen. William's responsories reflect key moments across his entire life, in chronological order. Did responsories reflect a didactic or ideological programme, or a logical order of presentation? Were they chosen (in contradiction of the established view) to complement a definitive set of lessons (rather than vice versa)? If the Advent Sunday lessons were ever in an order that created the pattern of, for instance, Sarum responsory series, this order has been lost. Most importantly, is it significant that responsory series are prescribed in the Ordinal as the definitive, apparently constitutive element of a feastday's liturgical observance?

In the case of the selection of sungtexts for Thomas, each of the secular Uses drew on the monastic original, with slightly different results, deriving nine responsories from twelve. The textual programme behind their selection is explored by Slocum.[53]

---

[53] Slocum, *Liturgies*, pp. 160–66.

For Advent Sunday and the Dead, the existence of several families of rubrics, in cases so different as to allow immediate discrimination between the principal textual patterns, also inevitably raises several questions: what were the perceived and actual functions of rubrics? for what reasons would they undergo modification? Surely not every instruction was ever given in a manuscript. The generic nature of most of the rubrics suggest that they may have been considered no more than precise suggestions for the preparation and planning of services (much like the directions in the Customary and Ordinal) rather than indications for performance, and certainly not records of existing practice in any real context. The rubrics do not, for the most part, give us performance directions specific to the potential venues in which they were used. Indeed perhaps this is to be assumed during later stages of development, i.e. of the well-disseminated Sarum office of the fifteenth century, when books were being produced according to some textual family with generic features, without the knowledge of where they would be employed, or by whom or for what reason. According to the accepted view, Sarum rubrics, at one time, represented the state of the liturgical act at Salisbury Cathedral at the moment they began to be more widely adopted, but this stage of rubrical development *for the breviary* seems not to have included any level of detail as to the practicalities of acting it out, and seems rather more focused on which persons were present, what they performed, and the pattern according to which services were enacted throughout the year. Specific details of performance were either recorded elsewhere or not codified in writing.

The laconic rubrics of the Short version of Sarum, of the York sources in general, and of the early Hereford manuscript offer similarly indistinct but consequently versatile instructions, and the absence of florid detail at the beginning (in comparison with the Long family) should be viewed as the rule, rather than the exception. No such prescriptive detail is required. The absence of an explicit instruction to do something may suggest that it is implied or even universal, whilst the appearance of such an instruction (even one indicating that something, like adding the *Gloria Patri* to a psalm, should not be done) may suggest the opposite.

Where rubrics are expanded or amended to include specific instructions for performance, as in the pairs BL Hatton 63 / Oxford St John's 179 and BL Addl 32427 / Salisbury Cath 152, compilers of manuscripts may have been motivated by the same need for precision in resolving an ongoing ambiguity, or by some need to set out unambiguously the totality of the performance act. While adherence to a textual family may be the result of an ordinary pattern of copying, distinctive modifications giving specific information, especially where they are unique witnesses to those data, must cause us to attempt to identify the reasons for the amendment.

The Sarum Ordinal

Much has already been said about the role of the Ordinal as a determinant of content, and possibly the repository of the consistent characteristics of a Use. It is a matter of brief visual comparison of the texts of the Sarum Adv-Long pattern and the texts of the Old and New Sarum Ordinals printed by Frere (that is, *The Use of Sarum*) to infer that the rubrics of Adv-Long are based on texts related to the Ordinals. It would, however, be difficult to establish that the rubrics are drawn from any known version of the Ordinal, whether Old or New or not yet edited, and somewhat easier to suggest that Frere's manuscript exemplars for *his* New and Old Ordinals and the rubrics of the manuscripts in the present study share a common inheritance from a textual tradition which, owing to the methods of its transmission and copying, after its outset never achieved a fixed, final form.

In fact, the Ordinal appears never to have existed in a precisely fixed form prior to its being printed for the first time in 1477.[54] The so-called New Ordinal, a hypothetical entity, was edited by Frere from two manuscripts, Oxford, Corpus Christi MS 44 and BL Harley 2911. Frere's 'edition' of the Old Ordinal is essentially a printing of the Risby Sarum Ordinal, BL Harley 1001, dated to the second or third quarter of the thirteenth century,[55] which resembles but is not identical to other manuscript Ordinals of a similar date, and indeed to the later printed text. Similarly, the 1278 *Addiciones* to the Old Ordinal by the succentor of Salisbury, a document giving amendments, clarifications, and new information found in a number of manuscript copies exists in more than one version with vastly differing amounts of information, despite its having been promulgated by a figure of authority.[56] If even these authoritative corrections were not accurately transmitted, the assumption that *the* Sarum Ordinal ever existed in a fixed form incapable of modification must be just as dubious as such an assumption in the case of the Breviary. One result of constant revision (already assumed to be the case) was that the results of reform were not

---

[54] STC 16228, printed by Caxton.

[55] Pfaff, *LME*, p. 376.

[56] The *Addiciones* were printed by Frere in *The Use of Sarum*. Manuscript copies of the *Addiciones* have been seen by the author in BL Royal 5 E. III and Edinburgh UL 27.

incorporated wholesale into a single, consistent, revised version. Assuming that the earliest version of the Ordinal to circulate more widely was accurate for the practices of Salisbury Cathedral, there is no suggestion that further copies, especially in succeeding generations, would emanate from the same venue, nor is it likely that there would be a unified process of amendment and correction of all succeeding Sarum Ordinals any more successful than the consistent text of the *Addiciones*, then or at any later date. Earlier comments that several liturgical books used in the same venue may not have had similar contents are supported by the example given by the record of the primary visitation of William Alnwick, bishop of Lincoln, in October 1437, that the *libri in choro* [...] *in capella beate Marie, et in capella* le pele *in cantu maxime discordant.*[57]

Pfaff concludes that those seeking a single text of the New Ordinal will 'look in vain': the general tenor of new ordinals would have been the same, and they would have been based on similar premises, but with little textual consistency.[58] If a consistent textual tradition developed through the re-production and amendment of the Ordinal, surely witnesses to its particular text would be extant. Perhaps, then, we should speak of 'new ordinals', rather than trying to impose some order and singularity on the development of a nonexistent authoritative version. The rubrics of the breviaries in our study underline the variability of the directions which may have also existed in ordinals, and with more study, may help to illuminate the processes of their development. This diversity of contents may indeed point to a diversity of editorial priorities.

On the basis of the evidence discussed thus far, the development of the texts of the Sarum breviary as the normative Office liturgy in the province of Canterbury seems to have been influenced by a number of competing impulses on the part of its redactors and transmitters. One of these is the promulgation of the habitual practices of Salisbury Cathedral more widely throughout the southern province. When this happened, and how successfully, is a contentious matter, and will be discussed in the next chapter. Another impulse, which may postdate the former or which may have happened at the same time, represents a standardizing of text and practice in order that Salisbury liturgy could be used anywhere. An example of the standardization of practice might be that which was augmented or trimmed considerably by Henry Chichele and/or those

---

[57] 'Contra precentorem', in 'Bishop W. Alnwick's Visitation Book (circa 1437–44)', *Lincoln Cathedral Statutes*, ed. by Henry Bradshaw, 3 vols (Cambridge: Cambridge University Press, 1892–97) II (1897), 404.

[58] Pfaff, *LME*, p. 416.

responsible for early fifteenth-century redaction of the Sarum liturgy. These texts were deliberately adapted for broad rather than local usage. Another editorial impulse, with which may be associated such manuscripts as Durham Cosin V. I. 3, BL Addl 32427, and the BL Hatton 63 / Oxford St John's 179 pair, is characterized by a number of efforts in favour of an increased level of detail in some cases, in others the re-promulgation of local features. These three impulses, among others, may have been coincident within the chronology of the dissemination of the Sarum liturgy, dependent on individual and specific circumstances. In chapter 4 we will examine some of the observable influences on liturgical practice which may explain the varied contents of manuscripts and textual families.

Conclusions: Explaining Variation in Liturgical Texts

The word-by-word analysis of three Offices from twenty-eight witnesses and another regional Office from a further sixteen has permitted a closer observation of the variation in manuscripts of the Office liturgy among representatives of the same liturgical Use; between different Uses; and, in terms of functional difference, between all of the witnesses. It is clear that textual families of reasonable stability are based on relative consistency in certain genres of texts (responsories and antiphons); and greater variation in others (lessons and rubrics). This is the case as much on a regional level, a fact witnessed by the variants in the Office for William, as it is across the province of Canterbury, demonstrated by the variants in the final forms of the Use of Sarum. These textual variants both illustrate the diversity of manuscript sources of the liturgy at a deeper level than the liturgical analysis in chapter 2 has shown, and underline the consistency of sungtexts and especially responsory series as principal constitutive characteristics of a Use.

Multiple influences on the manufacture and later redaction of a book may also explain the many nonsubstantive variants which do not appear to form or support relationships between sources. In general terms we can identify three different types of variation in English liturgical texts:

1. **Textual drift** of the sort common to all medieval books;

2. **Involuntary or instinctual changes**, on the part of the scribe;

3. **Deliberate changes.**

Unlike textual drift, which is essentially unpredictable, involuntary variation is based on context. It may be the product of the circumstances in which the scribe was working, or different experiences of the texts from the scribe or his community, or the process of copying or compiling liturgical books in some particular context. Deliberate change amounts to a textual change with an intentionally different performance result, and it is variants in this category which need to be scrutinized most closely in order to derive meaningful observations about the development, standardization, and speciation of the liturgy. Such changes appear to occur most frequently in lessons or rubrics, genres that are much more subject to local concerns and proclivities, and seem to have been viewed as the constitutive texts of an Office both by their contemporaries and by modern analyses.

Deliberate changes to the contents of liturgical books are entirely reasonable, in a way that such changes to named texts with named authors are not. This may result, at least in part, from the fact that it is not possible to glean the original intentions of the initiator/confector of some liturgical observance. This is true for numerous reasons, among them the absence of authorial intention from nearly every liturgical manuscript from the Middle Ages (empirically speaking) and the fluidity of written liturgy and its performance result. *Deus in adiutorium* is a less fluid text than a responsory, which is similarly less fluid than a lesson for St Everild: and functional, repeated texts well-established in the medieval user's consciousness are probably less likely to undergo change, either involuntary or deliberate. But pragmatic texts intended for performance and transmitted in part by acting them out are inevitably mutable. Similarly the focus or emphasis which some redactor may wish to promote may differ as much in the Office for Advent Sunday as it may in sources of the Office of St William.

A Sarum Breviary is not a Sarum Breviary in the same way that a copy of Augustine's *De civitate Dei* is a copy of that work. The compositional act for the latter canonical text is complete, and it is read and copied in order to transmit a finished product. Even if the first Sarum Breviary used as an exemplar outside the diocese of Salisbury (or the Cathedral close) was an accurate record of the liturgical acting-out which happened in the Cathedral, it would have been an accurate record based on only one fixed time and place in some way associated with the manufacture of that first exported book. It is in the nature of liturgical acting-out to be mutable — kalendars are witness to the wholesale adoption of entirely new observances, for one — and it is in the nature of the resulting manuscripts to record accurately the deliberate change to the practical result (or to be a fixed text which is deliberately amended). For this reason among others, each manuscript must be treated like a unique witness. Each is a product of a unique process of manufacture which can influence the contents, as discussed above. Sometimes several manuscripts can be associated with the same tradition because they were subject to the same influences, provoking shared features. It is now incumbent upon us to identify some of the influences on liturgical practice and the surveying and production of liturgical books, and to compare the evidence from manuscript sources with the documentary record of the development of the post-Conquest English Office liturgy.

Chapter 4

THE REGULATION AND TRANSMISSION OF SECULAR LITURGY

> Of course the Roman or Sarum Use sometimes covers whole districts, but on the other hand very many localities had their own special Antiphons and Lessons.
>
> Falconer Madan, 'The Localization of Manuscripts', p. 22.

Hᴏᴡ *and why was the liturgical pattern of medieval England modified from time to time*? The variation witnessed in the preceding chapters at different levels of organization within the liturgy demands that these questions be addressed. We have until now been concerned with the establishment and characterization of manuscript evidence, beginning in chapter 2 with the employment of a method both liturgically detailed and textually abstract, and shifting in chapter 3 to a model more scrupulous as to textual variation. It is now time to compare observations based on this body of evidence with the picture formed by more conventional sources for ecclesiastical history. Here the manuscript groupings and regional patterns observed in the preceding chapters are placed in their historical context.

This chapter presents the argument that in addition to a case for the provincial synod as a primary arbiter of the kalendar, there is evidence for liturgical consistency at diocesan and minuter levels in conjunction with documentary prescriptions, some featuring much liturgical detail. It appears that diocesan authorities may have had a larger role in the promulgation of feasts and the assurance of consistency than might be expected. The adoption of a pattern of saints and feastdays could be surprisingly successful with primarily diocesan authorization. Much of the second part of the chapter discusses the development of the Use of Sarum, employed as a model because it is the pattern for which the most evidence survives. Although the take-up of Salisbury Cathedral liturgy outside its own diocese and the establishment of a Sarum Ordinal may be seen as relatively unproblematic, the promulgation and development of the 'Use of Sarum' in disparate regions were influenced by a range of often competing factors. One of these was, evidently, a conscious imitation of patterns unambiguously associated with the Cathedral. Other forces were more interested in standardizing and making liturgical prescriptions generic and comprehensive, where they had before been tied to the specific case of Salisbury. There were also conscious movements to create or to recover local liturgical distinctiveness, a development surely linked to and enabled by the local or diocesan capacity to regulate liturgy. Different impulses may have at one time been influences on different aspects of the same rite; it should therefore not be thought that a process of redaction in one section of a manuscript should make us believe that such a policy was carried out across all sections, or indeed across witnesses of a particular observance. Instead, these 'impulses' lying behind the form of liturgical change should help to suggest motivations for action, not to predict or explain contents.

At the same time it is important for contextual reasons to survey some of the developments in ecclesiastical history that precede the existence of the 'Use of Sarum'. A brief conspectus of Anglo-Saxon and early Norman liturgy is provided, and its lasting effects by the time of the institution of New Sarum and the building of the new cathedral are assessed. The late medieval situation is considered first in the context of the adoption of saints and feastdays, illustrating the motivations and procedures behind the promulgation of a feastday and highlighting the role played by diocesan bishops.

The Early Regulation of English Liturgy

The evidence for the imposition of liturgical features on the Anglo-Saxon Church, at least of an obvious nature, is scant, and Billett argues that 'not a trace' of the Office prior to the Synod of Whitby has survived, let alone any indication of local practices. But there may be a case for a model of liturgical innovation centred on local principles. Against the assumption that the Church used a proto-Benedictine form based on the Rule of St Benedict from Augustine's mission onward, Billett proposes that the Roman form was 'enriched through various kinds of interchange [...] as well as through local innovation, while retaining its structural integrity'.[1]

---

[1] Billett, 'The Divine Office in Anglo-Saxon England', pp. 103–04.

More generally, Susan Rankin writes,

> The liturgy must [...] be in some way malleable. That implies not only that individual communities should be able to make the liturgy in their own image, but also that an individual community should be able to re-shape its own liturgy in changing circumstances [...]. The challenge [...] is to recognize where a set of liturgical instructions fixed in time by being codified in a book sits in the matrix of time and place.[2]

There are, of course, a few references to matters of worship in chronicles and accounts depicting the history of Christianity in Britain from Augustine's mission onward. Mainly, these accounts address uniformity of worship but also the existence of multiple, authorized versions.

Foremost and exemplary among these chronicles is the *Historia Ecclesiastica* (hereafter *HE*) of Bede the Venerable, which supplies a few cogent details. The second question of Augustine of Canterbury to Pope Gregory the Great seems to ask whether customs encountered in different geographical regions of the church ought to be adopted. Gregory replies that the Church in England should be taught 'from every individual Church whatever things are devout, religious and right'.[3] A mission sent to support Augustine brought 'many books'.[4] Bede also notes the appearance, somewhat later, of certain individuals who are noted for their skills: among these are Putta, bishop of Rochester, 'especially skilled in liturgical chanting *after the Roman manner*, which he had learned from the disciples of the blessed Pope Gregory',[5] and more pertinently 'the esteemed John', precentor of St Peter's. John had been brought to Britain by Benedict Biscop in order to instruct the monks of Wearmouth in:

> The mode of chanting throughout the year as it was practiced at St Peter's in Rome. Abbot John [...] taught the cantors of the monastery the order and manner of singing and reading aloud and also committed to writing all things necessary for the celebration of festal days throughout the whole year; these writings have been preserved to this day in the monastery and copies have now been made by many others elsewhere.[6]

---

[2] Susan Rankin, 'Making the Liturgy: Winchester Scribes and their Books', in *The Liturgy of the Late Anglo-Saxon Church*, ed. by Helen Gittos and M. Bradford Bedingfield, Henry Bradshaw Society Subsidia, 5 (London: Boydell, 2005), pp. 29–52 (p. 32).

[3] Bede, *The Ecclesiastical History of the English People*, ed. by Judith McClure and Roger Collins (Oxford: Oxford University Press, 2008), I. 27. Henceforth *HE*.

[4] *HE*, I. 29.

[5] *HE*, IV. 2.

[6] *HE*, IV. 18.

Whether or not this account bears relation to reality, several inferences can be made. Evidently for Bede (d. 735), authority in the performance of the liturgy derived from Rome; and, to the extent that it is possible, it also came by descent from Gregory. Bede's narrative suggests that it was possible to perform worship according to a specific pattern or techniques that could be learned from persons endowed with such authority. These references from Bede are admittedly limited, but they are nearly the sole source of information for this period.[7]

Here there is some correspondence with resolutions of the early English synods. The Council of *Clofesho* (747, roughly contemporary with Bede) made several prescriptions concerning worship, most notably that saints' days and various other matters were to be kept 'iuxta martyrologium eiusdem Romane ecclesie',[8] an observation which again hints at the existence of an authoritative Roman pattern of worship transmitted in kalendars and martyrologies which could be followed and copied by others. Sarah Foot concludes that the idea of the Anglo-Saxon cursus, in her particular case in minsters, 'must take us beyond the prescriptions and admonitions of the conciliar literature'.[9] But aside from that literature little can be known because of the near-complete absence of extant service books.

In *Anglo-Saxon Church Councils*, Catherine Cubitt shows that there was a major concern for uniformity with Rome: in the Mass, Office, Kalendar, and litanies at least; the minor litany was a non-Roman practice to be carried out 'according to the custom of our predecessors'. *Clofesho* should be seen, says Cubitt, as a means of consolidating the Romanizing project: the prescriptions 'are an expression of the movement within the Anglo-Saxon Church for unity and uniformity with Rome'.[10]

Stephen Allott's translation of a letter of Alcuin to archbishop Eanbald II in 801 emphasizes this Roman obsession:

> I don't know why you asked about the order and arrangement of the missal. Surely you have plenty of missals following the Roman rite? You also have enough of the

[7] Pfaff, *LME*, p. 30.

[8] *Councils and Ecclesiastical Documents Relating to Great Britain and Ireland*, ed. by Arthur W. Haddan and William Stubbs, new edn, 3 vols (Oxford: Clarendon Press, 1964), III, 366–68, canons 10–18. Hereafter Haddan and Stubbs.

[9] Sarah Foot, *Monastic Life in Anglo-Saxon England, 600–900* (Cambridge: Cambridge University Press, 2006), p. 188.

[10] Catherine Cubitt, *Anglo-Saxon Church Councils, c. 650–c. 850* (London: Leicester University Press, 1995), p. 149.

larger missals of the old rite. *What need is there for new when the old one is adequate?*[11]

Despite its early flourishing, monasticism in Britain was in decline by 900, regardless of the best efforts of King Alfred, who encouraged the repopulation of religious communities with Continental monks after the ravages of the Viking invasions. The Rule of St Benedict was for these communities a unifying element which transcended any regional peculiarities, although as has been mentioned, Billett contends this was not the case before *c*. 970.[12] Continental influence was also at the head of the English Church from the ascent to Canterbury of Dunstan, abbot of Glastonbury from 940; and the consecrations of bishops Ethelwold at Winchester and Oswald at Worcester. Dunstan had lived in Ghent and Oswald was late of the Cluniac monastery at Fleury. Ethelwold was reputed to have sent for a continental copy of the Rule of St Benedict from Fleury.

These three figures, particularly Ethelwold, were also responsible for the *Regularis Concordia* (*RC*), the definitive English expression of monasticism agreed upon at Winchester around 970. *RC*, too, involves allusions to Continental practices through similarity to other such texts from across Europe, and makes no attempt to hide its origins in the *Rule of St Benedict*. It has been associated, too, with the *Concordia Regularum* of Benedict of Aniane (Aachen, compiled 816).[13] But it includes a number of peculiarly English practices, inspired perhaps by an emphatic recollection of 'the customs of our fathers': the bell-pealing between Holy Innocents and the octave of Christmas; efforts to promote daily Communion; special prayers and psalms for the royal family; and notes on the status of the king were all important elements.

In principle, the *Concordia* was made in good faith with little in the way of punitive action in case elements of it were not followed. But how this could have remained the case is not entirely clear. In broad outline, it was an article of

---

[11] Stephen Allott, *Alcuin of York, c. AD 732 to 804: His Life and Letters* (York: William Sessions, 1974), letter 19, p. 27.

[12] Billett says that the idea of genuine Benedictine worship of the seventh century later destroyed by 'foreign invasions and native laxity' has gone unchallenged since the nineteenth century 'only because it has never been articulated so baldly'. Billett, 'The Divine Office in Anglo-Saxon England', p. 6.

[13] See *Regularis Concordia Anglicae Nationis Monachorum Sanctimonialiumque* [The Monastic Agreement of the Monks and Nuns of the English Nation], ed. by Thomas Symons (London: Nelson, 1953), pp. xlv–lii.

monastic law intended to standardize the customs of English monasteries and was formalized between 965 and 975. While this work was being completed,[14] Ethelwold re-established an abbey at Peterborough. As a newly formed community, it would surely have been receptive to the reform. Thomas Symons suggests that Peterborough had been reformed according to the *Concordia* around 966.[15] Yet David Knowles writes that 'we should [...] hesitate to suppose that the *Concordia* was in all cases taken to a monastery as its code [...] it was not in the genius of tenth-century England to conceive of a number of separate bodies as governed by an abstract code'.[16] Whether or not it may have been followed to the letter, the *Concordia* represents one of the only institutionally mandated efforts at standardization which survives from the Anglo-Saxon period, although it is most useful to us as a snapshot of liturgical preferences at one time and place, rather than as a more wide-ranging resource.

Another set of prescriptions, probably based on the *Regularis Concordia*, can be found in the letter of Aelfric to the monks of Eynsham, a letter which contains, among other things, liturgical observations which follow roughly the cycle of the Temporale. It contains large amounts of verbatim borrowing from *RC*, but it is clear that Ethelwold's text is a model which the author of this letter is trying to improve upon, developing or replacing elements of the *Concordia*.[17] Like several other prescriptive sources, it seems not to be tied necessarily with its obvious place of use: it lacks details such as the Dedication feast of Eynsham and the names of saints whose relics found a place at the high altar. This does not, evidently, suggest that the ascription to a place of use is wrong.

A series of essays has exposed some of the difficulties experienced in dealing with Anglo-Saxon worship.[18] In the absence of prescriptive documentary sources, efforts have been made to extract some of the fundamental or most frequently occurring constituents of the Anglo-Saxon liturgy from the evidence in the extant primary sources, that is, the manuscript service books that sur-

[14] David Knowles, *The Monastic Order in England: A History of its Development from the Times of St Dunstan to the Fourth Lateran Council* (Cambridge: Cambridge University Press, 1949), p. 50.

[15] Thomas Symons, 'Regularis Concordia: History and Derivation', in *Tenth-Century Studies: Essays in Commemoration of the Millennium of the Council of Winchester and Regularis Concordia*, ed. by David Parsons (London: Phillimore, 1975), pp. 39–42.

[16] Knowles, *Monastic Order*, p. 66.

[17] *Aelfric's Letter to the Monks of Eynsham*, ed. by Christopher A. Jones, Cambridge Studies in Anglo-Saxon England, 24 (Cambridge: Cambridge University Press, 1998), pp. 27, 34.

[18] *The Liturgy of the Late Anglo-Saxon Church*.

vive. In particular, attention has been paid to the kalendar (Anglo-Saxon kalendars exist in quantities in psalters, missals, and the like) by Francis Wormald and Rebecca Rushforth in two Henry Bradshaw Society volumes, and various attempts have been made to extract 'the' Anglo-Saxon kalendar, and the list of saints therein venerated, from the surviving sources.[19] Sally Harper and others have also reported a particular Marian devotion in the manuscripts, supported by the fact that most extant manuscripts do have the four principal Marian feasts.[20] But it has been questioned whether any such standard version existed prior to the standardizing efforts at the Conquest. Other than the kalendar, research has perhaps overemphasized the Mass to the detriment of the Office.

Save for these observations, the picture of the Anglo-Saxon liturgy is clouded by the passage of time, by the fact that Billett's model of regionalized Roman liturgy must never have been regulated or unified,[21] and by the reputed efforts of Norman authorities to blot out past practices which were seen to be overly superstitious and perhaps too pagan. The next logical step will be to survey the post-Conquest developments, altogether more deliberate and explicit.

Prescription in Secular and Monastic Liturgy after the Conquest

The history of Norman liturgy is the history of the institutions in which it was performed. Across the country new secular foundations, cathedrals with deans and chapters, were being founded on Continental models, and new or reformed monastic foundations had the rich background of English Benedictine practice for inspiration: monastic cathedrals were unknown in Northern France.[22] Perhaps as a consequence, the sources which depict liturgy or give instructions for its performance are closely linked to the statutes which provided for every aspect of institutional life. Monastic daughter-houses, for example, built upon practices established at and for the parent monastery, perhaps even to such an extent that across institutional boundaries, 'the' Benedictine liturgy did not exist.[23] Monastic houses, particularly older ones, were likely to have produced a unique interpretation of the Rule of St Benedict that was pertinent to their

[19] Francis Wormald, *English Kalendars before AD 1100*, Henry Bradshaw Society, 72 (London, 1934); Rebecca Rushforth, *Saints in English Kalendars before AD 1100*.

[20] Sally Roper, *Medieval English Benedictine Liturgy*.

[21] Billett, 'The Divine Office in Anglo-Saxon England', p. 60.

[22] Pfaff, *LME*, p. 101.

[23] A point which underlines Pfaff's concern about the idea of any broadly uniform rite.

circumstances, whose properties could vary greatly within the same country. Cluny and the monastic revival of the ninth and tenth centuries produced large congregations of monks through daughter-houses, all of which would have followed the same patterns for living and indeed for worship. In chapters 2 and 3, I have explored the consistency of sources of Benedictine origin and suggested parameters for their comparison. The liturgy of Augustinian foundations and their daughter-houses in particular has been evaluated in two recent theses by Timothy Morris and Anna Parsons which question the long-held belief that they normally adopted the local pattern. Morris argues for the existence of an 'Oseney Use' and Parsons for a 'Guisborough group Use': both are convincing, and the argument that the substantial community at Guisborough would have produced its own patterns is well supported by manuscript evidence including the responsory series discussed in chapter 2.[24]

The establishment of secular cathedrals was a new development in the Anglo-Norman period, initiated by Norman ecclesiastics seeking to perpetuate a familiar model. Conceptions of the secular liturgy are as a consequence tied to models established for these secular cathedral foundations, and the prescriptive sources dealing with liturgical matters generally need to be viewed in this light. It has been perceived that the considerable liturgical requirements of a cathedral would have been laid out by necessity in ordinals, customaries, and other such reference material.

Here, at a turning point in English history, one might also anticipate a sea-change as a result of which substantial and standardizing effects in the liturgy should be expected. It has been mentioned before that Norman authorities were wary of what they felt to be an overly superstitious and primitive form of liturgy. The *Monastic Constitutions* of Lanfranc, the document comparable to the *Concordia* for this period, shares some practices with its antecedent but rejects some of the slightly quainter ones. This document seems to have been written so that it was versatile enough to be used in various venues.[25] Popular thought, perhaps legitimately and certainly in practice, has it that Norman ecclesiastics would perpetuate a model familiar to themselves. These efforts might help to explain some of the Continental allusions in post-Conquest liturgy.[26] Lanfranc

---

[24] Parsons, 'The Use of Guisborough'; Timothy Meeson Morris, 'The Augustinian Use of Oseney Abbey: A Study of the Oseney Ordinal, Processional, and Tonale (Bodleian Library MS Rawlinson c. 939)' (unpublished doctoral thesis, University of Oxford, 1999).

[25] Pfaff, *LME*, p. 106

[26] The liturgical evidence for this is outlined in chapter 2.

and Thomas of Bayeux, the first properly Norman archbishops, are two likely candidates: the former, in addition to his *Monastic Constitutions*, apparently initiated a reform of the kalendar (a view now somewhat discredited in two independent efforts by Richard Pfaff and Jay Rubenstein).[27] Archbishop Thomas, it is said, was forced to supply York Minster with new books to make up for Viking vagaries. The new books (logically speaking) would in both cases transmit a form of liturgy familiar to the figure of authority. I have noted the comments of Hugh the Chanter's chronicle relating to Thomas elsewhere.[28] New heights of uniformity in both Canterbury and York might be a reasonable expectation, in contrast to the lack of uniformity which seems to have prevailed in the Anglo-Saxon Church. The consolidation at the Conquest of Canterbury and York with Rouen meant that three large and influential provinces were operating under a singular temporal administration. The liturgical features shared between the various Norman patterns, proposed by Edmund Bishop, W. H. Frere, and more recently by David Hiley, may well have been influenced by the movement of ecclesiastical personages from post to post across the Channel. Bishop suggested that Robert de Bethune, bishop of Hereford from 1131, may have been responsible for the Norman character of the Hereford liturgy.[29]

But the states of liturgy both prior to and after the years surrounding the Conquest are inadequately documented to argue such a case based on the primary evidence. In large part the early post-Conquest liturgy must be extrapolated from much later manuscripts, although it is likely that such consistent features as responsory series, attested both in early manuscripts and in their reputed Continental antecedents, would have survived.[30] The present state of editorial work is also faulty. In addition to the reprint of the 1531 'Great' Sarum Breviary by Procter and Wordsworth, F. H. Dickinson and J. W. Legg's

---

[27] Pfaff, 'Lanfranc's Supposed Purge'; Jay Rubenstein, 'Liturgy against History: The Competing Visions of Lanfranc and Eadmer of Canterbury', *Speculum*, 74 (1999), 279–309.

[28] Salisbury, *The Use of York*, p. 38.

[29] Edmund Bishop, 'Holy Week Rites of Sarum, Hereford, and Rouen Compared', in his *Liturgica Historica*, pp. 276–300; Walter Howard Frere, 'The Connexion between English and Norman Rites', in *Walter Howard Frere: A Collection of his Papers on Liturgical and Historical Subjects*, ed. by J. H. Arnold and E. G. P. Wyatt, Alcuin Club Collections, 35 (London: Oxford University Press, 1940), pp. 32–40; David Hiley, 'The Norman Chant Traditions – Normandy, Britain, Sicily', *Proceedings of the Royal Musical Association*, 107 (1980–81), 1–33.

[30] See Pfaff, *LME*, p. 358.

editions of the Sarum Missal and W. H. Frere's editions of the Ordinal and Consuetudinary do not seem to be representative of an early tradition.[31]

Again, our principal evidence for liturgy in this period ought to be the manuscripts themselves, an approach employed in previous chapters. In addition to breviaries and antiphonals, ordinals and customaries, as preservers of liturgical practice, may seem to be a tantalizing 'snapshot' which give a complete and useful summary. But it is perhaps questionable whether the more complex and seemingly well-established the model, the less likely that such detailed models ever reflected actual practice. I imagine that some of these, the most elaborate, were constructed optimistically by precentors and others who may have been attempting to compensate in writing for inadequate activities in reality. Indeed, that which is written down may never be equated with reality in any manuscript.[32]

Here again, where liturgical evidence fails to present a complete or convincing picture, documentary sources exist in quantities, though the information they supply may be somewhat less than adequate. The best sources of detailed information, by far, other than the service books, are the foundation statutes of secular cathedrals, chantry chapels, and collegiate churches, some of which are discussed later in this chapter. Among the substantial sections on the composition and duties of the chapter which are the preoccupation of many of these sets of statutes, often a number of liturgical observations are made: the number and types of feasts observed; the number and design of feasts with proper texts; the insertion of new observances; and specific matters relating to performance which betray more details about the services themselves. Aside from a well-known incident at Glastonbury in 1083 where deaths resulted from the introduction of a new method of chanting the liturgy,[33] various institutional mandates are extant. Statutes for York and Lincoln in 1090 are among the early exemplars with the *c.* 1223 Sarum Constitutions of Richard Poore among the most well known, and also among the first to use the formula 'according to the Use/custom of Sarum', an indicator of the adoption of the liturgical pattern at Salisbury Cathedral whose frequent presence in the documentary evidence is a likely reason that scholars have felt the adoption was widespread.

---

[31] *Breviarium ad usum insignis ecclesiae Sarum*, ed. by Procter and Wordsworth; *Missale ad usum insignis et praeclarae ecclesiae Sarum*, ed. by F. H. Dickinson (Burntisland, 1861); *The Sarum Missal: Edited from Three Early Manuscripts*, ed. by John Wickham Legg (Oxford: Clarendon Press, 1916); Frere, *The Use of Sarum*.

[32] I thank the Very Revd Keith Jones, Dean of York, for this observation.

[33] *The Anglo-Saxon Chronicle*, ed. by D. Whitelock with D. C. Douglas and S. E. Tucker (London: Eyre and Spottiswoode, 1961), p. 160.

Despite the fact that Anglo-Saxon developments have attracted strong (perhaps the strongest) interest from scholars of medieval England, Dumville maintains that it is difficult 'to speak with confidence about continuity or change in the liturgical practice of any specific church in [Anglo-Saxon] England [...] for sheer lack of evidence'.[34] Some of the problems faced by those investigating the earliest English liturgies — the lack of source material, especially a lack of supporting evidence for the imposition, redaction, or promulgation of rites — were equally faced by those investigating liturgy at the end of the Middle Ages. The narrative of ecclesiastical history must not be ruled by patterns of survival of unambiguous source material, however, and in both cases it is suggested that the analysis of as many liturgical sources as possible may result in an amelioration of the problem. The subsequent sections of this chapter attempt to reconcile what has been gleaned from every surviving, complete Office book with the limited documentary evidence for the regulation of late medieval liturgy in England, in an attempt to derive some reasonable conclusions.

The Adoption of Saints and Feastdays

The variable contents of the kalendars discussed in chapter 2 provoke a number of questions, for instance:

1. Why did some observances (for instance, those found in the normative and regional kalendars) enjoy widespread recognition or quick dissemination, while others appeared in only a few kalendars?

2. Who authorized the contents of (and additions to) kalendars, and by what process was this done?

3. How consistently were new feasts added, or old ones retained? How can the reliable local traditions linked to certain regions be explained?

In addressing all of these questions it will be shown that diocesan authority, whether through a personal act of the bishop or by the collective will of a synod, had enough influence to manipulate the patterns of feastdays, just as provincial or archiepiscopal proclamations did. This may help to explain why regional groups of feasts, and local observances in general, were both consistent and frequent constituents of kalendars, and may be a practical explanation of the variation among manuscript sources.

---

[34] David Dumville, *Liturgy and the Ecclesiastical History of Late Anglo-Saxon England* (Woodbridge: Boydell, 1992), p. 96.

The theoretical basis for the influence of the diocesan bishop on local affairs and especially the canonization of saints has been outlined by E. W. Kemp and C. R. Cheney. Nearly all of the 'honours of canonization' of Robert Cardinal Bellarmine (1542–1621) which are quoted by Kemp include many allusions to liturgical observance or at least the potential for veneration: these included the prescription of public recognition of the saint; public prayer through his intercession; the dedication of buildings to the saint; celebration of Mass and Office for the saint, and his festival observed; and the transferral of relics to reliquaries. Translations, Kemp points out, could be considered an early form of canonization.[35] The regulation of sanctity, namely the handing over of the authority for canonization to the pope from the thirteenth century onward, owed its existence to the abuse of episcopal privilege as concerned saints, mainly in reaction to the veneration of 'unworthy, unorthodox, or even mythical personages', or 'manipulations of [a] cult for financial gain'.[36] Kemp paints the newly exclusive privilege of the pope to canonize saints as a solution which ameliorated what was a *normative* role of the diocesan bishop. Papal intervention might help to resolve disputes over evidence for sainthood, or to arbitrate if the diocesan bishop refused to be responsible. More positively, the influence of an ecclesiastical personage of higher status than the diocesan would bring about greater splendour for the saint.[37] Cheney confirms some of these points, and seems tacitly to emphasize the local authority of the bishop. Often the evidence for the influence of a bishop is recorded in the statutes of a diocesan synod.[38] The bishop in synod could reinforce important statutes set by his superiors, or indeed add to them by making common-law statutes; similarly, the 'legal structure conformed to the diocese rather than the province'. The influence of the diocesan synod was most felt, Cheney wrote, in ritual and monetary matters, elements which could be better controlled in synod than in provincial council.[39] Not only was a synodal statute more efficient, but it might also have been required to ensure compliance, according to Pfaff, who wrote that papal

[35] E. W. Kemp, *Canonization and Authority in the Western Church* (Oxford: Oxford University Press, 1948), pp. 1–2.

[36] Kemp, *Canonization and Authority*, p. 169.

[37] Kemp, *Canonization and Authority*, p. 169.

[38] The authority of synods came from the divine authority of those present, and the divine authority of the bishop permitted him to call the synod. See Enrico de Botteo, *Tractatus de synodo episcopi* (Lyon, 1529), prima pars, esp. parts 11–20.

[39] C. R. Cheney, *English Synodalia of the Thirteenth Century* (Oxford: Oxford University Press, 1941), pp. 12, 33.

promulgation of a feast may not have been sufficient to ensure its observance.[40] Sometimes the enthusiastic re-promulgation of a papal bull seems to have been required, as will be demonstrated below for an entirely uncontroversial saint. It is perhaps unsurprising that local affirmation may have been required in order to ensure compliance with papal requirements: the doctrine of infallibility was in its early days and the geographical and social distance of the pope from the English parish church surely meant that a more local authority would have enjoyed more credibility. The authorities would in any case have been responsible for communicating any inclination of the pope. It must be remembered that the universal accessibility of the successor of Peter directly to the faithful is a very recent phenomenon.[41] While it might be expected that bishops did not often take the initiative in promulgating feastdays on their own authority, some of the variety in local practice might be explained by the transfer of ecclesiastical persons from diocese to diocese and indeed from country to country:[42] many bishops or future bishops spent time abroad.

Barbara Haggh in an analysis of the medieval liturgy of Cambrai Cathedral questions the assumption that there was a uniform pattern of liturgy even in a single institution 'and that the leaders of that establishment prescribed the use, seeking conformity if not imposing it.' She blames this assumption on 'post-Tridentine and post-Vatican II thinking' and argues that the feastdays of saints celebrated at Cambrai owed more to individual donors to the foundation than to its leaders.[43] A notable English example of a kalendar which incorporates disparate saints of significance to its owner is Oxford, Magdalen College 223, made for Thomas Wolsey while Archbishop of York, and which includes both the arms of his present and previous dioceses and saints associated with those localities.

Feasts Added by Statute

The evidence provided by provincial and diocesan statutes supplies some support for these arguments, suggesting that practical details of the liturgical observance of a feastday were mainly restricted to lower-level proclamations

---

[40] Pfaff, 'New Liturgical Observances in Later Medieval England', p. 8.

[41] See Jacques Derrida, *Foi et savoir* (Paris: Seuil, 2000), pp. 39–40.

[42] A. Hamilton Thompson, *The English Clergy and their Organisation in the later Middle Ages* (Oxford: Clarendon Press, 1947), p. 19.

[43] Barbara Haggh, 'Nonconformity in the Use of Cambrai Cathedral: Guillaume du Fay's Foundations', in *The Divine Office*, pp. 372–97.

and that diocesan provisions often repeated the texts of papal ordinances. The texts of the papal bulls canonizing Edmund of Abingdon (1246) and Richard of Chichester (1260) both include numerous proofs of the sanctity of the saint, and while each feastday is instituted, no liturgical details are given. In *c.* 1247 William Raleigh, bishop of Winchester, issued a synodal statute ordering the main feastday and translation of Edmund in his own diocese, and also reiterated a previous order of 1224 given by bishop Peter des Roches that Swithun and Birinus along with other saints *quae sancti patres et predecessores nostri in episcopatu nostro sollenniter celebrari sanxerunt* should be added to the kalendar and were to be celebrated liturgically.[44] The same provision, adding Richard, was promulgated by bishop John Gervais for Winchester in a statute 1262–1265.[45] An order to celebrate Edmund's main feast along with that of Nicholas was also added to a synodal statute of Walter de Cantilupe of 26 July 1240 for Worcester diocese, though *nolumus tamen per hoc opera laicorum fidelium impediri.*[46] It was also ordered that the feast of Edmund, along with those of Dominic and Francis, was to be celebrated with nine lessons. In a statute of 1245–1259 of bishop Fulk Basset, Edmund, Osyth, and Ethelburga were ordered for the diocese of London, along with Erkenwald, the Conversion of Paul, the Chair of Peter, and St Oswald *in civitate London.*[47] All of these statutes illustrate the concern and authority of the diocesan bishop, and it is interesting to note that several successive bishops promulgated the same saints in largely similar wording.

Similarly, the proclamation by Urban VI of the sanctity of St Anne in 1383 is framed, as printed by Wilkins, by words of William Courtenay, archbishop of Canterbury, to Robert de Braybroke, bishop of London. Having received letters from the pope (*ut ipsius beate Anne festivitatem in dicto regno [Anglie] solenniter et devote celebrari a prelatis et aliis Christi fidelibus in ipso regno commorantibus mandaremus*), William repeats the order specifically directed at the subordinates of the bishop of London.[48]

[44] *Councils & Synods, with Other Documents Relating to the English Church: AD 1205–1313,* ed. by F. M. Powicke and C. R. Cheney, 2 vols (Oxford: Clarendon Press, 1964), II, 127 (1224), 414 (1247). Henceforth *C&S.*

[45] *C&S,* II, 722.

[46] *C&S,* II, 318.

[47] *C&S,* II, 653.

[48] *Concilia Magnae Britanniae et Hiberniae, a synodo Verolamiensi AD 496 ad Londinensem AD 1717,* ed. by David Wilkins, 4 vols (London, 1737), II, 178–79. Henceforth *WC.*

In 1398 an order of Roger Walden, archbishop, is repeated in a letter from bishop Robert to the archdeacon of London. Walden had ordered the feastdays of David, Chad, and Winifred *cum novem lectionibus et ceteris omnibus ad officium sanctorum* [...] *de communi in locis ubi proprium servicium de sanctis huiusmodi non habetur*, a statement which both conveys the impression that proper liturgy may be disseminated only slowly (certainly more so than merely adding a name to a kalendar), and that the authorities were able to offer an alternative to them. It was also ordered that David, Chad, and Winifred should be added to the kalendars of Canterbury province. There was also to be a weekly commemoration for Thomas Becket on *die Martis sub regula commemorationis festi loci*. The whole was followed by a diocesan order for London to observe the same matters, including the addition of the saints to the kalendars of London diocese.[49]

The feast of George was amplified in 1415 by archbishop Henry Chichele to a major double feast, and a rest from work *sicut et prout in festo natalis Domini* was ordered, that the people might come to church to praise God. In addition the feastdays of David, Chad, and Winifred were liturgically amplified with nine lessons and were to be sung directed by 'rulers of the choir', who would lead the chanting. This seems to be a statute which institutes nothing, but produced a liturgical response for reasons that will shortly become clear.[50]

In 1415 St Paul's Use was suspended, in favour of the Use of Sarum, except for provisions which permitted certain local saints to be retained in the kalendar. More detail on this conversion appears later in this chapter.

By contrast in his 1416 statute Chichele first demonstrates the sanctity of John of Beverley, then illustrates the connexion of the saint with the battle of Agincourt. His main feast (the day after John Portlatin) was to be observed in the manner of the feast of one confessor in paschal time *secundum usum Sarum ecclesie* by the province of Canterbury. John's translation was also prescribed for 25 October, where it converged with the feast of Crispin and Crispinian, an observance of greater antiquity. To resolve this problem the two feasts were to be celebrated together. There were, ordered Chichele, to be three lessons for the martyrs, three middle lessons for John, and the last three *de exposicione evangelii plurimorum martyrum cum servicio secundum usum Sarum in talibus fieri consueto*. In this statute too there is an increased amount of specificity, and concern for liturgical detail.[51]

---

[49] *WC*, III, 234–35.

[50] *WC*, III, 376.

[51] *WC*, III, 379.

A similar concern for liturgy is seen in the 1481 record of the convocation of Canterbury which promulgated the feasts of Osmund, Frideswide, Translation of Etheldreda, and the Visitation of the BVM. In the familiar pattern, the virtues of the saints are first established, and they are added to the list of saints. The Visitation, with rulers of the choir, was to be a double feast *secundum usum Sarum cum pleno servicio*. The saints' days were to be celebrated throughout Canterbury province with an office of nine lessons with music led by rulers of the choir on the authority of the present council.[52]

Finally the feasts of the Transfiguration and the Holy Name of Jesus were promulgated between 1487 and 1489: an archiepiscopal order of 19 March 1487 conveyed by Thomas bishop of London to Robert Stillington, bishop of Bath and Wells, prescribes the Transfiguration on 7 August (*recte* 6 August) with nine lessons.[53] There were also to be solemn processions with Litany on Wednesdays and Fridays, and three proper collects at Mass.[54] The whole was promised with forty days' indulgence. The form of the feast of the Holy Name was prescribed in Canterbury convocation in 1488: four sheets which contained the order of service for the feast were presented, and their contents approved.[55] Both feasts were approved by the Northern Convocation on 27 February 1489.[56]

The final liturgical order relating to Canterbury province before the abolition of the Latin liturgy was one of Thomas Cranmer, which in 1542 prescribed the Use of Sarum for all clergy of the province as concerned the Divine Office.[57] It is not clear why this prescription was imposed, whether it was an attempt to prescribe a specific form of the Office for clergy who had been using variable and perhaps deficient forms, or a final attempt to promulgate a pattern which had in the sixteenth century still not been accepted, and which was now to represent Cranmer's first move toward a national liturgy for the Church of England. In any event this statute had been anticipated by the 1541 printing of a Sarum Breviary which omitted all mention of the Pope.

It may be an obvious conclusion that it seems to have been possible to control the liturgical result through episcopal statute. In general the statutory evidence

---

[52] *WC*, III, 613.

[53] Order paraphrased in *Registers of Robert Stillington*, ed. by H. C. Maxwell-Lyte, Somerset Record Society, 52 (London, 1937), pp. 144–45.

[54] The third of which was 'for the removal of pestilential air'.

[55] *WC*, III, 626.

[56] Order paraphrased in *Records of the Northern Convocation*, p. 203.

[57] *WC*, III, 861–62.

for the imposition of feasts from Anne onward shows an increasing concern for liturgical specificity. The papal bulls establishing feastdays were understandably concerned with establishing the sanctity of the saint; documents from lower-level authorities may have been more concerned with practical matters such as the number and source of lessons on a day where two feasts converged.

Another example of concern for liturgical problems surrounding feastdays can be found in the textual evidence from a number of manuscripts: a number of later breviaries, for instance Bodl. Lat. lit. b. 14, have rubrics explaining the course of action when First and Second Vespers for two adjacent feasts converge: these are found at First Vespers of *Decollatio* John Baptist (with Augustine on the preceding day) and Second Vespers of Michaelmas (Jerome is on the following day), Andrew (whose feast may be immediately followed by Advent Sunday), and Anne (followed by James). These rubrics also demonstrate a concern for the classification of feasts and their convergence, and the establishment of generic texts which were not customized at the point of manufacture for specific places of use.

While archiepiscopal prescriptions or provincial convocations by this stage always provided the impetus, the existence of documents from local bishops which re-promulgated these prescriptions may suggest that action from them was required. Nigel Morgan notes a number of instances where diocesan bishops, perhaps influenced by the centralizing impetus of the Fourth Lateran Council, expressed displeasure with the lack of uniformity in the kalendar.[58]

Given this exposition of the attempts to promulgate feastdays in English kalendars in the later Middle Ages, it is convenient to interrogate the manuscript evidence to determine how successfully these feasts were adopted, particularly as in at least a few cases saints may have been promulgated for pragmatic reasons. Jeremy Catto points out that the promulgation of saints George and John of Beverley by archbishop Chichele on behalf of Henry V, a 'master of the art' of propaganda, held significance: victory at Agincourt had been on the day of John's translation (a fact mentioned in the statutes) and George may have been a way to create an analogy involving the king and the archetypical *miles Christi*.[59] Kathleen Edwards suggested that the introduction of Osmund,

---

[58] Nigel Morgan, 'The Introduction of the Sarum Kalendar into the Dioceses of England in the Thirteenth Century', in *Thirteenth Century England VIII: Proceedings of the Durham Conference 1999*, ed. by Michael Prestwich et al. (Woodbridge: Boydell, 2001), pp. 179–206 (p. 186), referencing *C&S*, ii, 127, 414.

[59] Jeremy Catto, 'Religious Change under Henry V', in *Henry V: The Practice of Kingship*, ed. by G. L. Harriss (Oxford: Oxford University Press, 1985), pp. 97–115 (p. 107).

famed bishop of Salisbury, in the fifteenth century may have been an attempt at the popularization of the Use of Sarum (falsely) attributed to his institution.[60] By contrast, Pfaff has suggested that the feast of the Holy Name was popularized by private devotion, which suggests that private piety may have had an effect on official promulgation.[61] It is worthwhile to remember that some later saints may not be added to books of relatively late date as a result of the books no longer being in active use.

Edmund of Abingdon's feast on 16 November, the earliest of the feasts imposed on Canterbury liturgy to be studied here, is present in most secular and monastic kalendars. It is noticeably absent from Books of Hours and other manuscripts of Continental manufacture; and from several monastic kalendars (CB, of the thirteenth century, from Peterborough; and CY, from Barnwell). It is added to CL, the kalendar of the Coldingham OSB breviary. Richard of Chichester's main feastday is present in most Sarum manuscripts, and added to the manuscript Hereford breviary (kalendar CI), whose manufacture is roughly contemporary with Richard's canonization. It is absent from the York secular manuscripts and Augustinian books from Guisborough (CC, DB); and from many Books of Hours associated with Sarum by their Office of the Dead. Among prominent monastic books Richard is not present in CH, the late thirteenth-century Worcester antiphonal; and CK, the late thirteenth-century Muchelney breviary. Notably, it is also not in BU, the early fourteenth-century Springfield Sarum antiphonal.

The feast of Anne is said to have been instituted in England in 1383 to celebrate the marriage of Richard II to Anne of Bohemia, but there are widespread suggestions that it was observed in books of earlier date. Among notable examples which have been pointed out is a kalendar of the Queen's College, Oxford which was copied, not before 1340–41, from an exemplar from after 1295.[62] Owing to the late date of most of the extant kalendars it is in most Sarum, York, and Benedictine kalendars except several early examples (CP, *c.* 1300;

---

[60] Kathleen Edwards, *The English Secular Cathedrals in the Middle Ages: A Constitutional Study with Special Reference to the Fourteenth Century*, 2nd edn (Manchester: Manchester University Press, 1967), p. 80. The proposition is disproved in Diana Greenway's 'The false Institutio of St Osmund', in *Tradition and Change: Essays in Honour of Marjorie Chibnall*, ed. by Diana Greenway, Christopher Holdsworth, and Jane Sayers (Cambridge: Cambridge University Press, 1970), pp. 77–101.

[61] Pfaff, 'New Liturgical Observances in Later Medieval England', p. 257.

[62] *Liber Obituarius Aulae Reginae in Oxonia*, ed. by J. R. Magrath (Oxford, 1910). The dating is attributed to H. M. Bannister.

CR, *c.* 1200; CT, of the early fourteenth century). The feastday is added to X, Salisbury Cathedral 224 of the mid-fourteenth century and six other Sarum kalendars (AX, BB [Norwich], BC [Dublin], BI, BL, BU). Among Sarum books Anne's feast is nowhere in kalendar CW, BL Sloane 1909, of the fifteenth century.

The feast of David of Wales is in a large number of manuscripts, predominantly Sarum and Benedictine; it has been added to ten Sarum and three monastic manuscripts but is otherwise in the original contents. His feast is absent from three Sarum kalendars: BF (produced abroad); BR (Bodl. Laud misc. 3A), and BZ (BL Stowe 12, of the early fourteenth century). However no York manuscript has David, and these along with other manuscripts form a group of twenty-six which have Albinus on 1 March. Fifteen manuscripts have no saint on the day.

Chad's feastday is also in most Sarum and some Benedictine manuscripts. He has been added to a number of Sarum breviaries that predate the promulgation in 1398, and to three York kalendars (G, M, R). There is nothing on 2 March in a further thirty-seven kalendars, mostly Hours and psalters, but including two Sarum breviaries: Lambeth Palace 69, Henry Chichele's own breviary (made between 1408 and 1414); and BL Stowe 12 (of date noted above).

The feastday of Winifred is found in the original contents of 17 kalendars, and as an addition in a further twenty-five. There are no surprises here: most of these entries are in Sarum books, for in the province of York this is the feastday of Eustace. The only anomaly is the appearance of Eustace in BW, Bodl. Laud misc. 299, a late Sarum breviary.

John of Beverley's main feast is in most Sarum and York manuscripts, whilst it is added to twenty-five, and nothing appears on the day in thirty-one, a group which encompasses a wide range of manuscripts including some Sarum breviaries (BF, BH, BR, BZ), but primarily Hours and psalters. His Translation feast is included with that of Crispin and Crispinian, as suggested in the founding statute, in thirty-five kalendars of both York and Sarum manuscripts. The remainder have the Roman martyrs only.

The last saints to be added to the kalendar might be likely to be the least frequent to appear. However the feasts of Etheldreda (translation, 17 Oct) and Frideswide (19 Oct) seem to have benefited from their long institution, as they are present in forty-one and forty-eight kalendars respectively: thirty-two of these contain both feasts. Fourteen of the appearances of Etheldreda are original. Of these original entries, all but five are to be found in books associated with East Anglia: two (CG, DI) are from Gloucester, with the others from the Benedictine houses in Coldingham (CL), Chertsey (CT), and St Mary's

York (DC). Frideswide is original in twenty-nine kalendars, which represent a variety of traditions. By contrast, Osmund, bishop of Salisbury, is perhaps the least likely to have been picked up by kalendars: his main feastday is original in about five (late) kalendars, and added in seventeen. His translation is original in nine, and added in fourteen. In both cases all of these are Sarum books: the December feastday is the day of St Barbara in York.

The *Nova Festa*: Transfiguration, Holy Name, and Visitation

The three principal *nova festa*, which were investigated at length by Richard Pfaff in the 1960s,[63] were promulgated after 1450 and were well-established by 1500. Of one hundred and thirty-two kalendars, all three appear in ten. By numbers, the Visitation is the most likely to appear by itself (double the frequency of any other single feast), and indeed the most frequently occurring feast to appear, though not by a large margin (thirty-one occurrences to twenty-seven for the Transfiguration and twenty-four for the Holy Name). This may be a result of its having been separately promulgated at a different time, and consequently included alone in a new hand more frequently (eight instances to two for both Transfiguration and Holy Name). Indeed, fourteen kalendars containing the Visitation have neither of the other feasts, suggesting different patterns of influence and promulgation. But it is in seventeen cases in a kalendar with one or more of the others. The Transfiguration and Holy Name, by contrast, are found together in sixteen cases; in six of these they have been unambiguously added by the same hand. No manuscript has both feasts with one as original and the other added by a new hand.

Seven of the manuscripts containing *nova festa* in their kalendars also have additions for them in the contents: Camb. UL Dd. X. 66 has all three in kalendar and additions, BL Addl 4500(AU) has all three in the kalendar in a new hand, with Transfiguration and Holy Name as additions. Camb. Magdalen F. 4. 10, by contrast, has three additions to the kalendar, but none in the Sanctorale. Oddly BL Royal 2.A.XII has no Visitation in the Kalendar, but has an addition in the Sanctorale (Table 4.1).

How and why were saints and feastdays added to kalendars? Surveying all of the evidence it seems clear that manuscript kalendars consistently added new feasts according to statutory provision, with a few anomalies, especially con-

---

[63] This study began with his thesis, and was revised for the published version in Pfaff, *New Liturgical Feasts in Later Medieval England*. Judith Aveling, a PhD student at the University of Bangor, is at present exploring the reception of the feast of the Holy Name.

Table 4.1: Kalendars containing the *nova festa*. Numbers in brackets indicate the number of kalendars in each category.

Transfiguration[a]

Original in   J AL CA CJ CP CQ CS CW CY DC DO DX (12)

Added in   R Z AU AW AX AZ BA BG BI BW CK CT CZ DD DU (15)

[a] L (York Minster XVI. O. 23) has 'non Transfig. Dni'.

Holy Name of Jesus

Original in   J L AL BH BL BO BS CJ CP CW (10)

Added in   Q R Z AU AW AZ BG BW CC CT CU CZ DD DU (14)

Visitation of the BVM

Original in   W AA AC AL AQ BA CF CJ CU DK (10)

Added in   Z AT AU AW AY AZ BE BG BH BI BN BS BW BX CL CP CQ CZ DE DT DX (21)

Transfiguration alone

Original in   CA CS CY DC DO (5)

Added in   AX CK (2)

Holy Name alone

Original in   L BL BO (3)

Added in   Q CC (2)

Visitation alone

Original in   W AA AC AQ CF DK (6)

Added in   AT AY BE BN BX CL DE DT (8)

Visitation and Transfiguration

either original or added in BA BI BX CQ (4)

Visitation and Holy Name

either original or added in BH BS CU (3)

Transfiguration and Holy Name

either original or added in J R CW CT DD DU (6)

Kalendars which contain all three *nova festa*: Z AL AU AW AZ BG BW CJ CP CZ (10)

cerning the fact that before promulgation saints may have had existing cults.
This section confirms the assumption that the saints imposed by statute in the
later Middle Ages are the most likely to be added to any of the kalendars studied here, perhaps a testament to the success of diocesan orders for their institution. However, new feasts were very unlikely to be taken up in the kalendars of
Books of Hours and psalters which may have enjoyed little if any practical usage
in a liturgical context. For the feasts promulgated by authorities in the province
of Canterbury, compliance with documentary prescriptions is most complete
in late Sarum breviaries. By contrast York books are governed by their own sets
of saints and do not seem to be overly affected by developments in the southern province. Monastic books, of course, were governed by their own kalendars
which, within Order or region, had similarities. Sometimes, as with many of
the new saints but especially Anne, Etheldreda, and Frideswide, the existence
of an active cult before the statute may have inflated the number of kalendars
in which a saint appears. Osmund, who was only recently canonized when his
feast was imposed, appears to have been added most infrequently. Among the
nova festa the Visitation was the most frequent to appear, and to appear without the other two, probably a result of its promulgation at an earlier date with
Osmund and the two female saints. The Transfiguration and Holy Name seem
sometimes to be added together. It is worth mentioning that despite the existence of an approved form for Holy Name (discussed above) there are rarely
provisions in the Sanctorale for its performance.

Pfaff suggests that the dates on which feasts are prescribed to be added to
the kalendar may not concur with a gradual, successful process of introduction:
he gives the examples of the feasts of the Transfiguration and Visitation, which
both had a long history before their official promulgation: the Transfiguration
was commemorated in the patristic period, and certainly before the year 1000:
the late thirteenth-century Bodl. Univ. Coll. 101, a Cluniac book, is witness to
this. By the beginning of the fifteenth century, Pfaff says, the Transfiguration
was observed in some Benedictine and Augustinian houses: it gained greater
recognition in secular liturgy after the promulgation in 1457.[64] The Visitation
was originally instituted in 1389 by Boniface IX, 'a rare example of a new liturgical observance established solely by the fiat of authority'.[65] It saw relatively
low acceptance in the Church and was re-promulgated in 1475 by Sixtus IV,
and promulgated in England five years later, after which it saw more or less

---

[64] Pfaff, 'New Liturgical Observances in Later Medieval England', pp. 37, 54, 58.

[65] Pfaff, 'New Liturgical Observances in Later Medieval England', p. 77.

consistent observance. The feast of the Holy Name was spurred on by popular devotion, mainly centred on the proper Mass, and only after promulgation did the Office emerge as a consistent entity.[66] In this way, Pfaff argues, the *nova festa* exemplify some of these developments. Lists and dates may be artificial: he suggests that the introduction of feasts followed a process of 'germination, initial extension, and wider popularity'.[67] Holy Name proves that a *privately* popularized feast can gather sufficient steam to become mainstream. It may be most suitable to consider this pattern for all such feastdays added to kalendars.

* * *

Whilst it has been shown that a number of provincially mandated feastdays came to be observed in both ecclesiastical provinces and especially in areas where the Use of Sarum was prevalent, it seems that much of this uniformity can be ascribed to their imposition at the diocesan level. Chapter 2 outlined a number of patterns which could be ascribed to geographical regions, and it is here suggested that these too, at least in the secular cursus, are realizations of a model imposed on a diocese.

The appearance of provisions for saints is frequent in synodal statutes. The first of a series of orders in Winchester diocese, that the feastdays of Swithun and Birinus, patrons, should be celebrated solemnly by clergy and people, was issued by Peter des Roches in *c.* 1224. This order also stipulated that *festa aliorum sanctorum quorum corpora in ecclesia nostra vel aliis ecclesiis nostre diocesis requiescunt, in kalendariis scribantur, et quando contingunt denuncietur et in ecclesiis celebrentur.*[68] As noted above this prescription was repeated in *c.* 1247 by William Raleigh and 1262–1265 by John Gervais.[69]

In other situations it was noted that the lack of agreement in practice required correction: archbishop Stephen Langton (presumably acting as diocesan bishop) offered the following under the heading *De celebratione festorum* in additions to 1222–1228 statutes for Canterbury diocese: 'Quoniam turpis est omnis pars que non congruit suo universo statuimus quod festa consueta uniformiter [per diocesim] celebrentur, *nisi alicubi subsit causa specialis a diocesano approbata.*'[70] This passage emphasizes the idea that a standard set of obser-

---

[66] Pfaff, 'New Liturgical Observances in Later Medieval England', pp. 136, 147.

[67] Pfaff, 'New Liturgical Observances in Later Medieval England', p. 7.

[68] *C&S*, II, 127 (1224).

[69] *C&S*, II, 414, 722.

[70] *C&S*, II, 167: emphasis mine; passage in square brackets in one of three witnesses.

vances was desirable, but leaves the door open for special cases relating to saints to which particular devotion was offered in certain venues, on the same order as the Winchester statute above. In other synodal statutes it was more frequently the practice to supply lists of saints' days. This practice is exemplified in the 1240 statutes of Walter of Cantilupe for Worcester diocese, which include several such lists: the double feasts *in ecclesia Salusbur*;[71] the days when the choir was to be ruled; and the *festa ferianda* in Worcester diocese along with the lesser days when ploughing was permissible. Owing to their presence in only one witness the contents of these lists are suggested by Powicke and Cheney to be the work of William de Blois, Walter's predecessor, but evidently the latter found them suitable for re-promulgation.[72]

Further examples of lists are found in 1229–1241 statutes of bishop Roger Niger for the archdeaconry of London, and later much enlarged in bishop Fulk Basset's revised statutes for the diocese of London, 1245–1259. The author of the first set attempts to clarify doubts about whether certain feastdays were to be observed: these were Gregory (in March); Mellitus and Erkenwald (April); John Portlatin, Ethelbert, and Augustine of Canterbury (May); Barnabas, Alban, and Commemoration of Paul (June); Translation of Thomas Becket (July); Oswald (August); Giles (September); Osyth and Ethelburga (October); and Erkenwald (November). These were to be celebrated along with those saints whose veracity it was not necessary to mention.[73]

The second set of statutes for London, of slightly later date, also attempts to ensure that the right saints are being observed with the right honours.[74] The first category for each month indicates the saints to be celebrated by all; the second those feasts on which some work can be done by the laity (Table 4.2). The statute continues with a list of observances and the amount of work that was permissible for the laity on those days.

In the face of this statutory evidence, which seems to suggest that it was possible and indeed likely for precise groups of saints to be ordered in each diocese, it is striking that one of the most consistent patterns in the evidence from manuscript kalendars, the group of 'synodal' feasts in East Anglian books, appears to have no extant statutory confirmation whatsoever, and the only evidence for its apparent imposition is found in the kalendars themselves. Notwithstanding this there is, as chapter 2 has demonstrated, a uniform group of saints who were

[71] Table 2.8 in chapter 2 gives an account of the feasts mentioned in the statute.

[72] *C&S*, ɪɪ, 318–25.

[73] *C&S*, ɪɪ, 329.

[74] *C&S*, ɪɪ, 653–55.

Table 4.2: Feasts to be observed in the diocese of London (1245–1259).

January	Circumcision; Epiphany; Conversion of St Paul *cum honore et reverentia*; Fabian and Sebastian; Agnes; Vincent to be observed in churches.
February	Purification, Cathedra Petri *per omnia sollempnis*; Matthias.
March	Annunciation with solemnity; Gregory.
April	Mark, Erkenwald *ab omnibus*; Alphege, George, Mellitus.
May	Philip and James, Inventio Holy Cross *ab omnibus*; John Portlatin, Dunstan, Ethelbert *sint in civitate ista sollempnia propter reverentiam reliquiarum que ibidem continentur*.
June	Barnabas, Nat. John Baptist, Peter and Paul, Commem. Paul with solemnity; Alban *tantum in decanatu Middelsexiensi*.
July	Thomas Becket, Mary Magdalene, James with solemnity; Margaret.
August	Peter in Chains, Oswald *in civitate London*, Laurence, Assumption, Bartholomew, Decoll. John Baptist *ab omnibus*.
September	Giles by his pilgrims and churches. Nat. BVM, Exaltatio Holy Cross, Matthew, Michael *ab omnibus*.
October	Dedication of St Paul's Cathedral, Luke, Simon and Jude *ab omnibus*. Osyth and Ethelburga *in suis decanatibus*.
November	All Saints *sit summe solempne*; All Souls. Martin, Edmund king and martyr, Katherine, Andrew with solemnity. Edmund of Canterbury, Cecilia, Clement *post celebrationem misse agriculture non negentur*.
December	Nicholas, Thomas, Christmas and the following days *sit cunctis sollempne*.

identified consistently as synodals in Norwich manuscripts. This evidence must surely suggest that diocesan statutes imposing the synodals must have existed, although the documents do not appear to have survived. Taking into consideration some of the other regional kalendars from chapter 2, the statutory provisions do not always accord with the manuscript evidence, notably in the diocese of London, for which the regional kalendar established in chapter 2 does not accord completely with either statutory list. Some regional kalendars are entirely unsupported by statutory evidence, and vice versa. However successful the episcopal orders may have been, the attempt to regulate the celebration of feastdays at diocesan level must be noted.

The distinctiveness of the Use of Hereford, the only realistic diocesan Use in the South that was not by its own admission an obvious variant of Sarum, should be pointed out as a strong example of a diocesan pattern which covered more than the specific saints to be venerated. Whilst the liturgy of Wells adhered from an early date to the Use of Sarum associated with Richard Poore, bishop Jocelin of Wells was not hesitant to ensure the consistency of the details of liturgical ceremony particular to his own cathedral.[75] It is also worth highlighting that regional patterns could be enacted on a wider basis than a single diocese. Sally Harper has presented the case for a distinctive Welsh realization of the Use of Sarum, the normative liturgy there as in the rest of the province of Canterbury: the extant Welsh books illustrate, she says, an individualized pattern of saints and distinctive patterns of worship. Some Welsh saints were observed in the liturgy in the conventional manner, whilst others were accorded proper lessons collected from *Vitae*. She hypothesizes that there may have been a larger body of proper material for Welsh saints than the limited number of sources now extant may suggest.[76]

The region for which the clearest, and latest, evidence of liturgical innovation and monitoring by a diocesan bishop (or any single individual) survives is Exeter under John Grandisson (bishop 1327–69). He was not the first to offer prescriptive advice to the diocese: in addition to the fragmentary evidence for pre-Conquest Exeter liturgy provided by the so-called tenth-century Leofric Missal (s.x), bishop Peter Quivil (1280–91) discussed a number of distinctive liturgical matters in a very detailed set of statutes.[77] Shortly after his consecration Grandisson's concern for liturgical matters was made clear: on 24 February 1329 he asked the archdeacon of Salisbury to loan him *aliquem librum pontificalem, antiquum et veracem, ut [...] modum Saresburiensis ecclesie in nostra Exoniensi teneamus*.[78] In his first visitation of his cathedral (19 December 1328) Grandisson enquired about the Ordinal and Consuetudinary *in quibus discrepant ab usu Sarum vel aliarum ecclesiarum, necnon de collectario correspondente; qui remittantur ad nos ad examinandum, corrigendum, et approbandum*.[79] His own Ordinal and Consuetudinary (the *Ordinale Exon* edited by the Henry Bradshaw Society) were produced in the spring of 1337.[80] He also

---

[75] C. M. Malone, *Facade and Spectacle: Ritual and Ideology at Wells Cathedral* (Leiden: Brill, 2004), p. 131.

[76] Sally Harper, *Music in Welsh Culture before 1650: A Study of the Principal Sources* (Aldershot: Ashgate, 2007), pp. 201–16.

[77] Pfaff, *LME*, p. 396.

[78] *The Register of John de Grandisson, Bishop of Exeter (AD 1327–1369), with some Account of the Episcopate of James de Berkeley (AD 1327)*, ed. by F. C. Hingeston-Randolph, 3 vols (London: G. Bell, 1894–99), I, 214.

[79] *The Register of John de Grandisson*, ed. by Hingeston-Randolph, I, 436.

[80] Edited by John Neale Dalton in *Ordinale Exon*, Henry Bradshaw Society, 37, 38, 63, 79, 4 vols (London, 1909–39).

produced a martyrology or lectionary to be used for saints' days. Both follow the typical pattern of establishing the customs and duties of the various cathedral offices, and the Office for Advent Sunday provides an archetype for the rest of the year. Particularly notable are the prescriptions for Matins on Christmas Day.[81] Pfaff calls the Ordinal 'overwhelming', an assessment which can be confirmed by the start of the Henry Bradshaw Society edition, where Grandisson's extreme attention to detail is noted, with special care to address the convergence of feastdays and details of ceremonial. Except for these matters, or where there is a local difference, Grandisson expects that the Use followed would be that of Sarum.[82] Despite this, it seems he had hoped the 'Use of Exeter' would be observed at Ottery St Mary, if the foundation statutes of that church are an indicator:

> Statuimus quod ubicunque ordinale vel consuetudinarium vel statuta nostra non sufficiant forte in multis faciendis per totum annum, quod tunc recurratur ad ordinale et consuetudinarium Sarum, ita tamen, quod semper omnia per nos disposita firmiter observentur. Nolumus tamen, quod allegent vel dicant, unquam se usum tenere Sarum; sed magis Exonie, vel ut verius dicant, usum per nos eis traditum proprium et specialem.[83]

It is not clear to what extent Grandisson was trying to create or promote a distinctive Use of Exeter, or suggest that any such pattern of liturgy and customs should be imposed on venues other than his own cathedral church. It is evident from the specificity of his prescriptions, and the fact that he is said to have given personally a great number of volumes to the cathedral, that he *as diocesan bishop* was trying to effect substantive change on the liturgy of Exeter. As a consequence Grandisson has left for the modern reader one of the most substantial, datable witnesses to medieval liturgical practice in England.

While Exeter may be the diocese for which there is the greatest amount of evidence for liturgical resolutions, it was clearly not the only home of regionally distinctive patterns of saints. Prescriptions by diocesan bishops appear to highlight local saints, or saints of particular interest for the region, and single

---

[81] Described and translated in Nicholas Sandon, 'Medieval Services and their Music', in *Exeter Cathedral: A Celebration*, ed. by Michael Swanton (Crediton: Southgate for the Dean and Chapter of Exeter, 1991), pp. 127–36.

[82] Pfaff, *LME*, pp. 400–04.

[83] 'LXXV: *de observacione ordinalis et aliorum*', in *The Collegiate Church of Ottery St Mary Being the Ordinacio et Statuta ecclesie sancte Marie de Otery Exon. diocesis*, ed. by J. N. Dalton (Cambridge, 1917), p. 224.

them out for particular attention. Sometimes the order is simply to add the saint to the kalendar; or to celebrate 'with solemnity'. In the fifteenth century and later there was an increasing concern at this regional level to present the particular liturgical actions desired. It may be helpful to consider Alexander Hamilton Thompson's suggestion that parishes are to a diocese as a diocese is to the English Church, as the English Church is to the Western Church.[84] Morgan suggests that some of the regional patterns that have survived in otherwise Sarum kalendars may be a result of diocesan interference, attempting to retain saints with a substantial local connexion.[85]

Saints and Feastdays: Conclusions

Regional kalendars show consistency within themselves, though not always in accordance with written prescriptions. As with other forms of evidence previously described, when determining the importance of the appearance of a saint in an unknown kalendar it is suggested that reference must be made both to other examples of kalendars from the same region, if it is known, *in addition to* statutory evidence. Nevertheless it is clear that documentary prescriptions of liturgical acts did exist, especially at diocesan level. They strove either to repromulgate feastdays that had been provincially or universally instituted, or to clarify the veneration of known feastdays with additional liturgical details. It is certainly possible that such deliberate acts were the cause of the textual and kalendrical diversity associated with various dioceses and regions, namely self-consciously distinctive groups of saints associated with regions, and groups of kalendars associated by shared points of variance which agree with geographical and institutional assignments. The imposition of such regionally observed features was without doubt the objective of the statutory prescriptions, which were apparently enacted at a lower level of authority — the diocesan bishop — than might have been expected, although the theoretical basis for the authority of the diocesan bishop over liturgy and the veneration of saints also appears to be strong. The next section of this chapter deals with the imposition of identifiable patterns of wider liturgical observance in a single region: the province of Canterbury, where the Use of Sarum is said to have been adopted progressively throughout the Middle Ages.

---

[84] Hamilton Thompson, *The English Clergy*, pp. 9–10.

[85] Nigel Morgan, 'The Sanctorals of Early Sarum Missals and Breviaries, *c.* 1250–*c.* 1350', in *The Study of Medieval Manuscripts of England*, pp. 143–62 (p. 143).

The Regulation of Secular Liturgy

Documentary evidence may also permit the description of the process by which the concept of the Use of Sarum, in a more general sense, was adopted throughout the province of Canterbury. It will necessarily be shown that there was a clear *idea* that there was a Use of Sarum, but the understanding of what it entailed, and which of its features required adoption, was subject to variation. In general, it can be said that the statutes and documentary references to the adoption and regulation of liturgy demonstrate some of the same inclinations as those mentioned with respect to the redaction of the texts. The earliest references to the adoption of Sarum liturgy refer specifically to a pattern associated with the worship of the new Salisbury Cathedral from its origins in the 1220s under bishop Richard Poore and later set down in the Ordinals of that place. Other statutory instruments illustrate various attempts to produce a standardized, uniform version of the liturgy *once associated* with Salisbury. Still other, contemporaneous documents enact a regional character or special features, such as local observation of a feast.

Ignoring for a moment the development of the Ordinal, a matter that will require some discussion, we should rehearse some of the now-accepted chronology of the 'Use'. The first apparent evidence for a retrievable, distinctive set of liturgical practices at Salisbury seems to date from the episcopacy of Richard Poore, *c.* 1217–28; Frere wrote that Sarum manuscripts had 'considerable fixity' from the early thirteenth century 'and in fact were beginning also to acquire [...] prestige'.[86] The revised Ordinal is said to have come into existence *c.* 1350–1400, and the general impression of modern scholarship is that something known as the Use of Sarum was introduced, in some form, across the province of Canterbury excluding the diocese of Hereford by *c.* 1325. Despite this conclusion the Use of Sarum was definitively imposed on clergy of the southern province only in 1542.[87]

The earliest history of the 'Use of Sarum' was once intertwined with the nostalgic myth of the institution of the liturgy of Salisbury Cathedral along with its customs and ritual by St Osmund, first bishop of the see of Salisbury and founder of the establishment of canons. From the fourteenth century onward it was believed that Osmund had constructed the Ordinal and Consuetudinary of Salisbury, although modern belief holds this not to be the case as these texts

---

[86] Francis Procter and Walter Howard Frere, *A New History of the Book of Common Prayer: With a Rationale of its Offices*, 3rd impr. (London: Macmillan, 1905), p. 20.

[87] *WC*, III, 861–62.

date from at least a century after his death. Osmund's liturgy, then, remains a mystery, as does the extent to which he can be credited for the character of the cathedral foundation.[88] Morgan suggests some facets of Sarum Use may have seen wider adoption from 1250 up to 1400; at the outset of this period it is highly unlikely that parish churches outside the diocese of Salisbury would have had any Sarum affiliation.[89] Pfaff is more specific: by *c.* 1290, with the new cathedral complete, he feels the idea of a liturgical feature *secundum usum Sarum* would have been more widespread.[90]

The Role of the Sarum Ordinal(s?)

Interpreting the role of the Ordinal in the development of Sarum is complicated by the absence of any uniform text with which it can be identified. It is important to recall that complete texts of the Office liturgy — as witnessed in breviaries, books which contained not only sungtexts but also lessons, prayers, and dialogues — were, in the later Middle Ages, a relatively new innovation. Frere's well known edition (in *The Use of Sarum*) is a pastiche of several copies, and his use of 'Old' and 'New' to denote two stages of development of the Ordinal makes it difficult to avoid the idea that first an original version, then a revised version of the Ordinal were promulgated. In reality, it is not at all clear what might have been the features in which 'considerable fixity' existed in the thirteenth century. Nigel Morgan has attempted to disambiguate the spread of the contents of the Sarum Consuetudinary, a procedural and administrative document, whose contents were borrowed from an early stage by a number of cathedral foundations including Wells and Lincoln,[91] from the spread of the contents of the Ordinal (which he suggests may have taken place in the 1320s). He tries to demonstrate that the process of imposition of Sarum associated (whether rightly or wrongly) with archbishop Henry Chichele in the fifteenth century was but the latest in a long series of actions to promulgate the Use of Sarum. Morgan would argue that the process took place in the years 1200–1350, well before Chichele's archiepiscopate, and that the Sarum kalendar, at a minimum, was well established in the province of Canterbury by

---

[88] Diana Greenway has asserted that the so-called 'Institutio Osmundi', a document allegedly dated 1091 which gives details of the duties and life of the office-holders in the cathedral, is a forgery. See Greenway, 'The false institutio of St Osmund'.

[89] Nigel Morgan, 'The Sanctorals of Early Sarum', pp. 143, 158.

[90] Pfaff, *LME*, p. 374.

[91] Morgan, 'The Introduction of the Sarum Kalendar'.

1325–50. After this point, Morgan suggests, most users of the Sarum kalendar would have *developed* [i.e. not copied] 'Sarum' texts for the feasts they were supposed to be celebrating,[92] although I suspect these texts were 'Sarum' not by any alliance with texts used in the cathedral, but by association with the self-identified Sarum kalendar.

All of these unsubstantiated hypotheses seem to demand some comprehension of the role of Ordinals, the documents which were most likely to have been working models for the imposition of Sarum of any date. Yet few facts are agreed upon with respect to the origins and later development of an Ordinal for Sarum Use, as the previous discussion of the textual families of the Ordinal in chapter 3 will have made clear.

The earliest documentary mention of an Ordinal is in a statute of bishop Gervase for St Davids, which prescribed in 1223 that the Offices of the Blessed Virgin Mary and of the Dead should be sung *secundum ordinale Sarum*.[93] Both Frere and Pfaff agree that the Consuetudinary (but not the Ordinal) dates from some point between 1173 and 1220, as it includes provisions for the main feast but not the translation of Thomas Becket.[94] Frere held that four distinguishable stages of development of the Ordinal were discernible: first, the 'Old Ordinal' which he associated with a date of *c.* 1270; next, the *Addiciones* which he prints and which form functional appendices to his text of the Old Ordinal, dated at *c.* 1278; a third stage, reflecting further corrections; and finally various forms of the 'New Ordinal', for which one of the identifying features is a brief reference to a previous version, *secundum antiquum Ordinale*. But there are problems with this model, not least the fact that none of the four stages appears ever to have attained textual unity: two witnesses of the *Addiciones*, BL Royal 5 E iii and Edinburgh UL MS 27, contain vastly different amounts of material. Furthermore, no manuscript source suggests that either the 'Old' or the 'New' Ordinal follows a fixed form, except as edited by Frere. In fact, the Risby Ordinal (BL Harley 1001) from which Frere copied the texts of the Ordinal and Consuetudinary in his edition (again, really a transcription) is of the early fourteenth century, and it is the earliest known such Ordinal. Pfaff states that 'no manuscript witness to what can fairly be characterized as a Sarum ordinal dates from earlier than the fourteenth century'.[95]

---

[92] Morgan, 'The Sanctorals of Early Sarum', p. 144.

[93] Haddan and Stubbs, I, 459.

[94] Pfaff, *LME*, p. 365.

[95] Pfaff, *LME*, p. 379.

It may then fairly be asked whether this fourteenth-century Ordinal represents a later stage of development, for instance the one witnessed by the Long versions of Sarum Office texts described in chapter 3. On perusal of the Adv-Long texts, for instance, convincing connexions can be seen between rubrics in Frere's 'Old Ordinal' (the fourteenth-century Risby Ordinal) and in witnesses of Adv-Long, most notably the long opening rubric setting the scene for Advent Sunday. Yet most of the rubrics of Adv-Short, where they exist, can also be associated strongly with those in the 'Old Ordinal'. It is worth mentioning that Frere calls Procter and Wordsworth's edition of the 1531 Great Breviary 'defective' in that it does not include the long Advent Sunday rubric. It must be pointed out here that the 1531 print is closest to the Adv-Short text, a conclusion that Frere does not reach.[96]

Caught in this problematic and theoretical sequence of events it will be useful here to make reference to a number of documents which may help to outline aspects of the contemporary understanding of Sarum Use and how it was adopted in venues other than in Salisbury diocese. In Dugdale's collection of foundation charters and statutes of ecclesiastical establishments, three documents make reference to an ordinal: a 1420 statute of William Heyworth, bishop of Lichfield, reads 'Insuper statuimus et ordinamus, quod singulis horis diei dicendis, necnon in antiphonis ad matutinas et vesperas, in festis duplicibus inchoandis, et psalmis intonandis, de cetero servetur forma Ordinalis Sarum'.[97] A comparable statute for the College of St Bartholomew, Tonge, Shropshire issued in 1410 by John, bishop of Coventry and Lichfield, had ordered that collects should be said *prout intitulantur in ordine secundum usum Sarum ecclesie*,[98] and the 1444 foundation statute of St Mary Magdalen, Battlefield, Shropshire, gives a similar prescription for the Office of the Dead.[99]

Three further statutes refer to Mass and Office according to the Use of Sarum. Thomas Barnesley, dean of the college of St John Baptist in Stoke by Clare, Suffolk, in 1422 ordered:

---

[96] Frere, *Use of Sarum*, II, xii.

[97] *Monasticon anglicanum: A History of the Abbies and other Monasteries, Hospitals, Frieries, and Cathedral and Collegiate Churches, with their Dependencies, in England and Wales*, ed. by William Dugdale, revised by John Caley, Henry Ellis, and Bulkeley Bandinel, 6 vols (London, 1817–30), VI, 1263. Hereafter, Dugdale, all page numbers from volume 6.

[98] Dugdale, p. 1407–08.

[99] Dugdale, p. 1428.

Quod in dicta ecclesia quotidie dicantur, secundum usum Sarum, iuxta rerum et personarum facultatem, matutine, vespere, et alie hore canonice, cum missa de die et de beata virgine cum nota, nisi quando missa de die erit de beata virgine, tunc loco illius dicatur missa de Requiem pro defunctis.[100]

At a much earlier point, the 1226 statute for Merewell, Hampshire of Henry de Blois, bishop of Winchester, merely states that the *divina vero officia secundum Saresbiriam celebrentur*.[101] The nuns of St Clare, Brusyard, Suffolk, according to a 1354 statute of William bishop of Norwich, were to have some masses in the chapel of the Annunciation according to the Use of Sarum.[102]

The statutes are not always clear in referring to specific services which might be celebrated according to a textual pattern. Two statutes of Antony Bek, bishop of Durham, for St Andrew, Bishop Auckland (1292) and Chester-le-Street (1286), refer to the *modo psallendi secundum morem ecclesie Eborum vel Salesberie*, a direction that seems to suggest more that the colleges should adopt some accepted method of singing the psalms rather than that of a particular Use.[103]

Other statutes deal with specific items. The statutes of the college of St Mary in St Davids issued in 1372 by Adam, bishop of Menevia, provide one of the earliest statements including the prescription 'secundum *usum* Sarum': 'Quandocunque tamen dicentur matutine de festis duplicibus in estate, et tribus diebus ante pascha, secundum usum Sarum hora vesperarum.'[104] The college of St Elizabeth had a statute issued by John bishop of Winchester in 1300 relating to the Lady Mass:

Post primum matutinarum diei, celebrent missam gloriose Virginis cum nota et solempnitate decenti, secundum usum et consuetudinem Saresburiensis ecclesie, qua celebrata incipiant horas de die, et terminent omnes cum nota. Quibus dictis incipiant horas beate Virginis submissa voce, et eas similiter omnes dicant.[105]

In all cases (save Bek's note on the 'modo psallendi') it is not clear what the practical result of the imposition of Sarum might be, other than that, for instance, the Lady Mass might be said from a book identified with the Use of Sarum. It

[100] Dugdale, p. 1419.
[101] Dugdale, p. 1344.
[102] Dugdale, p. 1555.
[103] Dugdale, pp. 1335, 1338.
[104] Dugdale, p. 1388.
[105] Dugdale, p. 1340.

is also worth mentioning, recalling matters of authority from the preceding section, that the imposition of Sarum on these new foundations is generally authorized by the founder of the institution.

The earliest stage of development, then, is characterized by a subtle programme of promulgation based on practices clearly associated with Salisbury Cathedral. Statutory evidence suggests that Sarum may have been privileged: the 'Use of Sarum' is seen as a desideratum from the reference of St Davids onward. Few if any liturgical specifics are given, though it is worth underlining the fact that there are several mentions of a Sarum Ordinal. The evidence from the statutes suggests that at this stage, components of the Salisbury liturgy, generally without any detail specified in the statutes, were being taken up, especially in new foundations.

Other statutory evidence, by contrast, attempt to formulate or propagate detailed forms of Office texts which, although associated with the 'Use of Sarum', often consciously in the texts of rubrics, probably bore little relation to the contemporary liturgical practices of the eponymous Cathedral. These forms appear in breviaries of the late fourteenth and fifteenth centuries. It might be the case that the Adv-Long texts discussed in chapter 3 are associated with this pattern: they are comprehensive enough to include considerable detail in rubrics about practical matters, and it has been suggested that the contents are edited to reflect concerns about the veracity or appropriateness of some of the lessons for saints' days. It has further been proposed that these 'generic' texts were the basis for the breviary revisions associated with Archbishop Henry Chichele during his archbishopric, and with other attempts to reform or standardize the Sarum liturgy as it appeared across the Southern province.

Reasons for Change

It must be asked whether the revision, especially of rubrics and lessons, was a result of necessity, or a desire to refocus the message conveyed whether on the redactors' own initiative or by reason of criticism. Walter Howard Frere wrote that the revision of liturgy may be attributed to a practical need for change, often precipitated by the addition of new observances or the promotion of existing ones, or perhaps by a need for greater accuracy in prescribing the rites. He suggests that a pattern of more or less continuous modification was normative, and that the *Addiciones* and augmentations of the Old Ordinal represent distinct intermediate steps between it and the creation of the New text.[106]

---

[106] Frere, *Use of Sarum*, II, xiii.

The Adv-Long version, whose manuscript witnesses date from the later four-teenth century onward, therefore appear to have great consistency; however, these manuscripts fall into a number of textual families, as has been seen in chapter 3. These variant readings may be able to illuminate both the ways that different components of the later Sarum pattern was modified in different ways.

Chapter 3 has indicated that variance from breviary to breviary is most significant in lesson texts. Work carried out over a number of years by Sherry Reames has tentatively identified several attempts to produce a 'standard' lectionary from which the breviary lessons were taken.[107] She identifies one attempt, witnessed in BL Addl 32427 and Salisbury Cathedral 152, both fif-teenth-century books, whose contents for Advent Sunday also demonstrate a consistent programme of redaction. Another revised lectionary is found in manuscripts corresponding roughly to the Short group, and was reproduced in the folio printed editions of the Sarum liturgy. The earliest, fourteenth-cen-tury revision she terms the 'Chichele' group, solely on the basis that Chichele's book, Lambeth Palace 69, is one of the witnesses.

Table 4.3: Groups of manuscripts studied by Reames.

Reames's Folio Group	
Downside MS 48244	BL Addl 52359
Durham, Cosin V.I.3	BL Harley 1512–1513
Edinburgh, Advocates Library 18.2.13b	BL Harley 2785
Edinburgh, UL 26	Bodl. University College 22
Edinburgh, UL 27	

Chichele Group	
Camb., Emmanuel College 64	BL Harley 2946
Camb., Peterhouse 270	BL Sloane 2566
Camb., University Library Addl 4500	Lambeth Palace 69
Camb., UL Dd.X.66	Bodl. Hatton 63
Colchester, Castle Museum 1932.213	Oxford, St John's College, 179
Durham, Cathedral Library, A.IV.20	Stonyhurst MS 52
	York Minster, XVI.O.12

---

[107] For example, Reames, 'Late Medieval Efforts at Standardisation'.

Like Frere, Reames proposes that the revision of liturgical material arose out of necessity: the Office was too elaborate and in fact unreasonable for secular clergy; there were an increasingly impractical profusion of saints; and the lessons, as they stood, were without focus and incoherent.[108] Helpfully, Reames suggests that on the basis of their liturgical evidence the books of the Chichele group were edited and checked during the process of manufacture, perhaps at a single scriptorium, and that they contain only the relevant Sarum feasts according to the Ordinal.[109]

Again it is worth enquiring into the extent to which this 'Chichele' textual stage was associated with the various stages of the Sarum Ordinal. It may be suggested that Adv-Long and the standardized texts are associated with one or the other of Frere's texts of the Ordinal. However, it is very important to note that the New Ordinal antedates Chichele's archbishopric. The *origin* of at least some of the 'standardized' texts must not lie with archbishop Chichele and his reputed efforts to reform the breviary. Lambeth Palace 69, Henry Chichele's own breviary, may have been produced before his elevation to Canterbury, for the archiepiscopal arms are added over the border decoration. Marks and Williamson speculate that the volume dates from between 1408 and 1414, while Chichele was bishop of St Davids, for the royal arms on the first folio are those used after 1406 and David (but not Chad) is original in the kalendar.[110] Reames does not identify the confector of this textual pattern, but it is certainly not Chichele.

If Chichele was ever involved in a wider reform of the Sarum breviary, he might have adopted pre-existing standardized forms, conscious or not that at least one of these was in his own breviary, as a good and convenient model. It does seem a defensible view that Chichele was involved in *a* reform of the breviary in general, even if we owe many elements of the standardized Office in particular either to a unified text associated with the 'Old'/Risby ordinal or the new version, or to a mutual ancestor. Trying to identify any text specifically tied to the reputed revision of Sarum by Chichele would be even more challenging than attempting to reconstruct a uniform text of the New Ordinal.

While it may be impossible to tie Henry Chichele or indeed any other individual to the textual developments that produced the standardized form of the

---

[108] Reames, 'Late Medieval Efforts', p. 108.

[109] Reames, 'Late Medieval Efforts', p. 102.

[110] *Gothic: Art for England 1400–1547*, ed. by Richard Marks and Paul Williamson (London: V&A, 2003).

Long group, it may certainly be proposed that Chichele did actively promote the observance of the (or a?) Use of Sarum in the Southern province during his archiepiscopate. The idea of Sarum looms large in a number of his acts, most prominently the adoption of Sarum Use at Chichester, during a metropolitical visitation of the cathedral in the absence of the bishop. Chichele's *Register* reproduces the following document, dated 17 August 1423:

> Ultra hec tunc ibidem communicatu extitit per dominum et inter decanum ac canonicos predictos de mutacione usus divini servicii in ecclesia illa Cicestren' in usum ecclesie Saresberie, et tandem fuit finaliter concordatum quod bene placuit omnibus et singulis mutacio usus servicii antedicti, et sic dominus concessit eisdem certos libros de dicto usu Saresburiensi ad honorem dei et augmentum divini servicii prelibati.[111]

A further document from two years later permitted the Benedictines of Abergavenny to use books of Sarum Use which were to be provided by Lady Joan Beauchamp. Here Chichele speaks of Sarum as a privileged example of a Use.

> Nos igitur usum illum Saresburien' *famosum et laudabilem* reputantes, et ne cultus divinus in domo vestra predicta ex causa per vos suggesta totaliter abstrahatur quod absit seu quomodolibet minuatur, vestris supplicacionibus tanquam racioni consonis favorabiliter inclinati.[112]

A parallel might be seen in his statute for the feast of John of Beverley, seen above, which called for the feast *cum servicio secundum usum Sarum in talibus fieri consueto*.

Chichele would not have been the first or only individual to think of the Use of Sarum as a standard to be emulated or introduced. A sample of wills proved before him during his archiepiscopate serve to illustrate contemporary attitudes. Some testators provided for chantry clergy to say offices for them 'iuxta regulam usus Sarisburiensis'.[113] Others donated their books to churches and cathedrals, identifying service books especially with Sarum: 'unum novam portiforium vocatum liggere de usu Saresburiensi ad serviendem Deo'.[114] Robert Rede, bishop of Chichester, in 1415 gave to Langley convent all his books 'pre-

---

[111] *The Register of Henry Chichele, Archbishop of Canterbury, 1414–1443*, ed. by E. F. Jacob, 4 vols (Oxford: Oxford University Press, 1937–47), III, 505. Hereafter *Reg. Chichele*.

[112] *Reg. Chichele*, IV, 274. Italics mine.

[113] *Reg. Chichele*, II, 231; II, 347.

[114] *Reg. Chichele*, II, 245: will of Thomas Herlyng, canon of Chichester, 1423.

ter libros [...] qui sunt de usu Saresburiensi'.[115] Some of these prescriptions are similar to the foundation statutes prescribing Sarum for collegiate chapels seen above, but others provoke questions. The will of Gerald Braybroke, knight (written 1427, d. 1429) provided to the church of Horsyndon, Buckinghamshire, 'an antiphoner after the new ordinal noted, also a portous [portable breviary?] of two volumes not noted with *legendes after the new ordinal*'.[116] This raises several issues: why was the author of the will aware of the (a?) New Ordinal? When was this ordinal new?

Wills of Chichester ecclesiastics are also witnesses of the process of adoption of Sarum, perhaps as a result of the cathedral having taken up the Use. The will of William Milton, dean, bequeathed his great missal to the high altar of the cathedral 'si usus Saresburiensis in dicte ecclesia Cicestrensi observetur et si non, tunc volo quod dictum missale sit in disposicione decani et capituli ecclesie Cicestrensis'.[117] He died in 1424, just after the change to Sarum. By 1429 Simon Northew, canon, gave to the cathedral, 'quatenus ad usum Saresburiensem se converterint, duo gradualia et duo processionalia'.[118]

An earlier and rather more prominent adopter of Sarum during the office of Archbishop Chichele was St Paul's Cathedral, in 1415 (replacing the Use of St Paul's, for which there is limited evidence except that of the commemoration of particular saints noted elsewhere in this chapter). Richard Pfaff notes that a liturgical book associated with St Paul's, and now MS 1 in its library, contains 'a template for the divine office' (described as a psalter by N. R. Ker) which was annotated in the early fourteenth century, perhaps by Ralph de Baldock, successively archdeacon of Middlesex, dean, and bishop of London. Pfaff suggests that the annotations represent 'liturgical doodling', but is reluctant to consider either the possibility that the editor was trying to construct a 'distinctive St Paul's Use' or to cause this St Paul's book to cohere with the understood basis for Sarum.[119] A principal problem with making either statement is that there are no contemporary reliable St Paul's or indeed Sarum texts with which to compare the annotations.

---

[115] *Reg. Chichele*, II, 38.

[116] *Reg. Chichele*, II, 412.

[117] *Reg. Chichele*, II, 287.

[118] *Reg. Chichele*, II, 401.

[119] Richard Pfaff, 'Bishop Baldock's Book, St Paul's Cathedral, and the Use of Sarum', in *Liturgical Calendars, Saints, and Services in Medieval England*, chapter XI.

The eventual resolution of the question of St Paul's liturgy is much clearer. On 25 October 1414, Richard, bishop of London, issued a mandate following a visitation deploring various faults in the worship of the cathedral, including the fact that choir clergy in the cathedral said the Office 'secundum quemdam antiquum usum sancti Pauli vulgariter nuncupatum, alii vero, maxime extra chorum, secundum usum Sarisburiensis.' From Vespers on 1 December, he ordered, all would say divine service according to the Use of Sarum, with the whole, including certain local feasts not in Sarum, to be called the New Use of St Paul's.[120]

Returning to the matter of Chichele, there is no suggestion that he had an active hand in the promulgation of Sarum in London, but the timing is notable: he was elected in March and papally confirmed in April. More important is the fact that in various circles, including several prominent cathedrals, something known as the Use of Sarum was being adopted as a standard.

One other feature of some of the lesson-redactions which began to appear in the late fourteenth century and became ubiquitous not long after was that they attempted to reduce the fanciful and dramatic stories in the lectionary that had been bewailed by those who sought a return to the Bible. The pre-Wycliffite tract *Of feigned contemplative life, c.* 1370, criticizes many aspects of worship, but attacks in particular the Sarum Ordinal (seemingly more important than the Commandments) and, notably, the manufacture of new and expensive books, perhaps in response to mandates to commission new books reflecting the new liturgical consensus:

> Also the ordinal of Salisbury letteth [i.e. prevents] much preaching of the gospel, for fools charge that more than the commandments of God and to study and teach Christ's Gospel; for if a man fail in his Ordinal men hold that great sin and reprove him thereof fast, but if a priest break the hest of God men charge that little or nothing [...] but, Lord, what was the priest's office ordained by God before that Salisbury use was made of proud priests, covetous, lecherous and dronkelewe?

> [...] Ah, Lord, if all the study and travail that men have now about Salisbury use with multitude of new cost[l?]y portos, antiphonals, grails, and all other books were turned into making of bibles and in studying and teaching thereof, how much should God's law be furthered and known and kept.[121]

---

[120] William Sparrow Simpson, 'On a Mandate of Bishop Clifford', paper delivered to the Society of Antiquaries of London 7 April 1892, printed in *Proceedings of the Society of Antiquaries of London*, 2nd ser., 14 (1891/1982), 126–27.

[121] 'Of Feigned Contemplative Life', a tract edited in *The English Works of Wyclif, Hitherto*

Reames notes that whilst the reduction of the length of lessons, above other matters, was probably a priority of the redactors, the new lessons were also 'sober and restrained', managing to convey the details of the life and miracles of saints without unnecessary or graphic detail, 'greatly reducing both the indications of supernatural power and the defiant speeches and acts [...] that make other versions of these legends so entertaining and sometimes so subversive-looking in their social implications'.[122] She points in particular to the modification of the legend of Silvester, which gains much more realistic features: 'it is tempting to consider', writes Reames, 'that this recension was trying to meet the Wycliffites part-way, doing its best to prove Silvester's sanctity while ridding his legend of the kinds of stories that they considered most objectionable.'[123] While Reames is reluctant to ascribe the task of redaction entirely to this largely negative requirement Jeremy Catto has underlined the opposition of the Lollards, and argued that Sarum 'attests the vitality and importance of public communal worship in the Church's response to Lollardy'.[124] The new feasts which were added to the kalendar in the early fifteenth century were liturgical expressions of private devotion. It is Catto who suggests that 'in the interests of standardization Chichele may have encouraged the adoption throughout the province of Canterbury of the Sarum Use'.[125] He does not, as Morgan intimates,[126] suggest that this is when the promulgation of Sarum *started*.

In short, the efforts to standardize and make generic the Sarum Office were witnessed by the manufacture of breviaries containing an exceptionally rich selection of rubrics and with standardized, abridged lessons. Earlier manuscripts were altered to suit the new requirements,[127] whilst new volumes may have been manufactured in specific locations and according to the prescriptions of one recension of the Ordinal, for their contents (and often format)

Unprinted, ed. by F. D. Matthew (London: Published for the Early English Text Society by Trübner, 1880), pp. 192–94. Spelling has been modernized. Although Matthew thinks 'this is an early work of Wyclif's' (p. 187), Pfaff, in consultation with Anne Hudson, writes 'the treatise is now not thought to be Wyclif', and assigns it to the date supplied above. Pfaff, *LME*, p. 415.

[122] Reames, 'Standardisation and Reform', p. 108.

[123] Reames, 'Standardisation and Reform', p. 113.

[124] Catto, 'Religious Change', p. 109.

[125] Catto, 'Religious Change', p. 109.

[126] Morgan, 'The Introduction of the Sarum Kalendar'.

[127] Pfaff notes that in particular Longleat MS 10 and Bodl. Bodley 948 both have all the required additions. See Pfaff, *LME*, p. 441.

are nearly identical. Certainly the lists of saints provided for in the Ordinals achieved some esteem, and the appearance of consistent saints in the Sarum and York normative kalendars of chapter 2 seems to confirm this. These contents, a locally adaptable Office liturgy known as the Use of Sarum, eventually achieved general currency.

Was the new breviary an effort at reform? Yes, if one or both of the explanations are accepted: either the Lollard argument or the need for realistic working editions of the breviary with sufficient rubrical detail. Morgan writes that the revision of the breviary may, however, have simply been an attempt to introduce uniformity to the liturgy of the Southern ecclesiastical province, where we have no solid evidence of uniform diocesan Uses before Sarum.[128] Whether one of the forces behind the propagation of the 'generic' features of Sarum breviaries was Henry Chichele will not be known, although he was in a principal position of responsibility, and had concerns both for the adoption of Sarum liturgy and for the suppression of Lollardy. Both the 'Use of Sarum' as a concept and the standardized textual forms reflected by the Adv-Long rubrics were being promulgated by the time of Chichele's archiepiscopate.

* * *

Other probably conterminous editorial impulses, as has been stated, were preoccupied not with establishing total consistency but adding to an existing liturgical pattern. Some of the manuscripts which are witnesses to these inclinations are clearly linked to the Adv-Long rubrics and associated with the Ordinal, but contain textual or rubrical features associated with specific venues, and may be associated with an extreme attention to detail. The persistence of regional variation in the face of the imposition of uniformity, and the proliferation of new material, may be attributed to the persistence of local interests and devotions, and highlight the complex and interconnected influences on the final years of the Latin Office liturgy in England.

The appearance of localized content is not unexpected. Despite John Grandisson's 1329 request for an ancient and truthful exemplar from Salisbury which could be copied for Exeter, the resulting local pattern represented a conscious departure from Sarum, identified with Grandisson's own cathedral. The synodal feasts of Norwich (and the *constitutiones* of Dublin) draw attention to the fact that they, as a group, are not part of the typical kalendar and were believed to be instituted by a local decision-making process. One attempt

---

[128] Morgan, 'The Sanctorals of Early Sarum', p. 159.

to refocus the attention of clergy and to provide practical guidance was the *Directorium Sacerdotum* written by the Bridgettine Clement Maidstone in the 1440s. The *Directorium* attempted to determine and codify rules for the observance of feasts, their convergence, and their particular observances, especially where existing Sarum ordinals were deficient or contradictory.[129] The existence of tension between 'centralizing authority' and 'local traditions' as might produce local variants has been investigated by Reames, who notes several points in one early fourteenth-century manuscript, Edinburgh University MS 26, where a reader may choose between the Sarum version and a local variant.[130]

The establishment of local characteristics is complicated, not least because the wide variety of influences and circumstances which produced them makes their elucidation rather difficult. In addition, an apparently 'local' feature may appear in a manuscript corresponding in other areas to the 'standardized' texts, or influenced by other proclivities. By definition, no consistent pattern of saints develops or is promulgated in kalendar or Sanctorale; and casual perusal of the texts does not instantly reveal the differences. Chapter 3 discusses how one pair of books (Bodl. Hatton 63, of the fourteenth century, and the fifteenth-century Oxford St John's 179) seem to contain additional directions based on a common resource of new material, some of it from the New Ordinal. Another pair of fifteenth-century books, BL Addl 32427 and Salisbury Cathedral 152, contains similar detail and also provides additional liturgical texts in the form of extra prosas, perhaps to cover processions which resulted from some local circumstance; otherwise they may have been simply examples of the elaboration of the later liturgy. These books are also the only two witnesses of a vernacular aspersion chant, which may represent one of the earliest examples of the genre in English.[131] Finally Durham Univ. Cosin V. I. 3 and BL Royal 2 A XII, of the fifteenth century, are both (independent) examples whose idiosyncratic versions of the text may be the result of individual editorial rendering. The fact that the features which appear in these manuscripts bear no relation to any documentary rendering, and that they are apparently idiosyncratic in the manuscript tradition, suggest a decentralized approach to redaction.

---

[129] The several versions of Maidstone's *Directorium* are given in *The Tracts of Clement Maydeston, with the Remains of Caxton's Ordinale*, ed. by Christopher Wordsworth, Henry Bradshaw Society, 7 (London, 1894).

[130] Reames 'Unexpected Texts for Saints', p. 171.

[131] For which see Matthew Cheung Salisbury, 'A Fifteenth-Century Aspersion Chant', *Plainsong and Medieval Music Society*, online edns (2010). < http://plainsong.org.uk/assets/downloads/PMMS-Aspersio.pdf> [accessed 25 June 2013].

The local character of books may have also had an effect on patterns of veneration of saints. With respect to the kalendar, Morgan points to 'some persistence of local diocesan use' in Exeter, Ely, Norwich, and Chichester, normally meaning the retention of local saints, or their addition to the 'standard' Sarum kalendar as a group. This was especially likely if the relics of the saints were present. He points out that many local feasts were suppressed and that there was perceived reluctance to adopt the entirety of Sarum, including the kalendar. It might be the case that local saints continued to be venerated and that this is witnessed by their appearance in the kalendars of individual books.[132] Similarly, Reames reports that the appearance of Sarum lessons 'in more than a dozen textual families' — including one which she identifies in the lessons of BL Addl 32427 / ESC 152 — may also be evidence that there was some amount of local control over manuscript contents, and that at the imposition of Sarum users preferred to keep existing lessons, 'but in shorter forms'.[133]

In summary, both 'standardizing' and 'localizing' impulses may be seen at the same time in the history of the promulgation of the Use of Sarum throughout the fourteenth and fifteenth centuries, sometimes even in the same manuscripts. Among the more obvious local features are rubrics, often extended, providing for local celebration of the Office or specific points such as processions, personnel, or movement; the introduction of feastdays or patterns of saints not widely promulgated among the preponderance of English sources; and the presence of local texts or rubrics contrasted with those identified as 'Sarum'. Such manuscripts as Durham Cosin V. I. 3, BL Addl 32427, Salisbury Cathedral 152, BL Hatton 63, and Oxford St John's 179 are notable, identifiable examples which bear at least some of these characteristics.

The introduction of the Use of Sarum, or at least textual traditions associated with it, is clearly a development which is at least as old as the 1223 statute of Gervase, bishop of St Davids, which ordered the Lady Office and the Office for the Dead to be sung *secundum Ordinale Sarum* at St Davids.[134] But to say that a wholesale pattern was unambiguously adopted in all succeeding copies of the breviary would be to ignore a great deal of diversity and inconsistency which documentary records do not always reveal. Morgan demonstrates that the introduction of the Sarum kalendar took place over a longer period than has sometimes been suggested. He argues in his most recent work that

---

[132] Morgan, 'The Introduction of the Sarum Kalendar', pp. 184–93.

[133] Reames, 'Late Medieval Efforts at Standardisation', p. 92.

[134] Haddan and Stubbs, I, 459.

the introduction of the Sarum kalendar, above any other feature, is indicative of the taking-up of the Use, although it is impossible to tell when or how in any specific scenario on the basis of surviving evidence.[135] The 'Chichele' group of manuscripts, and any revision of the liturgy (or imposition of the pattern) contemporary with Chichele himself, may indeed be in line with the principles of some Ordinal. But, as Pfaff has written, Ordinals were inevitably an 'idealization', '[a] theoretical norm which a combination of innovation, laziness, and individualism rapidly made obsolete'.[136] This absence of an archetype helps to explain the profusion of variants, whether conservative differences from the Ordinal or wholesale change. As the first section of this chapter has suggested, a locally mutable liturgical pattern, which could be changed by the diocesan bishop or other authority, might be the context in which considerable textual variation, including local amendments, was allowed to exist.

Over three centuries of dominance, Sarum Use never took a form which was supported by official promulgation or an explicit list of features; instead, beyond the idea that some observance *secundum usum Sarum* was authoritative and theoretically associated with the mother cathedral, the form it took from place to place was moderated by friction between authoritative prescriptions and local practice.

It is worth mentioning that the 'codification' or adoption of Sarum, a process which varied in character on every occasion when the Use was taken up, is not directly comparable to the sixteenth- and twentieth-century codifications of the Roman rite or to the introduction of the Prayer Book. It has been demonstrated that the adoption of Sarum *characteristics* was far from comprehensive. Various versions of the Sarum Ordinal, an entity that changed measurably within even the surviving witnesses, provided a system of generally applicable guidelines and key contents (i.e. sungtexts and rubrics), whilst the specifics, found in the kalendar and Sanctorale as well as in the lessons of many feasts, may have been drawn from local tradition. It may be the case that editorial decisions (either for the production of books or the performance of liturgy) were necessarily constrained by local circumstances (including available exemplars) and by local preference, as well as by the functionality of the worship space, the number and skills of clergy and clerks, and other practical matters. It seems very unlikely that a parish church of even moderate size would have been able to produce cathedral-style liturgy according to the rubrics. Inevitably editorial

---

[135] Morgan, 'The Sanctorals of Early Sarum', pp. 143–44.
[136] Pfaff, 'New Liturgical Observances in Later Medieval England', p. 2.

decisions must also have been tied to the spirituality and particular practices of their users. An attempt to discuss difference among breviaries of a Use occupies the next part of this chapter.

Mouvance, Textual Stability, and the Copying and Revision of Liturgy

In chapter 3 I proposed three categories for the variation in English liturgical books: random textual 'drift'; unconscious, instinctual change; and deliberate change. Similarly, in her study of liturgical lessons for St Cecilia Sherry Reames suggests four categories for the transmission or reproduction of lessons: 1) a complete reproduction; 2) the employment of verbatim excerpts to replace a longer text; 3) the abridgment of an existing version with no new words; and 4) the abridgment by omission and/or rewording. Reames's categories offer more specificity to the variants encompassed by 'deliberate change'. These categories are all means of organizing the concept of expressive textual variation, informative and perhaps capable of revealing how a text has been transmitted. Derek Pearsall has written that the body of manuscript evidence becomes like a 'spoil-heap' or 'midden' from which archaeologists attempt to derive information about past civilizations. The information derived from individual witnesses may not normally be documented in the 'antiseptic operating theatre of the "critical edition"'.[137] More radically, Bernard Cerquiglini has written that with respect to the Middle Ages, since 'the variance of a medieval work is its primary character', 'every manuscript is a revision, a version'; 'every edition is a theory', proposals that not only suggest that the production of critical editions of medieval texts is flawed, but also that the texts themselves may not enjoy any noticeable stability whatever.[138] The applicability of these principles to the Sarum breviary, ostensibly a uniform text associated with the vicissitudes of a single venue but in fact one subject to myriad influences on its contents, not least the independent vicissitudes of every one of the innumerable venues in which the Sarum Office was celebrated, is unambiguous: Pfaff notes that 'the

---

[137] Derek Pearsall, 'Texts, Textual Criticism, and Fifteenth-Century Manuscript Production', in *Fifteenth-Century Studies*, ed. by Robert F. Yeager (Hamden, CT: Archon Books, 1984), pp. 121–36 (pp. 121–22).

[138] Bernard Cerquiglini, *In Praise of the Variant*, trans. by Betsy Wing (Baltimore: The Johns Hopkins University Press, 1999), pp. 38, 78. Despite this, critical editions are perceived as the zenith of all scholarship, writes Cerquiglini in his first chapter, since they are the foundation of most courses of literary and classical study.

variation among books nominally classed as of the Sarum rite is enormous.'[139] Even the Ordinals, guidelines for the carrying-out of services and models for service books, have an unclear lineage, but must have had an important role to play, especially in the take-up of the Sarum kalendar.

This type of meaningful textual variation has been discussed by Paul Zumthor and others in developing the concept of *mouvance*, meaningful textual mobility, a development which had been predicated by the anti-Lachmannian rhetoric of Joseph Bédier, who pointed out that the creation of a critical edition of an archetypical medieval text, one that had never necessarily existed, ought to be sidelined in favour of a more careful, scientific treatment of the extant textual traditions.[140] Zumthor suggested that an *œuvre*, a complete summation of the various *états du texte*, could not be defined as a static entity, but one which frequently changed its form and content over the period of its production and transmission, with each successive state an equally viable example around which an *apparatus criticus* could conceivably be constructed.[141] Any attempt to construct an edition of a medieval text would be foiled by the inaccessibility of the circumstances contemporary to any such recension of the work. We cannot produce parameters for the editing of a medieval text — the Divine Office — that has no author (we might ask with Barthes: has the author ever existed in this context?), which is preserved in copies for which we rarely have any information as to manufacture or motivations for scribal intervention, and which may or may not have had a role as script or prescription for actual performance.

Nevertheless some of the variance may be (to us) inexplicable. Stephen G. Nichols has pointed out some of the parameters of the 'manuscript matrix': discussing poetics, he notes that 'Scribal reworkings may be the result of changing aesthetic tastes in the period between the original text production and the copying [...]. The scribe's "improvements" imply a sense of superior judgment or understanding *vis-à-vis* the original poet'.[142] The scribes of late medieval liturgical manuscripts were not using their own judgement, but the statement is worth mentioning. The manuscript matrix is a series of 'gaps or interstices', writes Nichols, which are produced by scribal participation in the text, which

---

[139] Pfaff, 'Prescription and Reality in the Rubrics of Sarum Rite Service Books', p. 204.

[140] Discussed in Joseph Bédier, 'La tradition manuscrite du Lai de l'Ombre: Réflexions sur l'art d'éditer les anciens textes', *Romania*, 54 (1928), 161–96.

[141] Paul Zumthor, *Essai de poétique médiévale*, new edn (Paris: Seuil, 2000), p. 72.

[142] Nichols, 'Philology in a Manuscript Culture', p. 8.

he attributes, after Lacan, to 'pulsations of the unconscious'.[143] The employment of 'unconscious' change in my model of difference for liturgical text pre-
sumes that random drift (for instance, *ad* + accusative instead of employing the
dative) is not predicated by the particular scribe, rather that the character of the
unconscious changes made by a scribe is as much a product of his circumstances
as the conscious changes he may also make. This conclusion and the apparent
grounding of the unconscious variation in local circumstances serves to highlight the centrality and indeed viability of the local, and local preference, in the
continuing act of revising and reworking that is the transmission of liturgical
text. It will be no surprise for opponents of the *grand récit* or for those who
study the local character of the late medieval Church that under-examined copies of an ostensibly uniform text, when viewed as individuals, reveal that the
authority behind those copies can be found at a surprisingly local level.

The manuscripts of the York Office, writes Reames, are among the most
consistent as to textual uniformity, but within their contents are still examples
of *mouvance* which seem to abbreviate lessons by excerpting *verbatim* other,
longer examples of those lessons. With respect to Sarum, she writes that 'the
order of the day was obviously revision, not uniformity, and a remarkably large
number of people — from official and semi-official compilers to mere copyists
— seem to have participated in the process'.[144] Notably, Reames uses the term
'revision' here. Changes in text must not be attributed solely to 'drift' — they
are certainly a product of users' and scribes' habits *but also of their intentions*
which as a result of this study can sometimes be hinted at.

Chapters 3 and 4 have suggested how it may be possible to suggest some
of these intentions on the basis of the witnesses they have produced: in some
cases there seems to have been a need to provide more information, or more
locally specific information; or to reduce the length of the lessons; or to revise
their content. It is worth recalling that both 'standardizing' and 'localizing'
impulses are contemporaneous, and may also be subject to random or unconscious variation, or indeed *deliberate* variation, which may or may not affect the
performance result. Evidently copy-specific details caused by deliberate changes
are transmitted equally with components of the text — such as the rubric *ubi
vero dedicata est ecclesia in honore* — which permit a breviary to be used in any
venue, or at least not one specific venue. Morgan suggests that once Sarum
became widely used, Sarum breviaries would have been produced in large num-

---

[143] Nichols, 'Philology in a Manuscript Culture', p. 9.

[144] Reames, '*Mouvance* and interpretation', p. 169.

bers, 'easy to commission or [...] readily available for purchase',[145] presumably promulgating a relatively generic model of the text — though perhaps not.

Scribes certainly did not have a blank template upon which to impose their own preferences, nor were they likely to have no opinion about the established (and therefore correct) pattern in which the Office was rendered textually. It is far more likely that when Sarum was imposed, realistically from the fourteenth century onward, many features of existing local practice may have been retained. Local lessons, in particular, had a good chance of retention, as no Sarum Ordinal known to us contains full prescriptions for lessons, or even for the texts from which they should be drawn, merely an indication of how many proper lessons there should be, as Reames reminds us.[146]

Inevitably our conceptions of the priorities of scribes, local authorities, and national projects to standardize the liturgy must fall short of certainty. 'We lack a grasp', wrote David Chadd, 'of the *mentalité* which makes one course of events more likely', nevertheless *any* hypothesis for scribal participation in the creation and recreation of liturgical texts should be considered as 'much in history must eventually be reducible from theorems to people'.[147]

Rose Walker has aptly illustrated the fact that the idea of change, particularly in a liturgical context, might have been seen as problematic or even heretical.[148] Nevertheless it seems to have been authorized by a much decentralized process. Whilst the scribe was certainly responsible for random or unconscious change, he may not have been personally accountable for deliberate change. Books for service in a cathedral, a good example of decentralized authority, may have been checked by several senior figures either in the scriptorium or from the chapter: paraphrasing several prescriptive documents, Edwards suggests that this was the role of the precentor or cantor, while the Sarum New Customary includes this task in the role of the cathedral chancellor.[149] In any event the introduction of a new copy of a service book was the result of several processes, from the realization that a new book needed to be produced, to the

---

[145] Morgan, 'The Sanctorals of Early Sarum', p. 159.

[146] Reames, 'Unexpected Texts for Saints', p. 169.

[147] David Chadd, 'An English Noted Breviary of circa 1200', in *Music in the Medieval English Liturgy*, pp. 205–38 (pp. 224–25).

[148] Rose Walker, *Views of Transition: Liturgy and Illumination in Medieval Spain* (London: British Library and University of Toronto Press, 1998), p. 21.

[149] Edwards, *English Secular Cathedrals*, pp. 164, 319, and article 6 of the Salisbury New Customary.

commissioning of the volume and the search (if necessary) for an exemplar, to the choice of contents both before and during its manufacture, to the verification stage, if it existed. Neither extremity of scribal or other intervention is likely to have been the case, but the opportunities for deliberate redaction must be remarked upon.

Conclusions

The history of authoritative influence on Anglo-Saxon liturgical books neatly anticipates later developments. Other than general impressions of the contemporary understanding of liturgical patterns from historical accounts, and the large-scale organizing projects which sought to impose order on English monastic communities, it seems that the liturgical framework of the early Middle Ages in England was controlled at an institutional level. This is reasonable since the liturgies for which we have the most evidence are from monastic houses and other communities. There seem to have been few standardizing features (except perhaps a Benedictine inheritance common to most of the monastic sources), certainly not such features as regulated the later practice of the two ecclesiastical provinces. Dumville's comment about the lack of evidence for the Anglo-Saxon period may hold true until the end of the thirteenth century, for which even a reliable account of Sarum practice is lacking. The elements of uniformity seen in the later sources discussed in previous chapters, then, are striking.

There was certainly a measure of uniformity in the feastdays celebrated in the kalendars of the two principal post-Conquest Uses, a character demonstrated by the normative kalendars of chapter 2. In addition to long-standing observances these kalendars also included feasts of later date which had been endorsed by English hands at a number of levels. To answer one of the questions posed at the beginning of this chapter — who authorized saints for liturgical veneration? — the provincial authorization of feastdays was typical, but there is evidence that the diocesan bishop (or perhaps a still more local authority) moderated and sometimes determined the list of observances at local level, as Haggh has argued for Cambrai. John Grandisson and Exeter present an obvious candidate for this practice. Certainly the re-promulgation of orders by several levels (pope, archbishop, diocesan, suffragan, archdeacon) allowed for, and appeared to stimulate, the realistic provision for the observance in practical terms. In terms of how consistently feasts were added to kalendars by this process, it can be said that the feasts added from Edmund in 1246 onward to Osmund in 1481 are the most frequent addition to kalendars, and that they appear with considerable frequency. Whilst the saints appearing in the normative kalendars are witness to the consistency of the Sarum kalendar as a conception, the appearances of seemingly random feasts in individual kalendars have been associated with the persistence of regional observances which may have predated the Sarum kalendar.

More broadly, the adoption of the 'Use of Sarum', a pattern which nominally and conceptually has been understood to mean the adoption of a single, fixed text, apparently took place in different ways and with differing intentions. At the outset, and periodically thereafter, the adoption of Sarum meant the adoption of the real, contemporary pattern of liturgy at Salisbury; elsewhere and later it meant the imposition of a generic set of sungtexts and rubrics merely associated with the cathedral liturgy; in other places, local variation appeared, especially to provide detail in the rubrics or additional material. At no point, however, is it ever possible to say that the complete liturgical practice of Salisbury Cathedral was being adopted anywhere, in part owing to immense functional differences in the institutions which adopted it, from availability of personnel, to the presence of side-altars, to the length and direction of processions.

The medieval Church, Eamon Duffy has written, was a 'culture which was rooted in a repertoire of inherited and shared beliefs and symbols, while remaining capable of enormous flexibility and variety'.[150] Even the Ordinal, the text which ought to regulate and provide a model, was subject to several contemporary textual strains. But certainly a form of Sarum kalendar, consistent responsory series and other sungtexts, and several families of rubrics were being promulgated: not all witnesses of these were identical in other ways, however, and the kalendar and Sanctorale witness a variety of permutations of the adoption of later feasts.

The manuscript evidence suggests the coexistence, especially in the fifteenth century but also earlier, of standardizing impulses which sought to create a uniform, generic form for the Sarum breviary, and the concurrent persistence and, in cases, the creation of local characteristics, the latter probably helped by the fact that efforts toward standardization were also promulgated by local authorities. Both deliberate and 'unconscious'/instinctual change were likely to affect the contents of the books during the process of manufacture, and consequently any performance result.

Rather than condensing regional variation and copy-specific detail into a critical edition, an artificial process, the variants and individuated versions of the Office liturgy have given rise in this study to normative and regional

---

[150] Duffy, *The Stripping of the Altars*, p. 3.

liturgical kalendars and textual families; indeed, they permit some hypotheses about how and why liturgical texts changed from copy to copy. While they do not provide an unimpeachable critical edition for those who would desire one, these conclusions, proposing a set of tools for analysis, may be more useful than any putative edition for those who are interested in the development and reception of the late medieval English liturgy, and for those who need to know how to interpret its sources.

CONCLUSION

Having enumerated some of the difficulties with previous work on the English liturgy, chapter 1 proposes a model for studying all known, complete sources of the late medieval Office as unique witnesses. Pfaff's model of uniformity for medieval liturgical books provides a starting point for a quantitative approach to their study, attempting to assess both the common features of all books associated with a particular Use and the nature and significance of the variation within the same set of sources. It establishes that the variation among, for instance, Sarum breviaries is the enabler of their value as witnesses for ecclesiastical history. After an account of the historiographical situation in liturgical studies, it is shown that the analysis of these books required first a liturgical study of as many witnesses as possible, addressing the choice, order, and modification of liturgical contents based on their format and exploiting characteristic genres of text (responsory series, contents of kalendars). This analysis was followed by a more traditional textual analysis, word by word, of four selected feastdays which illustrate some of the textual families into which the sources can be sorted.

In chapter 2, the history of the responsory series as an analytical tool is given. It is shown that over 75% of series collected here conform to one of two patterns, associated with the Uses of Sarum and York. These series are absolutely consistent within books of those two Uses. The remaining series are compared with those collected in Hesbert's *Corpus Antiphonalium Officii* in order to identify a place of use, and the consistency of series within individual manuscripts, and within books associated with the same place of use, is underlined. Responsory series are proposed as a constituent of a Use's 'fingerprint'. The consistency of sungtexts in general and the centrality of responsories to the character of an observance, relating through text the significance of the saint or feastday celebrated, are likely to be the reasons for the stability of responsories and their viability as identifiers.

A method of transcribing and analysing the final-state contents of liturgical kalendars is then presented, allowing for the grouping of sources by shared variant from a 'base version'. Pairs and then groups of manuscripts are associated by their number of shared points of divergence from this version. Some kalendars associated in this way are shown to be related by geographical origin, others by Use, and others by various connexions, and it is suggested that closely allied kalendars may be a hint of a relationship among otherwise unrelated manuscripts. Comprehensive lists are given of all Dedication and Relics feasts (where possible identifying the venue or saint for which they are given). The phenomenon of the 'synodal' feast (an example of local influence, imposed by diocesan synod) is described and the extent of synodal feasts in kalendars is identified. It has always been assumed that a kalendar entry indicated at least some degree of observance. This is most likely true, but a kalendar entry alone should never be assumed to mean that there were any other provisions for the observance in the manuscript. In fact, it is rare for proper contents for a saint added to a kalendar to be added to the Sanctorale, perhaps beyond a proper collect. On the basis of more kalendars than have yet been studied concurrently, lists of characteristic 'regional saints' which exist in the majority of kalendars hailing from various geographical divisions are proposed for the first time. Comparative tables of the 'normative' Sarum, York, and Hereford observances are supplied, each a constitutive criterion of its Use.

Following this analysis, in chapter 3 results were presented from the word-by-word textual collation of three Offices (Advent Sunday, Thomas, the Dead) from twenty-eight manuscripts, and a further regional Office (William) from sixteen manuscripts. Having completed analysis of the texts in an abstract sense in chapter 2, this editorial task was undertaken to illuminate the types of variation in the actual texts. There appear to be a number of textual families within Sarum books; the reasons for this (changing preoccupations influencing the version of Sarum liturgy promulgated from time to time) are outlined. The case study of St William of York shows how the construction and promulgation of a proper office could be seen as an attempt to enhance the status of a saint. Each Office shows that while responsory series (and sungtexts more generally) are very consistent across witnesses, rubrics and lessons are most subject to variation from copy to copy such that no two witnesses are identical. It is suggested that this is because these two genres of text are most easily altered without damaging the coherence of the Office, and more importantly because they were the sections which local preoccupations would affect. The chapter ends by characterizing three categories of variants in the sources (random, inadvertent, and deliberate), and suggesting that deliberate changes, which result in demonstrably different performance results, can help to identify the motivations behind the development and redaction of the widespread 'Sarum' practice.

It was also necessary to situate the results from the liturgical and textual analyses in their historical context, and to evaluate to what degree they corresponded to the documentary record of influences on the practice of the liturgy. In chapter 4, it is suggested that the history of liturgical influence is, in fact, the history of the institutions in which it was performed. The individualistic patterns of the early Middle Ages, centred on the idiosyncratic practices of distinct religious houses, were eventually supplanted (at least in the secular cursus) by the adoption of wide-scale patterns, especially the Use of Sarum which, at least in principle, was promulgated first as the authoritative and praiseworthy liturgy of Salisbury Cathedral and then, more chaotically, on a much more extensive basis. The imposition of a Sarum kalendar, to give one example, was an attempt to clarify the veneration of saints across the Southern province, but in some cases the other saints in antecedent kalendars survived in local patterns. New features were added over time, either by authority or based on local preferences. The authority of the diocesan bishop as arbiter of these persistent local patterns, and of the introduction of newly canonized saints, is demonstrated by the local bishop's role in the documentary evidence. In general the adoption of the 'Use of Sarum' surely never meant the wholesale adoption of the precise practices of Salisbury Cathedral: for the most part, it meant the appearance of some textual pattern *secundum usum Sarum* (at least nominally) which was modified and added to as was felt necessary. The fact that no two Sarum breviaries may be entirely alike (and indeed that the very existence of two very similar Sarum breviaries, BL Addl 32427 and Salisbury Cathedral 152, was notable) must underline the importance of studying as many sources as possible, in order to enumerate the variation between sources, and to explore what that variation may mean.

In attempting to contextualize and clarify some of these observations, it might be timely to reconsider the five preconceptions which were described in chapter 1, in light of this new evidence.

1. *The English liturgy was, from copy to copy within a given time period, relatively static, particularly since much care was taken to produce apparently careful and conservative copies.*

There is much evidence for medieval attempts to ensure the consistency and uniformity of liturgical observances, especially at diocesan level and at episcopal visitations, where books were often inspected, but there appears to have been greater diversity than might be expected. The textual evidence from the manuscripts supports the idea that there were at least several textual families for Sarum, the most frequently observed Use, but that fundamentally these enjoyed a great deal of stability. Certain elements of the liturgy — sungtexts and sometimes rubrics — were less prone to variation than were lessons. Much greater regional diversity can be seen in the prescription and take-up of saints in the kalendar. It is unclear how and to what degree manuscripts were edited or checked on the fly during the act of copying. Some manuscripts show the effects of deliberate modification of a common pattern. Others vary in minor copy-specific details, but fundamentally provide the same information.

2. *The English liturgy was derived from a Roman model which itself derives from antiquity, and there is a clear line of organic development which shows that later versions are outgrowths and/or revisions of earlier ones.*

English kalendars, like all kalendars of the Western liturgy, contain feastdays and observances which have their origin in Roman practices. The Office had common features across Western Christianity. There is very little evidence for the Anglo-Saxon Office which can be illuminated by manuscript evidence; the post-Conquest Office is fundamentally Norman in character, a historical contention supported by evidence from liturgical manuscripts, especially responsory series, and the Sarum and York textual patterns no doubt derive their substantial common features from shared origins. It is not suitable to comment here on the apostolicity of the English Church or its liturgy.

3. *There were about five liturgical Uses in England at the Reformation, distinct enough to be identifiable, and they formed the basis of the Prayer Book liturgy that replaced them.*

There were two great secular Uses in England at the Reformation, Sarum and York. Witnesses of either Use can be identified by several diagnostic criteria, especially on the basis of a cumulative analysis of their kalendars and responsory series. Hereford Use shares a number of features, including responsories for Advent and the Dead, with Sarum. Whether these are a result of shared origins or the borrowing of material from Sarum is unclear. Nevertheless the medieval use of Hereford was something that was distinct (so much so that a printed breviary could be produced) and its textual pattern and self-identification are to be noted. There are no realistic witnesses to the Uses of Lincoln or Bangor although Exeter and St Paul's seem to have had self-designated diocesan (or at least cathedral) patterns.

4. *A liturgical text can be successfully edited by transcribing and comparing the texts (and possibly music) of several printed editions (or manuscripts, if any are present).*

It is again here repeated that every liturgical source, whether manuscript or printed, must be considered as a unique witness, in order to understand both the extent of variation and the degree to which that variation is significant, the latter only possible if the widest selection of sources is considered. Sometimes they may vary but little. Manuscripts are by nature, however, mutable by means of random, or unconscious, or deliberate variation. Printed books, as has been suggested above, must not be assumed to contain the best state of the text as it existed in manuscript form, nor should it be expected that the fullness of the manuscript tradition (in terms of variants) will be witnessed in print. Each printed book, too, must be treated as if each surviving copy of an edition might possess slightly different contents, not least because each copy may betray where and how it was used through annotations or other marks. If it is impossible to consider the entire contents of a book the scholar must be extremely careful to document modifications to its original state. These arguments, in conjunction with the fact that liturgical books (as prescriptions for performance) may change from copy to copy as a result of local preference, suggest that no such widely distributed liturgical text should be conventionally edited without major provisos: which version of 'the' Sarum breviary would form the base for such an edition? The Long and Short versions of the Sarum Office for Advent Sunday are consciously different, yet both versions are described as Sarum breviaries. Even the Ordinal, by rights the vehicle of unity, cannot successfully be edited as various interlocking versions give no sense of what was thought to be authoritative at any fixed point in time. Finally, it is to ignore half the evidence if the musical data are not at least considered. The insufficiency of the present text is acknowledged.

5. *A comparison of these modern editions can show where and how liturgical patterns differed from region to region or from time to time.*

As no edition of the Office for any Use can be said to be more than a transcription from one edition of an early printed book, with occasional reference to a few manuscripts, this is not a practical idea, despite the fact that such studies have dominated the study of the English Uses for the last one hundred and fifty years. At best, the modern editions give accessible texts of the printed breviaries.

Evidently, then, these preconceptions about the medieval English Office demand reconsideration. These observations may appear to have produced additional problems, and certainly more questions than answers relating to the development and transmission of liturgy. However light has been shed on a number of issues. The analysis of textual variants and the contents of kalendars and entire books has illuminated some of the influences on the construction of manuscript sources. It has been established that while random and inexplicable variants are present, few of them significant or the cause of groupings, substantive or apparently deliberate variance (usually with an effect on the performance result) can illustrate some of the priorities of the redactors of the manuscripts. Identifiable, quantifiable groups of saints found *together* in kalendars can help to identify the regional character of a manuscript.

It has been a long-term objective of my research to determine quantifiably the characteristics of an English liturgical book which would most easily permit it to be identified with one Use or another, or to differentiate between witnesses from different regions. Three principal categories for analysis have been identified in the preceding chapters, all of which should be considered in conjunction with one another.

1. There are consistent responsory series for Sarum, York, and Hereford Uses, as well as a number of groups of monastic manuscripts, for the Sundays and Ember Days in Advent, the Triduum, and the Office of the Dead. Responsory series for the secular Uses are absolutely consistent; no known witness has divergent responsories. However, it is vital to note that judgements must not be made on the basis of one or a few series, as individual series (and in the case of Hereford all of the series of Advent and the Dead) may be shared between two or more Uses or traditions. In the case of monastic books for certain houses or Orders, a similar consistency has been noted.

2. The kalendars of Sarum, York, and Benedictine manuscripts contain a great number of consistent feastdays which appear in distinctive patterns in books of each Use. These so-called 'normative kalendars' are discussed in chapter 2. It is equally important to remember that some of the 'characteristic' saints of a Use may also be characteristic of another Use, and that the comparison of *entire* kalendars, rather than the observation of one or a few allegedly diagnostic feasts such as that of William of York, must be the preferred method. Each normative kalendar gives only an indication of which saints are *most likely* to appear *as a group* in kalendars of a given Use. Regional kalendars, for the first time based on all of the surviving evidence, provide even greater specificity.

3. More conventional methods of textual analysis may also be helpful. Anyone may discover that the York and Hereford rubrics are much simpler than even the Short family of Sarum rubrics; the reader with more experience or time may discover that there are subfamilies identifiable within the Short and Long Sarum texts for both Advent Sunday and the Dead. Someone who only considers the lessons at Matins will discover that these may be drawn from different sources in books of different Uses: lessons for Thomas Becket in York books, for instance, are drawn from a sermon of Benedict of Peterborough rather than from the typical lesson text, *Gloriosi martyris Thome*. Chapter 3 has shown that books of the same Use, with lessons from the same source, may be identified with one another by means of the divisions of text. These methods of analysis, too, must be treated carefully and with reference to as many components of an Office book as it is possible to consider. Each section of a liturgical book, whether manuscript or printed — that is kalendar, Temporale and Sanctorale, psalter, and so on — needs to be considered as discrete and self-sufficient. If the study of various sections produces results that corroborate one another, any case for a relationship is strengthened.

The grouping of sources thus far in my work *has only been possible* as a result of cumulative evidence gathering, from several sections of each manuscript, at several levels of detail: inventory of contents, followed by choice and order of texts in the form of a number of responsory series from different parts of the liturgical year, followed by word-by-word comparison of complete offices. The common theme in each of these cases is that as a result of a myriad of influences on all parts of a manuscript, and the character of the sources themselves which may vary in copy-specific detail and on the basis of local circumstances, as much of a manuscript as it is possible to study should be included in the assessment of its liturgical Use, place of manufacture or use, and approximate date.

The concept of a liturgical Use, in practice, is one very different from the one envisaged by Thomas Cranmer at the termination of the Latin liturgy. But it is not in disagreement with the numerous documentary prescriptions that some observance should be sung *secundum usum Sarum*. By the early fourteenth century, when the idea of Sarum as an imitable standard became more widespread, it must have referred to the pattern of liturgy propagated in manuscript copies which found their way from Salisbury to other venues, rather than an accurate depiction of the contemporary state of affairs in the eponymous cathedral. The ascription 'Use of Sarum' was a mark of distinction, a signifier which established the authority and correctness of a pattern which, like its own initial textual state, was appropriated from Salisbury Cathedral. Subsequent versions remained associated with the venue, but various influences meant that the textual state of the 'Sarum breviary' was in fact approaching a uniform standard for the province of Canterbury. The term 'Use' may itself imply a greater uniformity than ever existed; the fact that from the outset until now it has been used as a descriptor of orthodoxy has undoubtedly contributed to the view that the liturgical pattern of the Use to which the descriptor refers did not change from book to book. To amend an aphorism which I have previously used for York alone,[1] if there is any lesson to be learned, it is that *usus Eboracensis* and *usus Sarisburiensis* obviously meant something to their contemporaries — although, despite the geographical ascription, what each meant undoubtedly varied from time to time and from place to place.

Whilst there may be no alternative at present, we ought as soon as possible to move on from using modern reprints of early printed books as the definitive texts of such and such a liturgical Use. The present data have been recorded in formats that would permit them to be uploaded to the Internet and made available for searching and comparison. New resources, based on the real contents of individual, identifiable liturgical books would free users in various disciplines from the need to use antiquated and unrepresentative editions of the liturgy or to be chained to ideas, like invariant Uses, whose importance has been artificially inflated, by allowing the consultation of contents and even full texts of real, individual books. Reliable, localized texts would be of use to cataloguers and bibliographers, art historians, auction houses, literary scholars, musicologists, historians, and the like. Of more general import is the fact that based on the success of similar such digital archives, a *bibliothèque imaginaire* of books of the liturgy, framed accessibly, could be of interest to the wider sphere of scholars of medieval studies. Such databases will supply for the next scholarly generation an easier introduction to these sources of central importance to Western Christendom.

A final suggestion is borrowed from M. R. James, who wrote, tellingly, in 1919 by which time many of his own descriptive catalogues were complete, 'See books for yourself. Do not trust that the cataloguer has told you everything.'[2] The study of the *actual* as opposed to perceived or reported contents of English liturgical books, it is hoped, ought to offer an abundance of useful information both for those whose concern is with liturgical manuscripts themselves and for

---

[1] Salisbury, *The Use of York*, p. 40.

[2] M. R. James, *The Wanderings and Homes of Manuscripts*, p. 95.

those for whom liturgical material from the Middle Ages is of importance. The rationalization of late medieval English liturgical patterns is not, in fact, the identification of a few common properties shared by scores of diverse books, but the recognition of the multifarious nature of texts, tunes, and directions that existed: a heterogeneity that, if illustrated with maps, wrote Richard Pfaff forty-five years ago, would be 'a nearly three-dimensional undertaking'.[3]

Ultimately it must be recalled what significance medieval liturgical manuscripts ought to have for our understanding of the medieval Church and Christianity in England. The human connexion to the texts has been mentioned: in fact every conscious decision and indeed every unconscious decision which changes the state of the text reflects on the predilections, preferences, and cultural understandings of a diverse public with varied and regional interests.

[3] Pfaff, 'New Liturgical Observances in Later Medieval England', p. 14.

BIBLIOGRAPHY

Manuscripts and Archival Documents

See Handlist 1 for an account of medieval manuscripts consulted.

Early Printed Sources*

STC 15793: *Breviarium secundum usum Herford* (Rouen: [n. publ.], 1505)
STC 15830: [Sarum breviary] (Paris: [n. publ.], 1531)
STC 15856: *Breviarium secundum usum ecclesie Eboracensis* (Venice: [n. publ.], 1493)

Modern Printed Primary Sources

The Anglo-Saxon Chronicle, ed. by Dorothy Whitelock (London: Eyre and Spottiswoode, 1961)

Bede, *The Ecclesiastical History of the English People*, ed. by Judith McClure and Roger Collins (Oxford: Oxford University Press, 2008)

The Book of Common Prayer (1549, 1559, 1662)

Breviarium ad usum insignis ecclesiae Eboracensis, ed. by Stephen W. Lawley, Surtees Society, 71, 75, 2 vols ([n. p.]: [n. publ.], 1880–83)

Breviarium ad usum insignis ecclesiae Sarum, ed. by Francis Procter and Christopher Wordsworth, 3 vols (Cambridge: Cambridge University Press, 1879–86)

Concilia Magnae Britanniae et Hiberniae, a synodo Verolamiensi AD 496 ad Londinensem AD 1717, ed. by David Wilkins, 4 vols (London: [n. publ.], 1737)

Councils and Ecclesiastical Documents Relating to Great Britain and Ireland, ed. by Arthur W. Haddan and William Stubbs, 3 vols, new edn (Oxford: Clarendon Press, 1964)

Councils & Synods, with Other Documents Relating to the English Church: AD 1205–1313, ed. by F. M. Powicke and C. R. Cheney (Oxford: Clarendon Press, 1964)

The Documents of Vatican II, ed. by Walter M. Abbott (London: Geoffrey Chapman, 1966)

[Hereford] See under Frere, Walter Howard

The Hereford Breviary, ed. by Walter Howard Frere and L. E. G. Brown, Henry Bradshaw Society, 26, 40, 46, 3 vols (London, 1904–15)

---

* For STC numbers, see Pollard, Alfred W., and G. R. Redgrave, eds, *A Short-Title Catalogue* [...]

Liber Obituarius Aulae Reginae in Oxonia, ed. by J. R. Magrath (Oxford, 1910)

[Lincoln] See under Bradshaw, Henry

Lincoln Cathedral Statutes, ed. by Henry Bradshaw, 3 vols (Cambridge: Cambridge University Press, 1892–97)

[Maidstone, Clement], *The Tracts of Clement Maydeston, with the Remains of Caxton's Ordinale*, ed. by Christopher Wordsworth, Henry Bradshaw Society, 7 (London, 1894)

Missale ad usum insignis et praeclarae ecclesiae Sarum, ed. by F. H. Dickinson (Burntisland: [n. publ.], 1861)

Monasticon anglicanum: A History of the Abbies and other Monasteries, Hospitals, Frieries, and Cathedral and Collegiate Churches, with their Dependencies, in England and Wales, ed. by William Dugdale, rev. by John Caley, Henry Ellis, and Bulkeley Bandinel, 6 vols (London: [n. publ.], 1817–30)

Ordinale Exon, ed. by John Neale Dalton, Henry Bradshaw Society, 37, 38, 63, 79, 4 vols (London: [n. publ.], 1909–39)

Patrologiae cursus completus: series graeca, ed. by Jacques-Paul Migne, 161 vols (1857–66)

Patrologiae cursus completus: series latina, ed. by Jacques-Paul Migne, 221 vols (Paris, 1844–64)

The Records of the Northern Convocation, Surtees Society, 113 (Durham: [n. publ.], 1907)

The Register of Henry Chichele, Archbishop of Canterbury, 1414–1443, ed. by E. F. Jacob, 4 vols (Oxford: Oxford University Press, 1937–47)

The Register of John de Grandisson, Bishop of Exeter (AD 1327–1369), with some Account of the Episcopate of James de Berkeley (AD 1327), ed. by F. C. Hingeston-Randolph, 3 vols (London: Bell, 1894–99)

Registers of Robert Stillington, ed. by H. C. Maxwell-Lyte, Somerset Record Society, 52 (London: [n. publ.], 1937)

The Registers of Roger Martival, Bishop of Salisbury 1315–1330, ed. by C. R. Elrington, Canterbury and York Society, 57 (Oxford: Oxford University Press, 1963)

Regularis Concordia Anglicae Nationis Monachorum Sanctimonialiumque [The Monastic Agreement of the Monks and Nuns of the English Nation], ed. by Thomas Symons (London: Nelson, 1953)

[Sarum] See under Procter, Francis

The Sarum Missal: Edited from Three Early Manuscripts, ed. by John Wickham Legg (Oxford: Clarendon Press, 1916)

Tolhurst, J. B. L., *The Monastic Breviary of Hyde Abbey, Winchester*, Henry Bradshaw Society, 69–71, 76, 78, 80, 6 vols (London: [n. publ.], 1932–42)

The Use of Sarum: The Original Texts Edited from the Manuscripts, ed. by Walter Howard Frere and L. E. G. Brown, 2 vols (Cambridge: Cambridge University Press, 1898–1901)

Viollet-le-Duc, Eugène-Emmanuel, *The Foundations of Architecture: Selections from the 'Dictionnaire raisonné'*, trans. by Kenneth D. Whitehead (New York: Braziller, 1990)

[Wycliffe, John], *The English Works of Wyclif, Hitherto Unprinted*, ed. by F. D. Matthew (London: Published for the Early English Text Society by Trübner, 1880)

[York] See under Lawley, Stephen

Secondary Studies

Abercrombie, N. J., *The Life and Work of Edmund Bishop* (London: Longmans, 1959)

Allott, Stephen, *Alcuin of York, c. AD 732 to 804: His Life and Letters* (York: William Sessions, 1974)

Arnold, J. H., and E. G. P. Wyatt, eds, *Walter Howard Frere: A Collection of his Papers on Liturgical and Historical Subjects*, Alcuin Club Collections, 35 (London: Oxford University Press, 1940)

[Arundel Castle, F. W. S.] *Bibliotheca norfolciana: A Catalogue of Selected Manuscripts and Printed Books in the Library of His Grace the Duke of Norfolk* [signed F. W. S] (Arundel Castle, 1961)

Bannister, A. T., ed., *A Descriptive Catalogue of the Manuscripts in the Hereford Cathedral Library* (Hereford: Wilson & Phillips, 1927)

Baumstark, Anton, *Comparative Liturgy*, rev. by Bernard Botte, trans. by F. L. Cross (London: Mowbray, 1958)

Bédier, Joseph, 'La tradition manuscrite du Lai de l'Ombre: Réflexions sur l'art d'éditer les anciens textes', *Romania*, 54 (1928), 161–96

Bergeron, Katherine, *Decadent Enchantments: The Revival of Gregorian Chant at Solesmes* (Berkeley: University of California Press, 1998)

Beyssac, Gabriel, 'Note sur un graduel-sacramentaire de St-Pierre-St-Denys de Bantz, du XIIᵉ siècle', *Revue Bénédictine*, 31 (1921), 190–200

Bishop, Edmund, *Liturgica Historica: Papers on the Liturgy and Religious Life of the Western Church* (Oxford: Clarendon Press, 1918)

Bond, Francis, *Dedications and Patron Saints of English Churches: Ecclesiastical Symbolism: Saints and their Emblems* (London: Oxford University Press, 1914)

Borland, Catherine R., *A Descriptive Catalogue of the Western Mediaeval Manuscripts in Edinburgh University Library* (Edinburgh: [n. publ.], 1916)

Brewer, E. Cobham, 'Use', *Notes and Queries*, 7th ser., IX (17 May 1890), 389

British Library Manuscripts Catalogue, accessed via <http://www.bl.uk/catalogues/manuscripts/INDEX.asp>

[British Museum] A Catalogue of the Harleian Collection of Manuscripts, in the British Museum, 4 vols (London: [n. publ.], 1808)

[British Museum] A Catalogue of the Lansdowne Manuscripts in the British Museum, 2 vols (London: [n. publ.], 1819)

[Cambridge University Library] *A Catalogue of the Manuscripts Preserved in the Library of the University of Cambridge. Edited for the Syndics of the University Press*, 5 vols and index (Cambridge: [n. publ.], 1856)

Catto, Jeremy, 'Religious Change under Henry V', in *Henry V: The Practice of Kingship*, ed. by G. L. Harriss (Oxford: Oxford University Press, 1985), pp. 97–115

Cerquiglini, Bernard, *In Praise of the Variant*, trans. by Betsy Wing (Baltimore: The Johns Hopkins University Press, 1999)

Chadd, David, 'An English Noted Breviary of circa 1200', in *Music in the Medieval English Liturgy: Plainsong and Medieval Music Society Centennial Essays*, ed. by Susan Rankin and David Hiley (Oxford: Clarendon Press, 1993), pp. 205–38

——, 'Liturgical Books: Catalogues, Editions and Inventories', in *Die Erschließung der Quellen des mittelalterlichen liturgischen Gesangs*, ed. by David Hiley, Wolfenbütteler Mittelalter-Studien, 18 (Wiesbaden: Harrassowitz in Kommission, 2004), pp. 43–74

Cheney, C. R., *English Synodalia of the Thirteenth Century* (Oxford: Oxford University Press, 1941)

——, 'Rules for the Observance of Feast-Days in Medieval England', *Bulletin of the Institute of Historical Research*, 34 (1961), 117–47

Colker, Marvin L., *Trinity College Library Dublin: Descriptive Catalogue of the Mediaeval and Renaissance Latin Manuscripts*, 2 vols and supplement (Aldershot: Ashgate, 1991)

Combe, Pierre, *The Restoration of Gregorian Chant: Solesmes and the Vatican Edition*, trans. by Theodore N. Marier and William Skinner (Washington, DC: Catholic University of America Press, 2003)

Coxe, H. O., ed., *Catalogus codicum MSS qui in collegiis aulisque Oxoniensibus hodie adservantur*, 2 vols (Oxford: [n. publ.], 1852)

Cubitt, Catherine, *Anglo-Saxon Church Councils, c. 650–c. 850* (London: Leicester University Press, 1995)

Dalton, J. N., ed., *The Collegiate Church of Ottery St Mary Being the Ordinacio et Statuta ecclesie sancte Marie de Otery Exon. diocesis* (Cambridge: [n. publ.], 1917)

Derrida, Jacques, *Foi et savoir* (Paris: Seuil, 2000)

Dobson, R. B., *Church and Society in the Medieval North of England* (London: Hambledon, 1996)

Dobszay, Laszlo, and Laurence Paul Hemming, *The Restoration and Organic Development of the Roman Rite* (London: T&T Clark, 2009)

Dondi, Cristina, *The Liturgy of the Canons Regular of the Holy Sepulchre of Jerusalem: A Study and a Catalogue of the Manuscript Sources*, Bibliotheca Victorina, 16 (Turnhout: Brepols, 2004)

Du Boulay Hill, Arthur, 'The Wollaton Antiphonale', *Transactions of the Thoroton Society*, 36 (1932), 42–50

Duffy, Eamon, *The Stripping of the Altars: Traditional Religion in England c. 1400–c. 1580* (New Haven: Yale University Press, 1992)

Dumville, David, *Liturgy and the Ecclesiastical History of Late Anglo-Saxon England* (Woodbridge: Boydell, 1992)

Edwards, Kathleen, *The English Secular Cathedrals in the Middle Ages: A Constitutional Study with Special Reference to the Fourteenth Century*, 2nd edn (Manchester: Manchester University Press, 1967)

Edwards, Owain Tudor, 'How Many Sarum Antiphonals were there in England and Wales in the Middle of the Sixteenth Century?', *Revue Bénédictine*, 99 (1989), 155–80

——, *Matins, Lauds, and Vespers for St David's Day: The Medieval Office of the Welsh Patron Saint in National Library of Wales MS 20541 E* (Woodbridge: Brewer, 1990)

Egbert, Donald Drew, *The Tickhill Psalter and Related Manuscripts: A School of Manuscript Illumination in England during the early Fourteenth Century* (New York: The New York Public Library, 1940)

Farmer, D. H., *Oxford Dictionary of Saints*, 5th edn (Oxford: Oxford University Press, 2004)

Fassler, Margot E., and Rebecca A. Baltzer, eds, *The Divine Office in the Latin Middle Ages: Methodology and Source Studies, Regional Developments, Hagiography* (Oxford: Oxford University Press, 2000)

——, 'Sermons, Sacramentaries, and Early Sources for the Office in the Latin West: The Example of Advent', in *The Divine Office in the Latin Middle Ages: Methodology and Source Studies, Regional Developments, Hagiography*, ed. by Margot E. Fassler and Rebecca A. Baltzer (Oxford: Oxford University Press, 2000), pp. 15–47

Flood, John, '"Volentes sibi comparare infrascriptos libros impressos...": Printed Books as a Commercial Commodity in the Fifteenth Century', in *Incunabula and their Readers: Printing, Selling, and Using Books in the Fifteenth Century*, ed. by Kristian Jensen (London: British Library, 2003), pp. 139–51

Floyer, John Kestell, and Sidney Graves Hamilton, *Catalogue of Manuscripts Preserved in the Chapter Library of Worcester Cathedral*, Worcestershire Historical Society (Oxford: Printed for the Worcestershire Historical Society by Parker, 1906)

Foot, Sarah, *Monastic Life in Anglo-Saxon England, c. 600–900* (Cambridge: Cambridge University Press, 2006)

French, Thomas, *York Minster: The St William Window* (Oxford: Oxford University Press for the British Academy, 1999)

Frere, Walter Howard, *Antiphonale Sarisburiense: A Reproduction in Facsimile from early Manuscripts*, Plainsong and Medieval Music Society (repr. Farnborough: [n. publ.], 1966)

——, *Bibliotheca musico-liturgica: A Descriptive Hand List of the Musical and Latin Liturgical Manuscripts of the Middle Ages, Preserved in the Libraries of Great Britain and Ireland*, Plainsong and Medieval Music Society, 2 vols (London: [n. publ.], 1894–1932)

——, *Graduale Sarisburiense* (London: Quaritch, 1894)

——, *The Principles of Religious Ceremonial* (London: Mowbray, 1928)

——, *Studies in Early Roman Liturgy*, Alcuin Club, 28, 30, 32, 3 vols (London: Oxford University Press, 1930–35)

Froger, Jacques, *La Critique des textes et son automatisation*, Initiation aux nouveautés de la science, 7 (Paris: Dunod, 1968)

Gittos, Helen, and M. Bradford Bedingfield, eds, *The Liturgy of the Late Anglo-Saxon Church*, Henry Bradshaw Society Subsidia, 5 (London: Boydell, 2005)

Granger, Penny, *The N-Town Plays: Drama and Liturgy in Medieval East Anglia* (Woodbridge: Boydell and Brewer, 2009)

Green, Everard, 'Cardinal Quignon's Breviary', *Notes and Queries*, 7th ser., 2 (11 December 1886), 464–65

Greenway, Diana, 'The False Institutio of St Osmund', in *Tradition and Change: Essays in honour of Marjorie Chibnall*, ed. by Diana Greenway, Christopher Holdsworth, and Jane Sayers (Cambridge: Cambridge University Press, 1985), pp. 77–101

——, *Fasti Ecclesiae Anglicanae 1066–1300* (London: Institute of Historical Research, 1968–2006), 12 vols

Guéranger, Prosper, *Institutions Liturgiques*, 3 vols (Mans: [n. publ.], 1840–51)

Haggh, Barbara, 'Nonconformity in the Use of Cambrai Cathedral: Guillaume du Fay's Foundations', in *The Divine Office in the Latin Middle Ages: Methodology and Source Studies, Regional Developments, Hagiography: Written in honour of Professor Ruth Steiner*, ed. by Margot E. Fassler and Rebecca A. Baltzer (Oxford: Oxford University Press, 2000), pp. 372–97

Halmo, Joan, 'A Sarum Antiphoner and Other Medieval Office Manuscripts from England and France: Some Musical Relationships', *Plainsong and Medieval Music*, 11 (2002), 113–26

Hanna, Ralph, and Thorlac Turville-Petre, eds, *The Wollaton Medieval Manuscripts: Texts, Owners and Readers* (Woodbridge: York Medieval, 2010)

Hamilton Thompson, A., ed., *The Surtees Society 1834–1934*, Surtees Society, 150 (London: [n. publ.], 1935)

Harper, John, *The Forms and Orders of Western Liturgy from the Tenth to the Eighteenth Century: A Historical Introduction and Guide for Students and Musicians* (Oxford: Clarendon Press, 1991)

——, 'Liturgy and Music, 1300–1600', in *Hereford Cathedral: A History*, ed. by Gerald Aylmer and John Tiller (London: Hambledon, 2000), pp. 375–98

Harper, Sally [see also under Roper], *Music in Welsh Culture before 1650: A Study of the Principal Sources* (Aldershot: Ashgate, 2007)

Hesbert, René-Jean, *Corpus Antiphonalium Officii*, Rerum Ecclesiasticarum Documenta Series Maior 7–12, 6 vols (Rome: Herder, 1963–79)

——, *Le Problème de la transfixion du Christ dans les traditions* (Paris: Société de Saint Jean l'Évangéliste, 1940)

Heslop, T. A., 'The Canterbury Calendars and the Norman Conquest', in *Canterbury and the Norman Conquest: Churches, Saints and Scholars 1066–1199*, ed. by Richard Eales and Richard Sharpe (London: Hambledon, 1995), pp. 53–85

Hiley, David, 'The Norman Chant Traditions – Normandy, Britain, Sicily', *Proceedings of the Royal Musical Association*, 107 (1980–81), 1–33

——, 'Post-Pentecost Alleluias in Medieval British Liturgies', in *Music in the Medieval English Liturgy: Plainsong and Mediaeval Music Society Centennial Essays*, ed. by Susan Rankin and David Hiley (Oxford: Clarendon Press, 1993), pp. 145–74

Hughes, Andrew, 'British Rhymed Offices: A Catalogue and Commentary', in *Music in the Medieval English Liturgy*, ed. by Susan Rankin and David Hiley (Oxford: Clarendon Press, 1993), pp. 239–84

——, 'Chants in the Rhymed Office of St Thomas of Canterbury', *Early Music*, 16 (1988), 185–201

——, 'Fifteenth-Century English Polyphony discovered in Norwich and Arundel', *Music and Letters*, 59 (April 1978), 148–58

——, *Late Medieval Liturgical Offices: Resources for Electronic Research*, Subsidia Medievalia, 23–24, 2 vols (Toronto: Pontifical Institute of Mediaeval Studies, 1994–95)

——, *Medieval Manuscripts for Mass and Office: A Guide to their Organisation and Terminology* (Toronto: University of Toronto Press, 1982)

——, with Matthew Cheung Salisbury, 'The Ideal Copy: Fallacies in the Cataloguing of Liturgical Books', *Notes and Queries*, 56 (December 2009), 490–96

——, with Matthew Cheung Salisbury and Heather Robbins, *Cataloguing Discrepancies: The Printed York breviary of 1493* (Toronto: University of Toronto Press, 2011)

Hughes, Dom Anselm, *Septuagesima: Reminiscences of the Plainsong and Mediaeval Music Society, and of other Things Personal and Musical* (London: Plainsong and Mediaeval Music Society, 1959)

Hunt, Richard William, 'Notes on the *Distinctiones monasticae et morales*', in *Liber floridus: Mittellateinische Studien: Festschrift Paul Lehmann*, ed. by Bernard Bischoff and Suso Brechter (St Ottilien: Eos Verlag der Erzabtei, 1950), pp. 355–62

James, Montague Rhodes, *A Descriptive Catalogue of the Manuscripts in the College Library of Magdalene College, Cambridge* (Cambridge: Cambridge University Press, 1909)

——, *A Descriptive Catalogue of the Manuscripts in the Fitzwilliam Museum* (Cambridge: Cambridge University Press, 1895)

——, *A Descriptive Catalogue of the Manuscripts in the Library of Lambeth Palace* (Cambridge: Printed for the Cambridge Antiquarian Society, 1930–32)

——, *A Descriptive Catalogue of the Manuscripts in the Library of Sidney Sussex College, Cambridge* (Cambridge: Cambridge University Press, 1895)

——, *A Descriptive Catalogue of the Manuscripts in the Library of St John's College, Cambridge* (Cambridge: Cambridge University Press, 1913)

——, *A Descriptive Catalogue of the Manuscripts other than Oriental in the Library of King's College, Cambridge* (Cambridge: Cambridge University Press, 1895)

——, *A Descriptive Catalogue of the McClean Collection of Manuscripts in the Fitzwilliam Museum* (Cambridge: Cambridge University Press, 1912)

——, *A Descriptive Catalogue of the Western Manuscripts in the Library of Clare College, Cambridge* (Cambridge: Cambridge University Press, 1905)

——, *The Manuscripts in the Library at Lambeth Palace*, Cambridge Antiquarian Society Octavo Publications, 33 (Cambridge: Printed for the Cambridge Antiquarian Society, 1900)

——, *The Wanderings and Homes of Manuscripts* (London: SPCK, 1919)

——, *The Western Manuscripts in the Library of Emmanuel College: A Descriptive Catalogue* (Cambridge: [n. publ.], 1904)

——, *The Western Manuscripts in the Library of Trinity College, Cambridge: A Descriptive Catalogue*, 4 vols (Cambridge: Cambridge University Press, 1900–04)

Kemp, E. W., *Canonization and Authority in the Western Church* (Oxford: Oxford University Press, 1948)

Ker, N. R, *Medieval Libraries of Great Britain: A List of Surviving Books*, 2nd edn (London: Royal Historical Society, 1964)

——, and A. J. Piper, *Medieval Manuscripts in British Libraries*, 5 vols (Oxford: Clarendon Press, 1969–2002)

Knowles, David, *The Monastic Order in England: A History of its Development from the Times of St Dunstan to the Fourth Lateran Council* (Cambridge: Cambridge University Press, 1949)

Lasko, Peter, and Nigel J. Morgan, eds, *Medieval Art in East Anglia, 1300–1520* (Norwich: Jarrold, 1973)

Lawrence, C. H., *The Life of St Edmund by Matthew Paris* (Stroud: Sutton, 1996)

Legg, J. Wickham, *A Second Recension of the Quignon Breviary*, Henry Bradshaw Society, 35, 42, 2 vols (London: [n. publ.], 1908–12)

Le Goff, Jacques, *La Naissance du Purgatoire* (Paris: Gallimard, 1981)

Le Roux, Raymond, 'Répons du Triduo Sacro et de Pâques', *Études grégoriennes*, 18 (1979), 157–76

Madan, Falconer, *Books in Manuscript: A Short Guide to their Study and Use*, 2nd edn (London: Kegan Paul, Trench, Trüber, 1920)

——, 'The Localization of Manuscripts', in *Essays in History Presented to Reginald Lane Poole*, ed. by H. W. C. Davis (Oxford: Clarendon Press, 1927), pp. 5–23

——, and others, *A Summary Catalogue of Western Manuscripts in the Bodleian Library at Oxford which have not hitherto been catalogued in the Quarto series*, 7 vols in 8 (Oxford: Clarendon Press, 1895–1953)

Malone, C. M., *Facade and Spectacle: Ritual and Ideology at Wells Cathedral* (Leiden: Brill, 2004)

Marks, Richard, and Paul Williamson, eds, *Gothic: Art for England 1400–1547* (London: V&A, 2003)

Martinez, Ronald L., 'Dante's Forese, the Book of Job, and the Office of the Dead: A Note on *Purgatorio* 23', *Dante Studies*, 120 (2002), 1–16

——, 'Mourning Laura in the *Canzoniere*: Lessons from Lamentations', *Modern Language Notes*, 118 (2003), 1–45

Maskell, William, *The Ancient Liturgy of the Church of England: According to the Uses of Sarum, Bangor, York, & Hereford and the Modern Roman Liturgy Arranged in Parallel Columns* (London: Pickering, 1844)

McLachlan, Laurentia, ed., *Antiphonaire monastique: XIIIᵉ siècle, Codex F. 160 de la Bibliothèque de la Cathédrale de Worcester*, Paléographie musicale, 12 (Tournai: Société de Saint Jean l'Évangéliste, 1922)

Morgan, Nigel, 'The Introduction of the Sarum Kalendar into the Dioceses of England in the Thirteenth Century', in *Thirteenth Century England VIII: Proceedings of the Durham Conference 1999*, ed. by Michael Prestwich and others (Woodbridge: Boydell, 2001), pp. 179–206

——, 'The Sanctorals of Early Sarum Missals and Breviaries, c. 1250–c. 1350', in *The Study of Medieval Manuscripts of England: Festschrift in Honor of Richard W. Pfaff*, ed. by George Hardin Brown and Linda Ehrsam Voigts (Turnhout: Brepols, 2010), pp. 143–62

Mynors, R. A. B, and Rodney M. Thomson, *Catalogue of the Manuscripts of Hereford Cathedral Library* (Cambridge: Brewer on behalf of the Dean and Chapter of Hereford Cathedral, 1993)

Möller, Hartmut, 'Research on the Antiphoner – Problems and Perspectives', *Journal of the Plainsong and Mediaeval Music Society*, 10 (1987), 1–14

Nichols, Stephen G., 'Philology in a Manuscript Culture', *Speculum*, 65 (1990), 1–10

Norton, Christopher, *St William of York* (Woodbridge: York Medieval, 2006)

Ottosen, Knud, *L'Antiphonaire latin au Moyen-Âge: Réorganisation des séries de répons de l'Avent classés par R.-J. Hesbert* (Rome: Herder, 1986)

——, *The Responsories and Versicles of the Latin Office of the Dead* (Aarhus: Aarhus University Press, 1993)

Paisley, William J., 'Identifying the Unknown Communicator in Painting, Literature and Music: The Significance of Minor Encoding Habits', *Journal of Communication*, 14 (1964), 219–37

Parkes, M. B., *The Medieval Manuscripts of Keble College, Oxford: A Descriptive Catalogue with Summary Descriptions of the Greek and Oriental Manuscripts* (London: Scolar, 1979)

Pearsall, Derek, 'Texts, Textual Criticism, and Fifteenth-Century Manuscript Production', in *Fifteenth-Century Studies*, ed. by Robert F Yeager (Hamden: Archon, 1984), pp. 121–36

Pearsall, Derek, ed., *Manuscripts and Readers in Fifteenth-Century England: The Literary Implications of Manuscript Study: Essays from the 1981 Conference at the University of York* (Cambridge: Brewer, 1983)

Pfaff, Richard, 'Lanfranc's Supposed Purge of the Anglo-Saxon Calendar', in *Warriors and Churchmen in the High Middle Ages: Essays Presented to Karl Leyser*, ed. by Timothy Reuter (London: Hambledon, 1992), pp. 95–108

——, *Liturgical Calendars, Saints, and Services in Medieval England* (Aldershot: Ashgate, 1998)

——, 'Liturgical Studies Today: One Subject or Two?', *Journal of Ecclesiastical History*, 45 (1994), 325–32

——, *The Liturgy in Medieval England: A History* (Cambridge: Cambridge University Press, 2009)

——, *Montague Rhodes James* (London: Scolar, 1980)

——, 'M. R. James on the Cataloguing of Manuscripts: A Draft Essay of 1906', *Scriptorium*, 31 (1977), 103–18

——, *New Liturgical Feasts in Later Medieval England* (Oxford: Clarendon Press, 1970)

——, 'Prescription and Reality in the Rubrics of Sarum Rite Service Books', in *Intellectual Life in the Middle Ages: Essays Presented to Margaret Gibson*, ed. by Lesley Smith and Benedicta Ward (London: Hambledon, 1992), pp. 197–205

Phillips, C. S., and others, *Walter Howard Frere, Bishop of Truro* (London: Faber and Faber, 1947)

Piper, A. J., 'Cataloguing British Collections of Medieval Western Manuscripts, 1895–1995', in *The Legacy of M. R. James: Papers from the 1995 Cambridge Symposium*, ed. by Lynda Dennison (Donnington: Shaun Tyas, 2001)

Pollard, Alfred W., and G. R. Redgrave, eds, *A Short-Title Catalogue of Books Printed in England, Scotland, and Ireland and of English Books Printed Abroad 1475–1640*, 1st edn (London: Bibliographical Society, 1926), and 2nd edn rev. and enlarged by W. A. Jackson, F. S. Ferguson, and Katherine F. Pantzer, 3 vols (London: Bibliographical Society, 1976–91)

Procter, Francis, and Walter Howard Frere, *A New History of the Book of Common Prayer: With a Rationale of its Offices*, 3rd imp. (London: Macmillan, 1905)

Pächt, Otto, and J. J. G. Alexander, eds, *Illuminated Manuscripts in the Bodleian Library, Oxford*, 3 vols (Oxford: Clarendon Press, 1966–73)

Raine, James, ed., *The Historians of the Church of York and its Archbishops*, Rerum Britannicum Medii Aevi Scriptores, 71, 3 vols (London: Longman, 1879–94)

Rankin, Susan, 'Making the Liturgy: Winchester Scribes and their Books', in *The Liturgy of the Late Anglo-Saxon Church*, ed. by Helen Gittos and M. Bradford Bedingfield, Henry Bradshaw Society Subsidia, 5 (London: Boydell, 2005), pp. 29–52

Rankin, Susan, and David Hiley, eds, *Music in the Medieval English Liturgy: Plainsong and Mediaeval Music Society Centennial Essays* (Oxford: Clarendon Press, 1993)

Reames, Sherry, 'Late Medieval Efforts at Standardization and Reform in the Sarum Lessons for Saints' Days', in *Design and Distribution of Late Medieval Manuscripts in England*, ed. by Margaret Connolly and Linne R. Mooney (Woodbridge: Boydell and Brewer, 2008), pp. 91–117

——, 'Lectionary Revision in Sarum Breviaries and the Origins of the Early Printed Editions', *Journal of the Early Book Society*, 9 (2006), 95–115

——, '*Mouvance* and Interpretation in Late-Medieval Latin: The Legend of St Cecilia in British Breviaries', in *Medieval Literature: Texts and Interpretation*, ed. by Tim William Machan (Binghamton: Medieval and Renaissance Texts and Studies, 1991), pp. 159–89

——, 'Origins and Affiliations of the Pre-Sarum Office for Anne in the Stowe Breviary', in *Music and Medieval Manuscripts: Paleography and Performance: Essays Dedicated to Andrew Hughes*, ed. by John Haines and Randall Rosenfeld (Aldershot: Ashgate, 2004), pp. 349–68

——, 'Unexpected Texts for Saints in Some Sarum Breviary Manuscripts', in *The Study of Medieval Manuscripts of England: Festschrift in Honor of Richard W. Pfaff*, ed. by George Hardin Brown and Linda Ehrsam Voigts (Turnhout: Brepols, 2010), pp. 163–84

Ridyard. S. J., '*Condigna veneratio*: Post-Conquest Attitudes to the Saints of the Anglo-Saxons', *Anglo-Norman Studies*, 9 (1986), 179–206

Ringrose, J. S., *Summary Catalogue of the Additional Medieval Manuscripts in Cambridge University Library acquired before 1940* (Woodbridge: Boydell and Brewer, 2009)

Roper, Sally, *Medieval English Benedictine Liturgy: Studies in the Formation, Structure, and Content of the Monastic Votive Office, c. 950–1540* (London: Garland, 1993)

Rubenstein, Jay, 'Liturgy against History: The Competing Visions of Lanfranc and Eadmer of Canterbury', *Speculum*, 74 (1999), 279–309

Rubin, Miri, *Corpus Christi: The Eucharist in late Medieval Culture* (Cambridge: Cambridge University Press, 1991)

Rud, Thomas, ed., *Codicum manuscriptorum Ecclesiae Cathedralis Dunelmensis* [...] (London: [n. publ.], 1825)

Rushforth, Rebecca, *Saints in English Kalendars before AD 1100*, Henry Bradshaw Society, 117 (Woodbridge: Boydell for the Henry Bradshaw Society, 2008)

Sandler, Lucy Freeman, 'An Early Fourteenth-Century English Breviary at Longleat', *Journal of the Warburg and Courtauld Institutes*, 39 (1976), 1–20

Salisbury, Matthew Cheung, 'An Alternative Office for St Thomas Becket and its Implications', *Anaphora*, 2 (2008), 57–68

——, 'A Fifteenth-Century Aspersion Chant', *Plainsong and Medieval Music Society* (2010) <http://plainsong.org.uk>

——, *The Use of York: Characteristics of the Medieval Liturgical Office in York* (York: Borthwick Institute, 2008)

Sandon, Nicholas, 'Medieval Services and their Music', in *Exeter Cathedral: A Celebration*, ed. by Michael Swanton (Crediton: Southgate for the Dean and Chapter of Exeter, 1991), pp. 127–36

Slocum, Kay Brainerd, *Liturgies in Honour of Thomas Becket* (Toronto: University of Toronto Press, 2004)

Sparrow Simpson, William, 'On a Mandate of Bishop Clifford', paper delivered to the Society of Antiquaries of London, 7 April 1892, printed in *Proceedings of the Society of Antiquaries of London*, 2nd ser., 14 (1891/92), 126–27

Stäblein, Bruno, *Schriftbild der Einstimmigen Musik*, Musikgeschichte in Bildern, 3: Musik des Mittelalters und der Renaissance, 4 (Leipzig: Deutscher Verlag für Musik, 1975)

Symons, Thomas, 'Regularis Concordia: History and Derivation', in *Tenth-Century Studies: Essays in Commemoration of the Millennium of the Council of Winchester and Regularis Concordia*, ed. by David Parsons (London: Phillimore, 1975), pp. 39–42

Thompson, Alexander Hamilton, *The English Clergy and their Organisation in the later Middle Ages* (Oxford: Clarendon Press, 1947)

Thomson, Rodney M., and Michael Gullick, *A Descriptive Catalogue of the Medieval Manuscripts in Worcester Cathedral Library* (Cambridge: Published on behalf of the Dean and Chapter of Worcester Cathedral by Brewer, 2001)

Tolhurst, J. B. L., *Introduction to the English Monastic Breviaries (The Monastic Breviary of Hyde Abbey, Winchester, vol. 6)*, Henry Bradshaw Society, 80 (London: [n. publ.], 1942)

Turner, D. H., 'The Penwortham Breviary', *British Museum Quarterly*, 28 (1964), 85–88

Treitler, Leo, *With Voice and Pen: Coming to Know Medieval Song and How it was Made* (Oxford: Oxford University Press, 2003)

Vogel, Cyrille, *Introduction aux sources de l'histoire du culte chrétien au Moyen Âge*, Biblioteca degli Studi Medievali, 1 (Spoleto: Centro Italiano di Studi sull'Alto Medioevo, 1966)

Walker, Rose, *Views of Transition: Liturgy and Illumination in Medieval Spain* (London: British Library and University of Toronto Press, 1998)

Watson, Andrew G., *Catalogue of Dated and Datable Manuscripts c. 435–1600 in Oxford Libraries*, 2 vols (Oxford: Clarendon Press, 1984)

West, Fritz, 'Baumstark's Tree and Thoughts after Harvest', in *Comparative Liturgy: Fifty Years after Anton Baumstark (1972–1948): Acts of the International Congress, Rome, 25–29 September 1998*, ed. by Robert F. Taft and Gabriele Winkler, Orientalia Christiana Analecta, 265 (Rome: Pontificio Istituto Orientale, 2001), pp. 163–89

White, James F., *The Cambridge Movement. The Ecclesiologists and the Gothic Revival* (Cambridge: Cambridge University Press, 1962)

Wormald, Francis, ed., *English Benedictine Kalendars after AD 1100*, Henry Bradshaw Society, 77, 81 (London, 1939–46)

——, ed., *English Kalendars before AD 1100*, Henry Bradshaw Society, 72 (London, 1934)

Zumthor, Paul, *Essai de poétique médiévale*, new edn (Paris: Seuil, 2000)

Unpublished Modern Material

Billett, Jesse D., 'The Divine Office in Anglo-Saxon England, 597–c. 1000' (unpublished doctoral thesis, University of Cambridge, 2009)

Chadd, David, 'Beyond the Frontiers: Guides for Uncharted Territory', delivered at Frontiers of Research in Medieval Music, Dartmouth College, USA, summer 1988 (revised typescript dated October 1999, unpublished)

Doyle, A. I., and A. J. Piper, *Draft Catalogue of Medieval Manuscripts*, housed in the Search Room in the Palace Green Library, University of Durham

Morris, Timothy Meeson, 'The Augustinian Use of Oseney Abbey: A Study of the Oseney Ordinal, Processional, and Tonale (Bodleian Library MS Rawlinson c. 939)' (unpublished doctoral thesis, University of Oxford, 1999)

Parsons, Anna, 'The Use of Guisborough: The Liturgy and Chant of the Augustinian Canons of the York Province in the later Middle Ages' (unpublished doctoral thesis, University of Exeter, 2004)

Pfaff, Richard William, 'New Liturgical Observances in Later Medieval England' (doctoral thesis, University of Oxford, 1965, published as Pfaff, *New Liturgical Feasts*, see above)

Thomas, Islwyn Geoffrey, 'The Cult of Saints' Relics in Medieval England' (unpublished doctoral thesis, University of London, 1975)

Van Dijk, S. J. P., *Handlist of the Latin Liturgical Manuscripts in the Bodleian Library*, 7 vols in typescript held at the Bodleian, 1953

Handlist 1

Manuscripts, Kalendar Sigla and Notes

The first section of this list, 'arranged by library', gives all manuscripts consulted, of all varieties. The accompanying Descriptive Catalogue only presents breviaries and antiphonals. Manuscripts with a liturgical kalendar are provided with the relevant alphabetical kalendar siglum in parentheses. The second section, 'arranged by kalendar siglum', permits the reader to associate a kalendar siglum with its manuscript. These sigla were assigned in no particular order.

Manuscripts Arranged by Library

Aberystwyth, National Library of Wales, MS 20541.E, antiphonal
Arundel Castle Archives, MS s.n., the 'York Antiphonal'
Blackburn Museum, MS 091. 21195, diurnal
Cambridge, Clare College, MS G. 3. 34 (olim Kk. 3. 7), breviary (BB)
Cambridge, Emmanuel College, MS 64, breviary (BC)
Cambridge, Fitzwilliam Museum, MS 369, breviary-missal (CA)
——, McClean 65, breviary (AT)
Cambridge, King's College, MS 30, breviary (AX)
Cambridge, Magdalene College, F. 4. 10, antiphonal (CB)
Cambridge, Peterhouse (deposited in University Library), MS 270, breviary (BA)
Cambridge, St John's College, D. 21 (James 96), antiphonal
——, F. 9 (James 146), breviary (AY)
——, H. 13 (James 215), breviary
Cambridge, Sidney Sussex College, MS 62, diurnal (DV)
Cambridge, Trinity College, O. 7. 31, breviary
——, O. 10a. 26, breviary
Cambridge, University Library, Additional 2602, antiphonal (BU)
——, Additional 3110, breviary (H)
——, Additional 3208, breviary

——, Additional 3474, 3475, breviary (AV, AW)
——, Additional 4500, breviary-missal (AU)
——, Dd. X. 66, breviary (AZ)
——, Ii. IV. 20, breviary-missal
——, Mm. II. 9, antiphonal
Colchester, Castle Museum, MS 1932. 213, breviary (ED)
Douai Abbey, MS 4, breviary-missal
Downside Abbey, MS 48244, breviary
Dublin, Trinity College, MS 85, breviary (EB)
——, MS 87, breviary
——, MS 88, breviary (EC)
Durham, Cathedral Library, A. IV. 20, breviary
Durham, University Library, Cosin MS V. I. 2 (R)
——, Cosin MS V. I. 3 (Z)
Edinburgh, National Library of Scotland, Advocates MS 18. 2. 13A
——, Advocates MS 18. 2. 13B
Edinburgh, University Library, MS 26, breviary
——, MS 27, breviary (EF)
Hereford, Cathedral Library, MS P. IX. 7, breviary (CI)
Liverpool, Cathedral Library (deposited in University Library), Radcliffe 37, breviary (EA)
London, British Library, Additional 17002, breviary (DD)
——, Additional 17009, breviary
——, Additional 22397, breviary (BI)
——, Additional 27631, offices
——, Additional 28598, antiphonal
——, Additional 30511, breviary (J)
——, Additional 32427, breviary (DE)
——, Additional 33381, collection, Ely Priory (CD)
——, Additional 34190 and Egerton 2025, breviary
——, Additional 35285, antiphonal and missal (CC)
——, Additional 36672, breviary (CN)
——, Additional 38624, breviary (I)
——, Additional 43405, 43406, breviary, CK
——, Additional 49363, breviary-missal
——, Additional 52359, breviary, BM
——, Additional 59862, breviary, CZ
——, Arundel 130, ordinal
——, Burney 335, breviary (DL)
——, Harley 587, breviary (BH)
——, Harley 1512, breviary
——, Harley 1797, breviary (BG)
——, Harley 2785, breviary (BV)
——, Harley 2856, psalter, diurnal (CO)

——, Harley 2946, breviary
——, Harley 4664, breviary (CL)
——, Harley 4958, breviary
——, Harley 5037, breviary
——, Harley 5284A, breviary
——, Harley 5334, psalter
——, Lansdowne 431, psalter *cum canticis* (CY)
——, Lansdowne 460, antiphonal
——, Lansdowne 461, antiphonal
——, Lansdowne 463, antiphonal (BN)
——, Royal 2 A X, psalter/breviary hybrid (CM)
——, Royal 2 A XII, breviary (BF)
——, Royal 2 A XIV, breviary (BD)
——, Sloane 1909, breviary (CW)
——, Sloane 2466, breviary (BZ)
London, Lambeth Palace Library, MS 69, breviary (Y)
——, Sion College MS, breviary (G)
Warminster, Longleat, MS 10, breviary-missal (DZ)
Nottingham, University Library, MS 250, the Wollaton Antiphonal (DU)
Oxford, Bodleian Library, Auct E. 1. 1
——, Barlow 41, breviary (CS)
——, Bodley 68, kalendar (DP)
——, Bodley 547, breviary (DH)
——, Bodley 637, processional
——, Bodley 948, antiphonal (BJ)
——, Bodley 976, breviary (BQ)
——, Canon. lit. 215, breviary (DJ)
——, Digby 3, breviary
——, Douce 88 (DS)
——, Douce 293, psalter (DA)
——, e Musaeo 126, processional
——, e Musaeo 127, psalter
——, e Musaeo 185, psalter (DT)
——, e Musaeo 188, Hours (AP)
——, e Musaeo 226, Hours (AK)
——, Gough lit. 1, breviary, F
——, Gough lit. 3, Hours (AL)
——, Gough lit. 5, manual
——, Gough lit. 6, Hours (AI)
——, Gough lit. 8 and Rawl. lit. e. 1*, breviary (CV)
——, Gough lit. 9, Hours (AM)
——, Gough lit. 10, Hours (AJ)
——, Gough lit. 17 = Gough Missals 47, Diurnal (CU)

——, Hatton 4, psalter (BK)
——, Hatton 63, breviary
——, Hatton 106, psalter (BL)
——, Jesus Colleg 10, antiphonal (DI)
——, Lat. lit. b. 14, antiphonal (BS)
——, Lat. lit. c. 36, breviary (CR)
——, Lat. lit. d. 42, e. 6, e. 37, e. 39, the Chertsey Abbey breviary (CT)
——, Lat. lit. f. 2, Hours
——, Lat. lit. f. 21, Hours
——, Lat. lit. f. 29, breviary
——, Lat. lit. g. 1, psalter (DC)
——, Laud lat. 5, psalter (DB)
——, Laud lat. 15, Hours (BY)
——, Laud lat. 81, psalter
——, Laud misc. 3A, breviary (BR)
——, Laud misc. 84, breviary (E)
——, Laud misc. 204, Hours
——, Laud misc. 299, breviary (BW)
——, Laud misc. 666, vita et epistolae Thome Archepi'
——, Lit. 132, hours (DK)
——, Lyell empt. 4, psalter (CX)
——, Rawlinson C. 73, breviary
——, Rawlinson C. 466 (DQ)
——, Rawlinson C. 489, breviary
——, Rawlinson C. 553, hours (T)
——, Rawlinson C. 558, Hours (AO)
——, Rawlinson C. 781, Hours
——, Rawlinson D. 1218 (DO)
——, Rawlinson G. 127, psalter
——, Rawlinson G. 170, psalter (DN)
——, Rawlinson lit. d. 1, Hours (AH)
——, Rawlinson lit. d. 4, processional
——, Rawlinson lit. e. 1, Hours (AQ, AR)
——, Rawlinson lit. e. 3, Hours (CE)
——, Rawlinson lit. e. 4, Hours (CF)
——, Rawlinson lit. e. 5, Hours
——, Rawlinson lit. e. 6, Hours (AF)
——, Rawlinson lit. e. 7, Hours (AG, AS)
——, Rawlinson lit. e. 9, Hours
——, Rawlinson lit. f. 1, Hours (CG)
——, Rawlinson lit. f. 2, Hours (BX)
——, Rawlinson lit. f. 3, Hours (AE)
——, Rawlinson lit. f. 5, Hours

——, Rawlinson lit. g. 1, Hours (AD)
——, Rawlinson lit. g. 2, Hours (AB)
——, Rawlinson lit. g. 3, Hours (AC)
——, Rawlinson lit. g. 6, Hours (AA)
——, St John's College 179, breviary (BO)
——, University College 9, breviary-missal (CQ)
——, University College 22, breviary (BP)
——, University College 25, Hours and psalter
——, University College 101, breviary (CP)
——, Wood C. 12, Hours, BT
——, Wood empt. 20, commemorations (U)
Oxford, Keble College, MS 32, breviary (CJ)
Ranworth, St Helen's Church, MS s.n, the 'Ranworth Antiphonal' (W)
Salisbury, Cathedral Library, MS 152, breviary (DY)
——, MS 224, breviary
Stonyhurst College, MS 40, breviary
——, MS 44, breviary (DW)
——, MS 52, breviary
Worcester, Cathedral Library, F. 160, antiphonal (CH)
——, Q. 10, breviary (DG)
——, Q. 86, breviary (DF)
York, Minster Library, Additional 68, breviary (P)
——, Additional 69, breviary (Q)
——, Additional 70, breviary (O)
——, Additional 115, breviary (N)
——, Additional 383, breviary (M)
——, XVI. O. 9, breviary-missal (K)
——, XVI. O. 12, breviary
——, XVI. O. 23, breviary (L)

All printed books consulted are listed in the Bibliography.

HANDLIST 2

Manuscripts Arranged by Kalendar Siglum

Sigla A–D are not used in this system, which is not to be confused with the sigla assigned to witnesses of the Office to St William in Chapter 3.

E	Bodl. MS Laud misc. 84	Breviary	York Minster, perhaps
F	Bodl. MS Gough lit. 1	Breviary, noted, incomplete	Province of York
G	London LP MS Sion College 1	Breviary, noted	Skelton parish church
H	Camb. UL MS Addl 3110	Breviary	Province of York
I	London BL MS Addl 38624	Breviary	Province of York
J	London BL MS Addl 30511	Breviary	unknown, Province of York
K	York ML MS XVI. O. 9	Breviary – Missal	Province of York
L	York ML MS XVI. O. 23	Breviary (summer vol.)	Province of York
M	York ML MS Addl 383	Breviary	Province of York
N	York ML MS Addl 115	Breviary	Province of York
O	York ML MS Addl 70	Breviary	Harewood parish church (near Leeds)
P	York ML MS Addl 68	Breviary	Province of York
Q	York ML MS Addl 69	Breviary, noted	
R	Durham UL Cosin V. I. 2	Breviary, noted	Rudby parish church
S	Arundel Castle Archives, the York Antiphonal (s.n.)	Antiphonal	York Minster, St Sepulchre's chapel
T	Bodl. MS Rawlinson C. 553	Hours	St Mary's York, possibly
U	Bodl. MS Wood empt. 20	Commemoration	Diocese of York
V	1493.pr		
W	Ranworth Antiphonal	Antiphonal	St Helen's Church, Ranworth
X	Bodl. e Musaeo 2 = ESC 224, returned permanently	Breviary, noted	Prebend of Bedwin
Y	London Lambeth PL MS 69	Breviary	Henry Chichele
Z	Durham UL Cosin V. I. 3	Breviary, noted; composite	Norwich?
AA	Bodl. Rawl. lit. g. 6	Hours	E England?
AB	Bodl. Rawl. lit. g. 2	Hours	E or SE Counties England
AC	Bodl. Rawl. lit. g. 3	Hours	Diocese of Lincoln?
AD	Bodl. Rawl. lit. g. 1	Hours	Lincoln

AE	Bodl. Rawl. lit. f. 3	Hours	London, Sheparde family
AF	Bodl. Rawl. lit. e. 6	Hours	East Anglia?
AG, AS	Bodl. Rawl. lit. e. 7	Hours	
AH	Bodl. Rawl. lit. d. 1	Hours	London?
AI	Bodl. Gough lit. 6	Hours	England
AJ	Bodl. Gough lit. 10	Hours	Flanders?
AK	Bodl. e Musaeo 226	Hours	
AL	Bodl. Gough lit. 3	Hours	NE England?
AM	Bodl. Gough lit. 9	Hours	Kent?
AN	Bodl. Gough lit. 19	Hours	Farley, Hampshire
AO	Bodl. Rawl. C. 558	Hours	vD: Worcester – Droitwich?
AP	Bodl. e Musaeo 188	Hours	Diocese of Norwich?
AQ, AR	Bodl. Rawl. lit. e. 1	Hours	Kalendar from Richmond, Yorkshire
AS	*see* **AG**		
AT	Camb. Fitzwilliam Museum MS McClean 65	Breviary	EW? an area that venerated (Wulfstan erased) / quiriaci / trans. Aldelm
AU	Camb. UL MS Addl 4500	Breviary – Missal	
AV, AW	Camb. UL MS Addl 3474, 3475	Breviary	Norwich St George's
AX	Camb. King's MS 30	Breviary	
AY	Camb. SJC MS F. 9 (James 146)	Breviary	MRJ assignment dubious as it stands; see Pfaff, *LME*
AZ	Camb. UL MS Dd. X. 66	Breviary	
BA	Camb. Peterhouse MS 270	Breviary	East Anglia
BB	Camb. Clare MS G. 3. 34 (olim, MRJ, Kk. 3. 7)	Breviary	Norwich?
BC	Camb. Emmanuel MS 64	Breviary	Dublin?
BD	London BL MS Royal 2 A XIV	Breviary	Bridgettines (Syon, Isleworth), possibly
BE	London BL MS Sloane 2466	Breviary	
BF	London BL MS Royal 2 A XII	Breviary	England, produced abroad
BG	London BL MS Harley 1797	Breviary (temporale only)	
BH	London BL MS Harley 587	Breviary (temporale only)	Worcester associations
BI	London BL MS Addl 22397	Breviary (temporale only)	
BJ	Bodl. Bodley 948	Antiphonal	Langton; then London
BK	Bodl. Hatton 4	Psalter	Windsor
BL	Bodl. Hatton 106	Psalter	Sarum, Hereford, Llandaff

BM	London BL MS Addl 52359	Breviary, noted	orig. East Anglia? used in Lancashire
BN	London BL MS Lansdowne 463	Antiphonal, imperfect	Norwich/East Anglia
BO	Bodl. MS St John's College 179	Breviary (winter part)	found in Combe Martin
BP	Bodl. MS University College 22	Breviary	
BQ	Bodl. Bodley 976	Breviary	
BR	Bodl. MS Laud misc. 3A	Breviary (temporale only)	
BS	Bodl. Lat. lit. b. 14	Antiphonal	Denchworth parish, Oxfordshire
BT	Bodl. MS Wood C. 12	Hours	Beverley, possibly
BU	Camb. UL MS Addl 2602	Antiphonal	Springfield church, Essex
BV	London BL MS Harley 2785	Breviary	
BW	Bodl. MS Laud misc. 299	Breviary	East Anglia or Worcester (Ddr), possibly, then Launton parish church
BW	Bodl. MS Laud misc. 299	Breviary	East Anglia or Worcester (Ddr), possibly, then Launton parish church
BX	Bodl. Rawl. lit. f. 2	Hours	Henham Hall ? Suffolk
BY	Bodl. Laud lat. 15	Hours	NE England?
BZ	London BL MS Stowe 12	Breviary	adapted/used in Norwich
CA	Camb. Fitzwilliam Museum MS 369	Breviary, noted – Missal	Lewes
CB	Camb. Magdalene College F. 4. 10	Antiphonal	Peterborough
CC	London BL Addl 35285	Antiphonal and Missal	Guisborough priory, Yorkshire
CD	London BL Addl 33381	collection, the Priory of Ely 'ELY PRIORY TRACTS AND PRAYERS' (spine)	Ely, priory
CE	Bodl. Rawl. lit. e. 3	Hours	Norwich?
CF	Bodl. Rawl. lit. e. 4	Hours	England? Folkestone Kent?
CG	Bodl. Rawl. lit. f. 1	Hours	Gloucester abbey OSB
CH	Worcester Cathedral Library MS F. 160 (the 'Antiphonale Sarisburiense')	Antiphonal	for Worcester Cathedral and probably made in Worcester
CI	Hereford Cathedral Library MS P. IX. 7	Breviary, noted	for Hereford cathedral, used at Mordiford
CJ	Oxford Keble MS 32	Breviary	Walsingham
CK	London BL MS Addl 43405, 43406	Breviary	Muchelney
CL	London BL MS Harley 4664	Breviary	Coldingham; Durham, OSB cathedral priory St Cuthbert

CM	London BL MS Royal 2 A X	Psalter/Breviary hybrid	St Albans
CN	London BL MS Addl 36672	Breviary	Terouanne; 'belonged to S Saviour's Ch, Southwark'
CO	London BL MS Harley 2856	Psalter, Diurnal	
CP	Bodl. MS University College 101	Breviary	Cluniac priory, Pontefract, Yorkshire
CQ	Bodl. MS University College 9	Breviary – Missal	O. Carm., Cambridge?
CR	Bodl. MS Lat. lit. c. 36	Breviary (sanctorale), noted	Diocese of Bath
CS	Bodl. MS Barlow 41	Breviary (winter part)	Evesham abbey
CT	Bodl. Lat. lit. e. 37, Lat. lit. e. 6, Lat. lit. e. 39, Lat. lit. d. 42 (the Chertsey Abbey Breviary)	Breviary	Chertsey abbey, Surrey
CU	Bodl. Gough lit. 17 = Gough Missals 47	Diurnal	Peterborough abbey
CV	Bodl. MSS Gough lit. 8 (A) and Rawl. lit. e. 1* (B)	Breviary, monastic	Hyde abbey OSB, Winchester
CW	London BL MS Sloane 1909	Breviary	
CX	Bodl. MS Lyell empt. 4	Psalter	Croyland, Lincolnshire
CY	London BL MS Lansdowne 431	Psalter 'cum canticis'	Barnwell priory
CZ	London BL MS Addl 59862	Breviary	Norwich
DA	Bodl. Douce 293	Psalter, choir	N or NE England
DB	Bodl. MS Laud lat. 5	Psalter	Guisborough Aug.
DC	Bodl. MS Lat. lit. g. 1	Psalter	St Mary's York
DD	London BL MS Addl 17002	Breviary, noted	Norwich?
DE	London BL MS Addl 32427	Breviary, noted, choir	probably for Diocese of Worcester
DF	Worcester Cathedral Library MS Q. 86	Breviary	Hereford
DG	Worcester Cathedral Library MS Q. 10	Breviary	
DH	Bodl. Bodley 547	Breviary	Beckford priory Aug., Gloucester
DI	Bodl. MS Jesus College 10	Antiphonal (Diurnal?)	Gloucester abbey?
DJ	Bodl. Canon. lit. 215	Breviary	'Irish Breviary of the Sarum type'
DK	Bodl. MS Lit. 132	Hours	unknown
DL	London BL MS Burney 335	Breviary	O. Cist.
DN	Bodl. MS Rawlinson G. 170	Psalter	Province of York
DO	Bodl. MS Rawl. D. 1218		

DP	Bodl. MS Bodley 68	Kalendar	
DQ	Bodl. MS Rawl. C. 466		
DS	Bodl. MS Douce 88		
DT	Bodl. e Musaeo 185	Psalter	Benedictine, possibly
DU	Nottingham UL s.n. (the Wollaton Antiphonal)	Antiphonal	Notts; then St Leonard's Church, Wollaton, Nottinghamshire
DV	Camb. Sidney Sussex MS 62	Diurnal	N England, Aug.?
DW	Stonyhurst College MS 44	Breviary, summer part	Ashridge Aug., Buckinghamshire
DX	Blackburn Museum 091. 21195	Diurnal	Charterhouse, London
DY	Salisbury Cathedral MS 152	Breviary, noted	Arlingham, Gloucester
DZ	Longleat MS 10	Breviary – Missal	Kynbauton (orig.), Spaulding
EA	Liverpool, UL (Cathedral) Radclife 37	Breviary	unknown
EB	Dublin Trinity College, 85	Breviary	Province of York
EC	Dublin Trinity College 88	Breviary	unknown
ED	Colchester Castle Museum 1932. 213 (Ker 213. 32)	Breviary	Norwich
EE	London BL MS Harley 1513	Breviary	England: Clopham/Clapham?
EF	Edinburgh UL MS 27	Breviary, noted	used in Scotland

INDEX

Specific manuscripts and liturgical observances may be located using the Tables and Handlists.

1505 Hereford Breviary, printed book: 47, 116–17, 122, 132, 138
1531 Sarum Breviary, printed book: 8, 64–65, 67, 93, 110, 179, 202

Advent Sunday, office for: 9, 106, 107, 109–23, 127, 129, 136, 138–39, 140, 164, 197, 205, 224, 228
  Lessons: 119–22
  Vespers: 17, 19
Alcuin of York: 174
Anglo-Catholic liturgical revival: 25
Anne, saint: 88, 89–90, 184, 187–89, 192
Anthony Bek, bishop: 143, 203
Augustine of Canterbury: 173, 194

Bangor: 21, 22n, 226
Bede, the Venerable: 120, 173–74
Benedict Biscop: 173
Benedict of Peterborough: 106, 132, 229
Benedictine liturgy: chapters 2 and 3 *passim*, 172, 219
Beyssac, Dom Gabriel: 32, 33, 39–40, 48
Birinus, saint: 184, 193
Book of Common Prayer: 21, 22, 23, 26, 214, 226
Book of Hours: 42, 135, 192
Bradshaw, Henry: 32

Cambrai cathedral: 183
Canonisation: 182–83

Canterbury, ecclesiastical province of saints' days promulgated in: 10, 34, 85, 89–90, 94, 167–68, 179, 185–86, 188, 192, 193, 196, 199–200, 210, 230
Cathedrals, *see* individual entries
Chad, saint: 64, 87–90, 96, 98, 100–01, 185, 189, 206
Chichele, Henry, archbishop: 10, 34, 167, 185, 189, 200, 204, 206, 208, 211
'Chichele group', manuscripts: 34, 67, 103, 107, 112–14, 129, 136, 205–11, 214
Chichester, 10, 207–08, 213
Coldingham/Battle group (Benedictine liturgy): 53–55
Common of Saints: 16, 20, 146, 151–52, 162
Corpus Christi, feast of: 151
Council of *Clofesho*: 174
Council, Fourth Lateran: 187
Cranmer, Thomas, archbishop: 186, 229

David of Wales, saint: 87–89, 98, 101, 189, 206
Dead, office of the: 33, 35, 39, 42, 47, 51, 66, 106, 133–39, 164, 188, 201, 224, 228
Dedication, feast of the: 32, 51, 72n, 66, 88, 90–94, 102, 142, 176, 182, 224
Dominican liturgy: 58

Ecclesiological Society: 25
  Ecclesiologist, publication: 26
Edmund of Abingdon, saint: 86, 89, 153, 161, 184, 188, 219

Egwin, saint: 57, 86, 94–95
Ely: 144
Etheldreda, saint: 85, 88–89, 96, 98, 186, 189, 192
Ethelwold, saint: 86, 175–76
Erkenwald, saint: 64, 96, 184, 194
Exeter: 196–98, 219

Frere, Walter Howard: 31, 38, 66, 72
Frideswide, saint: 85, 88, 89, 96, 98, 186, 189–90, 192
Fulk Basset, bishop: 184

George, saint: 89, 185, 187
Glastonbury: 175, 180
Gloucester: 67, 93–94, 189
Guéranger, Prosper: 27
Guisborough Group Use (Augustinian liturgy): 51–53, 67, 178, 188
Gregory the Great, pope: 86, 94, 173–74, 194

Henry Bradshaw Society: 23
Hereford, use of: 5, 47–48, 59, 61, 94, 102, 116, 165, 179, 188, 195, 199, 224, 226, 228, 229
Hesbert, Dom René-Jean: 29, 39–40, 58
Historia Ecclesiastica: 173
Honorius III, pope: 141
Hugh the Chanter: 179

James, Montague Rhodes: 31, 38, 62, 102
John of Beverley, saint: 88–89, 90, 98, 123, 141, 185, 187, 189, 207
John Gervais, bishop: 184, 193
John Grandisson, bishop: 117, 196–98, 211, 219
John of Hexham: 142

Kalendar, liturgical: 38, 61–103, 216, 220, 223–25
    assessment of the use of a kalendar: 90
    Diocesan observances: 98
    normative kalendars for Sarum, York, and Benedictine liturgy: 72–90, 129
    regional kalendars: 93–98

Lanfranc, archbishop: 178
Legg, John Wickham: 24
'Leofric Missal': 196

Leroquais, Victor: 39
Lichfield: 64, 202
Lincoln: 21, 86, 153, 167, 180, 200, 226
liturgical books, types and structure: 18–20
Liturgical Movement: 27
London: 194–95

Madan, Falconer: 31, 38
Maidstone, Clement: 212
Mary, Blessed Virgin: 38, 92, 112, 177
    Lady Mass: 203
    Lady Office: 201
Mocquereau, Dom André: 28
monastic liturgy, *see also* Benedictine liturgy
    groupings of manuscripts by responsory series: 48ff
    Thomas Becket, original monastic form of office: 125–27
    Triduum monastic group: 55–56
music: 2, 6, 10, 12, 15–16, 18, 23–24, 28–29, 58, 109, 124, 144, 145, 152, 155, 158, 160–61, 164, 186, 227

Neale, John Mason: 26
Norman influences on insular liturgy: 13, 33, 85, 87–89, 102, 172, 177–79, 226
Norwich, as liturgical region: 57, 65, 93, 98–101, 112, 194–95, 211, 213
nova festa, Transfiguration, Visitation, and Holy Name: 14, 98, 186, 190–93

Oseney, use of: 178
Osmund, bishop: 187–88, 199
    liturgical observance: 85, 88, 89, 96, 98, 186–90, 192

parish church, as liturgical context: 14, 62, 93, 183, 200, 214
Peter des Roches, bishop: 184
Peterborough Abbey: 176
Pius X: 28
Plainsong and Medieval Music Society: 24
Pontefract priory: 51
popes, liturgical influence of: 182
Pothier, Dom Joseph: 27
Purgatory: 133

Quignon, Cardinal Francis: 22

Reginald of Durham: 142
Regularis Concordia: 15, 175–76, 178
relics, feast of: 90–93
responsory series, liturgical pattern: 33,
    37–61, 220, 223, 228
Richard of Chichester
    observance of feast: 184, 188
    Office: 158–62
    Vita: 160
Richard Poore, bishop: 180, 195–99
Ripon: 142
Robert de Bethune, bishop: 179
Robert de Braybroke, bishop: 184
Robert Rede, bishop: 207
Robert Stillington, bishop: 186
Roger Walden, archbishop: 185
Rouen, liturgical practices of: 179
rubrics (liturgical instructions): 110, chapter
    3 *passim*, 165–66, 202, 204, 210, 211,
    213–14, 220, 224, 226, 229
Rule of St Benedict: 15, 172, 175, 177–78

Salisbury Cathedral: 2, 9, 34, 85, 165, 167,
    172, 180, 189, 199, 204, 220, 225, 230
Sanctorale: 5, 8–9, 19, 20, 42, 63–64, 106,
    135, 141, 190, 229
    lessons: 34, 110, 120, 163, 215
Sarum Missal, modern editions: 24, 34,
    179–80
Sarum, use of, *specific concepts only*
    Addiciones to the Ordinal: 166–67,
        201, 204
    Customary: 9, 19, 165, 218
    Ordinal: 88, 111–12, 115, 165, 166–68,
        172, 199, 200–16, 218
Second Vatican Council, 1962–1965:
    28–29
Shropshire: 202
Solesmes, Abbaye-de-St-Pierre: 27–29, 32
St David's: 201, 203–04, 206, 213
St Paul's (London): 10, 21, 185, 208–09
Stephen Langton, archbishop: 193
Surtees Society: 23
Swithun, saint: 184, 193
Synod: 171
    'Synodal' feasts: 20, 63, 66, 93, 98–102,
        182, 184, 193–95, 211, 224
    Synod of Whitby: 172

Temporale: 9, 15, 19, 47, 51, 106, 176, 229
Thomas of Bayeux, archbishop: 179
Thomas Becket, saint: 60, 88, 106, 123–33,
    153, 161, 164, 201, 224
    monastic form of office: 125–27
    secular form of office: 127
transmission, of liturgy: 164, 168–70;
    215–19, 225

Wales: 94, 189, 196
Walter de Cantilupe, bishop: 73, 95,
    184, 194
Wells: 186, 195–96, 200
William Alnwick, archbishop: 167
William Courtenay, archbishop: 184
William Raleigh, bishop: 184, 193
William of York, saint: 106, 141–63,
    224, 228
    Office: 144–63
    Vita: 143, 153
Wilfrid, saint: 59, 85, 87, 95, 98, 141
Winchester: 85, 95, 175, 193, 203
Winifrid, saint: 88–89, 98, 185, 189
Wollaton Antiphonal: 58, 100
Wolsey, Thomas, archbishop: 162, 183
Worcester: 95
Wycliffite criticism: 209–10
York Minster: 142, 146

MEDIEVAL CHURCH STUDIES

All volumes in this series are evaluated by an Editorial Board, strictly on academic grounds, based on reports prepared by referees who have been commissioned by virtue of their specialism in the appropriate field. The Board ensures that the screening is done independently and without conflicts of interest. The definitive texts supplied by authors are also subject to review by the Board before being approved for publication. Further, the volumes are copyedited to conform to the publisher's stylebook and to the best international academic standards in the field.

Titles in Series

Megan Cassidy-Welch, *Monastic Spaces and their Meanings: Thirteenth-Century English Cistercian Monasteries* (2001)

Elizabeth Freeman, *Narratives of a New Order: Cistercian Historical Writing in England, 1150–1220* (2002)

The Study of the Bible in the Carolingian Era, ed. by Celia Chazelle and Burton Van Name Edwards (2003)

Text and Controversy from Wyclif to Bale: Essays in Honour of Anne Hudson, ed. by Helen Barr and Ann M. Hutchison (2005)

Lena Roos, *'God Wants It!': The Ideology of Martyrdom in the Hebrew Crusade Chronicles and its Jewish and Christian Background* (2006)

Emilia Jamroziak, *Rievaulx Abbey and its Social Context, 1132–1300: Memory, Locality, and Networks* (2004)

The Voice of Silence: Women's Literacy in a Men's Church, ed. by Thérèse de Hemptinne and María Eugenia Góngora (2004)

Perspectives for an Architecture of Solitude: Essays on Cistercians, Art and Architecture in Honour of Peter Fergusson, ed. by Terryl N. Kinder (2004)

Saints, Scholars, and Politicians: Gender as a Tool in Medieval Studies, ed. by Mathilde van Dijk and Renée Nip (2005)

Manuscripts and Monastic Culture: Reform and Renewal in Twelfth-Century Germany, ed. by Alison I. Beach (2007)

Weaving, Veiling, and Dressing: Textiles and their Metaphors in the Late Middle Ages, ed. by Kathryn M. Rudy and Barbara Baert (2007)

James J. Boyce, *Carmelite Liturgy and Spiritual Identity: The Choir Books of Kraków* (2008)

Studies in Carthusian Monasticism in the Late Middle Ages, ed. by Julian M. Luxford (2009)

Kevin J. Alban, *The Teaching and Impact of the 'Doctrinale' of Thomas Netter of Walden (c. 1374–1430)* (2010)

Gunilla Iversen, *Laus angelica: Poetry in the Medieval Mass*, ed. by Jane Flynn, trans. by William Flynn (2010)

Kriston R. Rennie, *Law and Practice in the Age of Reform: The Legatine Work of Hugh of Die (1073–1106)* (2010)

After Arundel: Religious Writing in Fifteenth-Century England, ed. by Vincent Gillespie and Kantik Ghosh (2011)

Federico Botana, *The Works of Mercy in Italian Medieval Art (c. 1050–c. 1400)* (2011)

The Regular Canons in the Medieval British Isles, ed. by Janet Burton and Karen Stöber (2011)

Wycliffite Controversies, ed. by Mishtooni Bose and J. Patrick Hornbeck II (2011)

Nickiphoros I. Tsougarakis, *The Latin Religious Orders in Medieval Greece, 1204–1500* (2012)

Nikolaos G. Chrissis, *Crusading in Frankish Greece: A Study of Byzantine-Western Relations and Attitudes, 1204–1282* (2012)

Demetrio S. Yocum, *Petrarch's Humanist Writing and Carthusian Monasticism: The Secret Language of the Self* (2013)

The Pseudo-Bonaventuran Lives of Christ: Exploring the Middle English Tradition, ed. by Ian Johnson and Allan F. Westphall (2013)

Alice Chapman, *Sacred Authority and Temporal Power in the Writings of Bernard of Clairvaux* (2013)

Religious Controversy in Europe, 1378–1536: Textual Transmission and Networks of Readership, ed. by Michael Van Dussen and Pavel Soukup (2013)

Monasteries on the Borders of Medieval Europe: Conflict and Cultural Interaction, ed. by Emilia Jamroziak and Karen Stöber (2014)

M. J. Toswell, *The Anglo-Saxon Psalter* (2014)

Envisioning the Bishop: Images and the Episcopacy in the Middle Ages, ed. by Sigrid Danielson and Evan A. Gatti (2014)

Kathleen E. Kennedy, *The Courtly and Commercial Art of the Wycliffite Bible* (2014)

David N. Bell, *The Library of the Abbey of La Trappe: A Study of its History from the Twelfth Century to the French Revolution, with an Annotated Edition of the 1752 Catalogue* (2014)

Patronage, Production, and Transmission of Texts in Medieval and Early Modern Jewish Cultures, ed. by Esperanza Alfonso and Jonathan Decter (2014)

Devotional Culture in Late Medieval England and Europe: Diverse Imaginations of Christ's Life, edited by Stephen Kelly and Ryan Perry (2014)